Sabbath Soup

Kathi Lipp

*Prayers, Liturgies, and Sabbath Experiences
by Bethany Howard and Hope Lyda*

TEN PEAKS PRESS®
EUGENE, OR

Published in association with Rachelle Gardner, Gardner Literary Agency.

Cover and interior design by Dugan Design Group
Photography by Jay Eads

The Angel Food Cake, Apple Cake, Charcuterie Board, Chocolate Chip Cookies, Interpretive Vegetable Soup, Pulled Pork, Queso Dip, Tomato Gin Soup, and Turkey Chili recipes were previously published in *The Accidental Homesteader* by Kathi Lipp. Copyright © 2023 by Kathi Lipp.

For bulk or special sales, please call 1 (800) 547-8979. Email: CustomerService@hhpbooks.com

TEN PEAKS PRESS is a federally registered trademark of the Hawkins Children's LLC. Harvest House Publishers, Inc., is the exclusive licensee of this trademark.

Sabbath Soup

Copyright © 2024 by Kathi Lipp
Published by Ten Peaks Press, an imprint of Harvest House Publishers
Eugene, Oregon 97408

ISBN 978-0-7369-8862-9 (pbk.)
ISBN 978-0-7369-8863-6 (eBook)
Library of Congress Control Number: 2024931387

Printed in China

24 25 26 27 28 29 30 31 32 / RDS / 10 9 8 7 6 5 4 3 2 1

To my dear friend Susy Flory.

This book is a tribute to the spirit of giving, the joy of living out of abundance, and the unbreakable bonds forged in the warmth of a kitchen and the sharing of a meal.

It is dedicated to you, Susy: my neighbor, my mentor, my friend, and the embodiment of community at its best.

May these pages reflect the love and wisdom you've shared with me, and may the soups we share continue to be a symbol of our enduring connection and the countless ways our friendship nourishes our lives.

Contents

Why Sabbath?

The further the soul is from the noise of the world, the closer it may be to its Creator, for God, with his holy angels, will draw close to a person who seeks solitude and silence.

THOMAS À KEMPIS

Beneath the loud hum of our hustle, there is the still, small voice that invites us to step away from producing and rushing so we can spend time in His presence being restored and blessed.

God, being the kind guide and Abba that He is, asks us to commit to something for our own wellness and wholeness. You won't hear an argument from me—not one problematic peep—when God tells me to step away from the computer and curl up for a midday nap instead! Setting aside and respecting a holy time of rest is more than a command; it is a gift.

"The Sabbath was made for man, not man for the Sabbath." MARK 2:27

Because it was made for us, embracing Sabbath shifts a daily "nothing special" experience into a mysteriously divine one. We transform a time of renewal into a spiritual practice. We bring meaning to the smallest of routines. We elevate a simple meal to a sacred ritual of connection and gratitude. And those changes have nothing to do with what we wear, serve, do, or the social status of who we feed. It has everything to do with the state of our heart.

And believe me, I understand that it isn't always easy to get to that state of heart and mind. I mean, we're living full lives that are demanding on even the slow days, right? My prayer for this book with its recipes, ideas for Sabbath living, practical steps, and compassionate prayers is that it will help you enter that state of the heart and mind with surprising ease. As you personalize routines and rituals, you will uncover a Sabbath way of going about your week. You'll find new ways of viewing tasks and priorities, serving your family, cultivating your own wellness, and connecting with the Creator who is eager for you to rest in Him.

I can wholeheartedly say I wish I had answered God's invitation to Sabbath living much earlier in life.

* * *

My husband, Roger, and I honor Sabbath from Saturday evening to Sunday evening. When my kids were little, I remember pausing during my Sunday tasks and thinking, "If Sabbath is supposed to be my day of rest, why am I so exhausted?"

Not only did we have church in the morning, but everyone was home and expected to be fed.

Three times.

So, I'd make breakfast before we went to church.

And then lunch right after we got home from church.

And then dinner.

And while everyone else in the family was resting, I was either prepping, making, or cleaning up after some meal.

A few things have changed since those early days of Sunday chaos with little kids: To start, my kids are grown and are only here on occasional Sundays when they make the trip (we live three hours from each other). Additionally, I have an amazing husband; while he doesn't love cooking, he is happy to not only BBQ, smoke meat, and make pizza, but he also believes deeply that if I cook, he should do the dishes. (This is only one of the many reasons I am deeply in love with this man.) And most importantly, I've changed my whole approach to Sabbath.

I no longer spend my Sundays cooking, or doing any other kind of work, really. I take the day truly as rest. The reason I'm able to do that is because I spend a few hours on Friday or Saturday preparing food for Sunday.

Sometimes, I buy some food ahead of time, make a couple of dishes on Saturday morning, and we are set. Other times, I'm cooking up a storm, pulling out all my culinary creativity, and cooking everything we'll eat from Saturday night to Sunday night plus enough leftovers to last until Tuesday or Wednesday.

But the most important part of all of this is that it is planned and prepped ahead so that I, the main cook of the house, get a Sabbath rest like everyone else.

I get to read a book or play in my garden.

I get to watch a movie or hang out with friends.

In other words, I get a break. A real break. When Monday comes rolling around and I'm back to work, I have had actual rest.

And friend? It is glorious.

It is what I want for you and your family.

The Sabbath

When I post about Sabbath, often the comments I get are "Sabbath should be on _____, not _____ when you are celebrating it."

So let me give you permission here to honor the day your way.

If you celebrate on Sunday? Great.

If you celebrate on Saturday? Great.

If you celebrate on Tuesday because you are a medical professional who saves lives on the weekends? Great. (And oh, by the way, thank you. You know, for saving lives…)

Whether done on the seventh day or not, honoring the principle of Sabbath is a worthy habit. Not only because it feeds our souls but because God calls us to this practice:

> *"Remember the Sabbath day by keeping it holy…For in six days the LORD made the heavens and the earth, the sea, and all that is in them, but he rested on the seventh day. Therefore the LORD blessed the Sabbath day and made it holy." EXODUS 20:8,11*

Why Soup?

Prepare a Sabbath meal, alone or with friends or family...
This food is not so much for survival as for sheer, savory delight. Put on some music, turn off the
phone. Take as much time as you like to feel, taste, smell each ingredient, every spice, bread,
and vegetable...Give thanks for the bounty of the earth.

WAYNE MULLER, SABBATH: *FINDING REST, RENEWAL,*
AND DELIGHT IN OUR BUSY LIVES

Why not Sabbath casserole or Sabbath BBQ?
I would 100% stand behind any of those ideas, but there are a few reasons why I have decided to make soup for almost every Sabbath, and I would encourage you to consider the same.

It's a one-pot meal.
The one-pot meal is the least fussy of all the meals. When I am done making my recipe in my trusty soup pot, I wait for it to cool down and then put the pot directly into my fridge on my "soup shelf" until after church, when I can simply pull it out, put it directly onto my burner, and heat up our meal. No fuss is my favorite kind of food. (And let's be honest, way fewer dishes is a total bonus.)

I often add a salad and a bread to that soup, but it's not required. Soup can be, and often is, a full meal on its own. It is enough.

I can use up a lot of food from the week before.
Sometimes I follow a recipe to the letter when trying a new soup. But more often I take one of two different approaches: the "anything can go in a soup" approach, or the "what do I need to use up?" approach.

When making "anything goes in" soup, I start with a recipe and beef up my base by adding whatever foods I have around that seem like they would make a great addition to that soup. At the start, I might add fresh vegetables (sometimes sautéed first). Cooked leftovers can be added near the end of a soup (so they don't cook too long), like extra chicken, ground beef, chorizo, sausage, chopped steak, or cooked beans. I can add some extra broth to have a "brothier" soup, or some cream or leftover mashed potatoes to have a thicker soup. I might even add cooked vegetables, rice, or pasta at the end.

If one of my leftovers isn't great to go into soup, how about on top of it? I've enjoyed great soup toppers like toasted bread, croutons, shredded cheese, chopped bacon, sour cream (or crème fraiche or Greek yogurt), fresh herbs, sautéed onion and mushrooms, nuts and seeds, tortilla chips, or crackers.

With the "use it up" approach, I see what I have on hand and decide my plan from there. Do I have some shredded chicken left over from the bird I roasted on Tuesday, along with some heavy cream from the cake

I baked last weekend? That sounds like a great start to a cream of chicken soup. Leftover steak and some stewed tomatoes? A beef and tomato stew recipe can use up all those bits and pieces.

Making soup is one of my favorite ways to use up leftovers. And it's one of my favorite ways to be creative. Some people have paint, I have chorizo.

Soup is stretchable.

One of our favorite Sabbath pastimes is to have family and friends around the table. I know I can always stretch soup to accommodate a larger crowd. Sometimes it's adding more chicken broth or cream; other times it's sautéing some veggies and adding some meat from the freezer, along with some salt, pepper, and herbs. I can always make a soup stretch to fit a few more people around the table.

The soup recipes in this book will provide four dinner servings or eight side dish portions. It is simple to reassign soup's role in the meal. If we have a lot of people coming, I can make a huge salad and serve cups of soup instead of bowls. I've even been known to run by the store after church and grab a couple of loaves of bread to accommodate a few friends and make a soup seem like it's more than it is.

The other thing I love about soup's stretchability is I will never make a small amount of soup. If it's not enough to fill the pot, it's not enough. I tend to make a whole soup pot, eat what we will on Sunday, and then have leftovers on Tuesday. If there are still leftovers after that (and when it's just me and Roger, there often are), I will freeze that soup in quart freezer bags or plastic containers for "fast food" lunches during the week. (When freezing in quart freezer bags, I freeze the bags lying down on a cookie sheet so they freeze flat and store well. Be sure to label all freezer bags because all frozen soup looks pretty much the same.) I love having a block of soup to defrost the night before, then I just plop it into a pan for lunch that day. It's still homemade, just not homemade that morning. But it counts.

Soup is easy to reheat or keep warm.

Reheating soup is a Culinary Level One skill. I have some kids who love to cook, and others who are grateful they have a Chipotle around the corner. But all of my kids can be trusted to reheat a pot of soup.

One of my favorite ways of reheating soup doesn't involve the stovetop at all. I love making soup in a slow cooker with a removable pot, letting it cool down, and putting that whole pot in the fridge. Sunday morning, our Sabbath, I plop that pot back in the base of the slow cooker, turn the knob to low, and arrive home at lunchtime with soup ready to eat. Soup, in my opinion, is the best "getting home from church" meal ever invented.

Soup is easy to level up or down.

Depending on your time, energy, and budget, you can make soup as simple or as fancy as you want. There are plenty of elaborate soups you can make, but my favorites tend to be the ones made with pretty humble ingredients and given time for the flavors to develop into something magical.

Sure, you can make a sophisticated soup topped with fresh herbs and a crostini and a bit of shaved, imported cheese on top. And I bet it will taste amazing. But you know what will also taste amazing? A humble chicken noodle soup with leftover shredded chicken, canned broth, dried noodles, onion, and chopped carrots and celery that have been lingering in your veggie drawer just a little too long.

Soup can be made ahead. (And actually tastes better when it is.)

This is my number one reason why I love having a soup routine each week. I can make this soup on Friday or Saturday (depending on what my week looks like), and just when I need a meal that is prepared and ready for me to serve, it's there waiting for me. I don't need to do a lot of extra work to get it on the table. (Plus, making it ahead forces me to clean out my fridge so I can keep that big soup pot in there until Sunday. It's a win-win.)

I have never met a soup that didn't taste better the second day. It's the law of soup.

Soup is easy to repurpose.

I love a good chili on Sunday, but I love it even more on Tuesday when I can put that same chili over a baked potato with some shredded cheese, chopped onion, and sour cream. This is one of my favorite meals ever. Besides chili, I've done the same with beef or chicken stew.

You can also thicken a brothy soup by adding noodles or dumplings, or ladle soup like a gravy over mashed potatoes, noodles, or rice.

Soup is flexible.

Soup can be a meal that feeds the multitudes—even those friends and family members who have different dietary preferences, restrictions, or allergies. I love to make a basic vegetable-based soup with vegetable broth, which most people can eat, and then have bowls or plates of meat, cheeses, rice, noodles, bread, and crackers (both classic and gluten free). People can use these additions to create a personalized soup. As a time-saving bonus, I provide a big bowl of fresh greens so people can use all the same side ingredients to create a one-of-a-kind salad to complete a hearty, customizable meal.

Soup is magical.

There's just something about soup that slows us down, makes us feel cozy, and forces us to linger. And the best stories are told around a bowl of soup. What other simple meal invites us to the practices that make Sabbath so good for the soul, our families, and our lives?

In our home, where we have plenty of "celebration" foods (steaks, ice cream, shrimp, and cake come to mind for birthdays and holidays), soup is our slow-down food. There is nothing fancy about the soups we make, but there is something special. Just like the best soups require the pot to linger on the stove, they also require people to linger a little longer around the table. You can't rush the cooking of soup, and you can't rush the eating of soup. You have to wait for it to cool down…so it's enjoyed one spoon at a time, between conversations.

And that? Simply magical.

The Gift of Preplanning
{Why This Works}

There remains, then, a Sabbath-rest for the people of God; for anyone who enters God's rest also rests from their works, just as God did from his.

HEBREWS 4:9-10

As you'll see reflected in the structure of this book, Roger and I and our faith tradition celebrate Sabbath on Saturday evening through Sunday afternoon. We make our biggest celebration meal for Saturday night, and don't work on Sunday. (This means we are just popping dinner into the oven, tossing a salad, and so on. All the heavy lifting is done on Friday or Saturday morning.)

If your schedule is different, adjust accordingly.

Okay, now the process.

The Weekly Process

Monday—Meal Plan

Hopefully, you will find some meal plans in this book that you love.

I cook on Friday or Saturday, depending on what we have going on that week. If Saturday is going to be busy, I either do all the cooking on Friday, or at least get a huge head start on that day. I love making things from scratch, but I also love getting a roast chicken from Costco, a batch of muffins from my favorite bakery, or, when my life is extra crazy, buying all the prepared food for a week and calling it a day.

This is the day I look at what food we have on hand, what needs to be used up, and what we are running short on, and then meal plan accordingly.

Tuesday—Fridge Clean Out and Shopping List

This is the day that I clean out my fridge, throw anything that looks iffy to the chickens, and make my shopping list. I tend to order groceries online on Tuesday night to pick up on Wednesday. It saves me time and money because I'm not buying impulse items. (It's easy to go into Sam's Club looking for spinach and end up with a six-piece outdoor dining set.)

Wednesday—Shopping Day

This is when I go and get everything I'll need for my cooking session on Friday or Saturday.

Thursday—Veggie Prep

This is when I do all my salad and vegetable prep. Washing, spinning, chopping. (Because if I don't prep vegetables, I don't eat vegetables.)

Friday or Saturday—The Big Cook

Sometime on Friday or Saturday, I do all my cooking. It usually takes a couple of hours, but I can cut down on that time by prepping vegetables on Thursday, and buying prepared foods (like shredded chicken, precut vegetables, etc.).

Menus—A Week at a Glance

Now, let's look at menu planning. Developing your own ideal routine will become simpler in time. To ease you into the possibilities, I share eight weeks of menu themes per season. My hope is that you'll find a few new favorites, and you'll be inspired to create some of your own menus with dishes you and your family are eager to gather around no matter the night.

Straightforward menu items like grilled veggies or grilled cheese don't have a recipe listed because many people already have a favorite way to do these. I hope I've included many new-to-you ideas to refresh your personal menus.

Sabbath Menus

Saturday Dinner—Our Big Meal

This is usually our biggest meal of the week. It typically involves a meat of some kind (pork roast, roast chicken, pot roast—as you can tell, we love a roast), a vegetable side, and some kind of starch. This is also the only meal of the week when I'm making a dessert.

I make enough of the meal so that there are leftovers for dinner on Monday, which I usually repurpose into something else. (Roast chicken with green beans and mashed potatoes becomes Shepherd's Pie. Brisket becomes BBQ sandwiches, etc.)

Sunday Breakfast

This is a different breakfast (pancakes, waffles, muf-

Leftover Salad to Love

You'll notice many times in the meal plans when I suggest a salad for Sunday, and I have leftover salad planned for Tuesday. If you've ever taken home leftover salad from a restaurant, you may consider this a terrible idea.

The key is to prep the salad, but don't mix the ingredients. And don't let your dressing touch any ingredients until you are ready to eat. Dressing, while delicious, destroys the structural integrity of salad.

fins, egg dish, etc.) than we have Monday through Friday (protein shakes, yogurt, quick oatmeal). Sometimes, if we know we're going to be in a rush on Sunday morning, we may eat this on Saturday.

Sunday Lunch

This is soup, salad, and usually some kind of bread. It's simple but delish enough that if we have people coming over after church, it's still special.

I make enough soup to have leftovers on Tuesday night.

Sunday Dinner

For this meal, I usually choose a family favorite: enchiladas, casserole, or chicken wings with dipping sauce. This is often fun food. I try to think of meals that can be prepped on Saturday morning and then popped into the oven/air fryer/slow cooker when appropriate on Sunday. Because on our chosen Sabbath day, while we're resting, we still want something amazing to eat.

Weeknight Dinners

Monday
Today, I take the leftovers from Saturday and make something quick but delicious. This is Monday Magic night where that Saturday roast chicken becomes transformed into Monday's chicken tostada. *Voilà!*

Tuesday
Because we need an easy night, this is just straight up leftovers that are going to be amazing but take no mental energy whatsoever. Dine on leftover soup and salad. Use ingredients you have on hand and want to use up.

Wednesday to Friday
The following three meals can be served in any order. If we're already running errands in town on Wednesday, that will be our "eat out" night, and we'll do something from the freezer on Thursday. Or sometimes we like a pizza on Wednesday. It's all up to you and how you live your life. This is our typical plan:

Wednesday
Enjoy leftovers from the week. If there are no leftovers, I will pull a prepped meal from the freezer. Trader Joe's is my go-to for these meals, but you may live near an Aldi or H-E-B (lucky you!) and find amazing things there. Your local grocery store will have plenty of options.

If Wednesday is when you're already out doing your shopping for the week, check and see if your store has a Wednesday special. For example, our local grocery store has a five-dollar summer special on sushi, and the sushi is amazing.

Thursday
Eat out. When you're choosing to eat out only once a week, make it worth it. Plan ahead so you choose an enjoyable experience and have time to look for specials if you're on a budget. This is the night to try foods that you wouldn't normally cook at home. While I'm trying to improve my international cooking, I love to try new foods by the people who know how to cook them. We've found the best Thai, Indian, Chinese, Italian, Mexican, and Japanese food in the city closest to our home, and we rotate through those cuisines.

Friday
Pizza night! We normally make one in our outdoor pizza oven, but sometimes we take one home from a local shop or buy a take-and-bake pizza. If you want to make your own or even turn it into a family activity, you'll find a homemade pizza dough recipe on page 30.

* * *

This schedule means I'm doing heavy meal prep only a couple hours each week on Saturday morning, and then the rest of the time it's pretty much assembling our dinners from ingredients and meal elements that are already prepared. Plus, I get all of Sunday off.

And my friend—that is a gift.

Fall

Rhythms, Rituals, and Routines

Within more restful rhythms we start to slow down—to walk without rushing, eat without gulping, and pray without looking at our watches.

RUTH HALEY BARTON

Several years ago, I wrote a book with my friend Cheri Gregory called *Overwhelmed: How to Quiet the Chaos and Restore Your Sanity*. One of the main concepts we talked about in that book was predeciding: how to make decisions in advance instead of in the moment to remove a lot of the stress from your daily life.

And this concept of meal planning and preparing for Sabbath (both from a food and rest aspect)? This is all based on predeciding.

What will we eat on Sunday after church? That was decided a week ago when I put together my meal plan for the week.

We are living this part of our lives by design ("Here are the meals we are having this week." "I will not be cooking on Sunday so that we can rest and enjoy ourselves.") and not by default ("I need to get home and start making something for lunch, but first I need to stop by the store…" "I don't have anything planned for lunch. Let's just drive-through somewhere…").

And by the way, I love a good meal out (even good drive-through food once in a while), but I want to do it because it is fun and I will enjoy the food, not because we are going for the lowest common denominator of what everyone can agree on.

The first time you work this Sabbath system, it will probably feel completely overwhelming: planning those meals, planning for the leftovers, creating your shopping list, shopping in advance, cooking in advance? It's going to feel like a lot.

But once you do it a few times, once you create that rhythm and ritual? You'll be wondering why you haven't been preparing food this way your whole life.

When you have Sunday to concentrate on how to love your people instead of how to feed them? You'll never turn back.

And another part I love about this plan? It's not all done on the same day. There is a planning day, a list-making day, a shopping day, a prep day, a cooking day, and a resting day. Everything gets done, and it just becomes part of your routine.

When I was a young mom, I spent a Saturday every month cooking 30 frozen meals. The problem was that I was *exhausted* after cooking that many meals, and it wasn't very strategic. Thirty separate dishes were overwhelming, lots of leftover ingredients went to waste, and to be honest, my family wasn't crazy about the recipes that were in the book I was following.

But doing this once a week allows me to see our schedule, plan ahead, and not stress out each and every night. It allows me to confidently plan other activities and events because I know that dinner is taken care of.

And if there's a meal or item on this plan that doesn't work for you—no problem. Swap it out for another from the recipe section or one of your family favorites. It's easier to swap out one meal than to create a week's worth of meals from scratch.

I love that I'm doubling the main meal on Saturday to have enough leftovers to reimagine them into something else on Monday. It's such a gift to not have to really cook on my busiest workday of the week, but rather just assemble a meal.

I savor the rhythm of taking a full day off on Sunday (and the Saturday night before it) to rest. I feel like I've not only done the hard work of feeding my people, but I've done the soul-nourishing work of feeding myself with wholesome, thoughtful, and flavorful food without the side order of hustle that normally accompanies it.

Whether you use the weekly menus I've provided or use your family favorite meals and prep and cook in advance, you are predeciding, and if you live your life in any sort of overwhelm, this will be a huge step in lessening that.

As you start to find your own rhythms, rituals, and routines for fall and for Sabbath, give yourself grace to experiment and adjust. Allow the specific bounty your geographic area offers to influence your menu choices and modifications. Figure out which days have enough margin for you to do more preparing and predeciding, and then go for it.

When you sit down on Sabbath and have your first spoonful of soup, my prayer is that you will feel nourished in every possible way.

Here's to a season of new beginnings, my friend.

The Freedom of Predeciding

Since moving from Silicon Valley to an area that looks remarkably like Pooh's Hundred Acre Wood, our varied collection of strange tools has grown quickly.

We now own a log splitter, a wrench the length of a dachshund, a winch and lift for getting things on and off our truck without a hernia, and, to Roger's great delight, a flame thrower.

But the tool that elicits the most questions from guests must be the fruit picker with basket and extendable pole.

In our area, there are hundreds of acres of abandoned fruit trees. Our friend Susy invited us to go apple picking with her one fall afternoon. (This was after inviting her to come blackberry picking on our property. We have formed a mutual picking society, apparently.) If you get to the trees early enough in the season, you will be rewarded with the proverbial "low hanging fruit."

But if you're a little later in the season and looking for fall's harvest of apples, pears, and apricots, you're going to need that telescoping pole to get to the fruit that you want.

And it is a joy, an absolute *joy*, to go and collect those apples, pears, and apricots, and to plan our fall breakfasts, desserts, and dishes around the abundance of the season.

The other advantage? The season is deciding for us what we are going to eat.

In a world where we are making a thousand decisions a day, it's a gift to let our gardens, our farmers markets, and the prices at the supermarket determine what we'll be eating (and not eating).

Eating seasonally is just one aspect of predeciding. In the dead of winter, we eat apples instead of having strawberries flown in from exotic locations. I'd rather save my money and one day visit those exotic locations.

So as you decide to create one of the menus listed in this book, do the predeciding that is going to cause you the least amount of stress. Seasonal eating is one great way to employ predeciding; in spring, eat the strawberries, not the apples. In October, eat the pears, not the blueberries.

Another great way to lessen overwhelm and employ predeciding is to think about your four resources of time, space, money, and energy. I like to think of my four resources anytime I'm feeling overwhelmed and see which of those resources I have the most—and the least—of today.

I have been in short supply of each of these resources at one point in my life or another. From my tiny kitchen in Uji, Japan, where my "counter space" was a cutting board balanced on my lap, to those times as a mom of elementary kids when I was working full time and trying to keep all the balls in the air. Our resources change all the time—but that means that predeciding can help us meet those changing needs and take care of our people and ourselves, no matter what the circumstances are.

Here are some predeciding strategies so that you can figure out what you're going to eat early enough so that you're not having to panic at the last minute:

1. **When I'm feeling low on time: follow the menus exactly, in order, through the seasons.** You don't have a bunch of time to figure out a new menu plan, but you need to have food in the house that is easy to prepare and will get you through the week without a lot of hassle. Follow the menu down to the whipped cream on the dessert. Sometimes having someone (even if it's a book) boss you around is the lowest stress factor you can experience. Just make your meal plan, see what you already have on hand, buy the rest at the store, and don't stress.

2. **When I'm feeling low on space: figure out your abundance, and then pick a menu.** There have been times when I've overbought tomatoes, or our garden won't quit when it comes to zucchini. Maybe I bought a family pack of ground beef at Costco last week, and the budget is looking a little tight this week, so ground beef it is. Look through the menus and find one that uses up what you have on hand and then shop for the rest.

3. **When I'm feeling low on money: adjust.** Just because the menu plan calls for carrots doesn't mean that's the best choice for you and your people. Green beans are a fine choice to substitute for what's in the menu plan. Especially if they are already in your fridge.

4. **When I'm feeling low on energy: cook half a menu.** Sometimes having a whole morning of cooking is just too much. In those instances, I would suggest that you decide in advance that you'll just make the main, meaty meal for Saturday dinner, and the soup for Sunday lunch, and then buy a few dishes to put around those couple of meals.

Fall
Sabbath Experiences

Delicious autumn! My very soul is wedded to it, and if I were a bird
I would fly about the Earth seeking the successive autumns.

GEORGE ELIOT

1. Make a fall Sabbath altar or centerpiece to build the practice of noticing and honoring the season. Over the weeks add written prayers, golden leaves, and other objects you gather on walks.

2. Write a thought, psalm, poem, or your own Sabbath prayer.

3. Set out a gratitude jar and a pen and paper for your family to use during the month. Every couple of weeks, read the expressions of thanksgiving when you gather for your Sabbath day soup.

4. Light a candle and say a prayer for a friend who is hurting.

5. Invite your family, roommate, friends, or neighbors on a group walk. So many topics and thoughts rise up during a stroll. Savor this time of connection and mutual listening.

6. Get out the colored pens or crayons and coloring books or plain paper. Turn on background music and give yourself permission to doodle and play for 30–60 minutes. Invite your family to join in.

7. Take five minutes for a breathing meditation or breath prayer each day. Here is a simple breath prayer to get you started: inhale as you think, "I take in God's grace" and exhale as you think, "I breathe out compassion for myself and others." Another option: "I breathe in God's hope" and "I breathe out my fear today." Create your own.

8. Listen to an audiobook on an inspiring topic or a story that captures your imagination. Let words wash over you while you do nothing but enjoy the chance to receive refreshment. I love Wendell Berry.

9. Sabbath journaling for fall: Spend moments this season writing about the rhythms you want to bring into your life. How do you want to rest and nest to serve your body, mind, and spirit?

10. Fall, with its back-to-school vibe, is a great time to learn a new hobby. I bought a beginning crochet kit and spent some of my Sabbath day being bad at a new hobby I thoroughly enjoy.

Week One
Football

F ootball in a book about Sabbath? Yep. It's happening right here. I love a big gathering of friends in the fall. If a football game happens to be on in the background, as long as I can still talk with the rest of the non-fans in the kitchen, I think it's a lovely way to spend an afternoon. Joy, celebration, and community score big.

For this week, I made sure all the food for lunch and dinner could run together to cover both meals—and if you're hosting guests, consider whether you need to double the soup recipe. Warming devices, such as slow cookers, can help you feed the grazing multitudes with ease.

Week 1 Menu

Saturday
Oven-Baked Meatloaf
Creamy Yukon Gold Mashed
    Potatoes
Roasted Green Beans
    (no recipe)
Dessert:
Nutella-Stuffed Brownies

Sunday
Breakfast:
Overnight French Toast
Lunch:
White Bean Chicken Chili
Apple Almond Salad
Air Fryer Baked Potatoes
Dinner:
Green Chile Enchilada Casserole
Queso Dip with Corn Chips
Cucumber, Tomato, and
    Avocado Salad

Monday
Remixed Meatloaf Spaghetti
Cheesy Garlic Bread
Italian Chopped Salad

Tuesday
Air Fryer Baked Potatoes with
    White Bean Chicken Chili
Cucumber, Tomato, and
    Avocado Salad

Wednesday
Leftovers or frozen meal of choice

Thursday
Dinner out

Friday
Pizza night!

Sabbath Soup

White Bean Chicken Chili

Prep Time: 5 minutes • Cook Time: 25 minutes • Yield: 4 bowls or 8 cups

Ingredients

2 T. vegetable oil

1 yellow onion, chopped

3 cloves garlic, minced

2 (14.5 oz.) cans chicken broth

4 (10 oz.) cans Ro*Tel mild diced tomatoes and green chilies

½ tsp. dried oregano

½ tsp. ground coriander seed

¼ tsp. ground cumin

1 lb. diced cooked chicken

1 (16 oz.) can cannellini beans

2 ears fresh corn, cut from the cob, or 1 (15 oz.) can corn (drained), or 1 ½ cups frozen corn kernels

Salt and pepper, to taste

Directions

1. In a soup pot, heat the vegetable oil and sauté the onion over medium heat until soft, about 5 to 7 minutes. Add in the garlic and continue to sauté for 1 additional minute.

2. Pour chicken broth into the pan. Then add the tomatoes, oregano, coriander, and cumin. Bring to a boil and simmer for 10 minutes.

3. Add in chicken, beans, corn, and salt and pepper. Simmer on low for 10 minutes. Taste, and add more seasoning if desired.

4. Serve with tortilla chips, lime, and avocado slices.

Oven-Baked Meatloaf

Prep Time: 15 minutes
Cook Time: 55 minutes
Yield: 8 servings

Ingredients

1 tsp. unsalted butter
1 medium yellow onion, diced
2 large eggs (or 3 small)
¾ cup whole milk
¾ cup Italian breadcrumbs
2 lbs. lean ground beef (80/20)
2 tsp. dried parsley
1 tsp. Italian seasoning
1 tsp. kosher salt
1 tsp. black pepper, adjust to taste
½ cup ketchup
1 tsp. Worcestershire sauce
2 T. brown sugar

Directions

1. Preheat the oven to 350°F. Prepare a rimmed baking pan by lining it with aluminum foil and lightly coating it with cooking spray.
2. In a small pan, melt the butter over medium-low heat and sauté the onion until tender and lightly browned. Remove from heat and allow to cool.
3. In a separate bowl, whisk together the eggs, milk, and breadcrumbs. Let this mixture sit for approximately 5 minutes to thicken slightly.
4. To the egg mixture, add the ground beef, cooled onion, parsley, Italian seasoning, salt, and black pepper. Mix until just combined.
5. Shape the meat mixture into an 8 × 4-inch loaf on the prepared baking pan.
6. Bake the meatloaf in the preheated oven for 40 minutes.
7. While the meatloaf is in the oven, prepare the sauce by mixing together the ketchup, Worcestershire sauce, and brown sugar.
8. After the initial 40 minutes of baking, remove the meatloaf from the oven and evenly spread the sauce over the top. Return to the oven and bake for an additional 10 to 15 minutes, or until the meatloaf reaches an internal temperature of 160°F.
9. Allow the meatloaf to rest for about 10 minutes before slicing.

Creamy Yukon Gold Mashed Potatoes

Prep Time: 15 minutes
Cook Time: 20 minutes
Yield: 8 servings

Ingredients

3 lbs. Yukon Gold potatoes
1 cup whole milk (or half-and-half for a richer texture)
½ cup unsalted butter
Salt and freshly ground black pepper, to taste
Optional: minced garlic, fresh herbs (like chives or parsley) for garnish

Directions

1. Start by washing and peeling the potatoes. Cut them into uniform chunks, about 2 inches in size.
2. Place the potato chunks in a large pot and fill with enough water to cover them. Add a generous pinch of salt to the water. Bring the water to a boil over high heat, then reduce to a simmer. Cook the potatoes until they are fork-tender, usually around 15 to 20 minutes.
3. While the potatoes are boiling, gently heat the milk and butter in a small saucepan over low heat. Stir occasionally until the butter is melted. Keep this mixture warm.
4. Once the potatoes are cooked, drain the water and return the potatoes to the pot.
5. Slowly add the warm milk and butter mixture to the potatoes while mashing. Use a potato masher or ricer for best results.
6. Season with salt and pepper, to taste. If you're using minced garlic, you can add it here.
7. Gently mix all the ingredients until you achieve a creamy texture. If the mixture seems too dry, you can add a little more milk.
8. Transfer the mashed potatoes to a serving bowl. If desired, garnish with freshly chopped herbs.

Nutella-Stuffed Brownies

Prep Time: 10 minutes
Cook Time: 40 to 45 minutes
Yield: 8 servings

Ingredients

Brownie Batter

   1 cup unsalted butter
   2 cups granulated sugar
   4 large eggs
   1 tsp. vanilla extract
   1 cup all-purpose flour
   ½ cup cocoa powder
   ¼ tsp. salt
   ½ tsp. baking powder

Nutella Filling

   1 cup Nutella
   ½ cup cream cheese, softened
   1 egg
   2 T. sugar

Directions

1. Preheat your oven to 350°F. Grease a 9 × 13-inch baking dish or line it with parchment paper.
2. Start by making the brownie batter: In a medium saucepan, melt the butter over low heat. Remove from heat and stir in the sugar. Once the sugar is incorporated, stir in the eggs and vanilla extract.
3. In a separate bowl, combine the flour, cocoa powder, salt, and baking powder. Gradually add this to the butter mixture and stir until well combined.
4. Make the Nutella filling: In a separate bowl, combine the Nutella, cream cheese, egg, and sugar. Stir until everything is smooth and well mixed.
5. Pour half of the brownie batter into the prepared baking dish. Spread the Nutella filling over the batter, then pour the rest of the brownie batter on top, spreading it to cover the Nutella filling as best as you can.
6. Using a butter knife, gently swirl the layers together to create a marbled effect.
7. Bake for about 40 to 45 minutes, or until a

toothpick inserted into the center comes out with a few moist crumbs.
8. Let the brownies cool completely in the baking dish before cutting them into squares.

Overnight French Toast

This recipe is great to make with a crusty bread. Sourdough or French breads are great, but my favorite is brioche. For an extra special treat, serve this French toast with fresh berries and a side of bacon.

Prep Time: 10 minutes, plus 4 hours or overnight in the fridge
Cook Time: 45 to 60 minutes
Yield: 8 servings

Ingredients

   1 loaf crusty bread
   8 large eggs
   2 cups whole milk
   ½ cup heavy cream
   2 T. vanilla extract
   1 tsp. cinnamon
   ½ tsp. nutmeg
   ½ tsp. salt
   ¼ cup sugar
   ½ cup brown sugar

Topping

   ½ cup all-purpose flour
   ½ cup packed light brown sugar
   1 tsp. ground cinnamon
   ¼ tsp. salt
   ½ cup cold unsalted butter, diced
   Warm maple syrup and butter, for serving

Directions

1. Grease a 9 × 13-inch pan with cooking spray. Cut bread into 1-inch chunks and spread evenly in pan.
2. In a medium bowl, mix together eggs, milk, cream, vanilla, cinnamon, nutmeg, salt, and sugars. Pour evenly over bread. Gently squish down the bread (using a food prep glove if you like) so that it's completely soaked in the mixture.
3. Cover the pan with plastic wrap and place in the fridge overnight (or for at least 4 hours).
4. Combine all the topping ingredients except

butter in a medium bowl. Using a pastry blender or a large fork, cut the butter into the mixture until it resembles small pebbles. Cover and refrigerate overnight.

5. The next day, preheat the oven to 350°F.

6. Uncover the baking dish and place the topping evenly over the bread.

7. Bake for 45 to 60 minutes or until a clean tooth-pick comes out.

Apple Almond Salad

Prep Time: 15 minutes
Yield: 4 main servings or 8 side servings

Ingredients

6 cups mixed greens
2 apples, cored and thinly sliced
½ cup almonds, sliced and toasted
¼ cup dried cranberries
¼ cup blue cheese or feta cheese, crumbled
¼ cup Balsamic Vinaigrette

Directions

1. In a large salad bowl, combine the mixed greens, apples, almonds, and dried cranberries.

2. Sprinkle the cheese on top.

3. Drizzle the Balsamic Vinaigrette dressing over the salad and gently toss to combine. Serve immediately.

Balsamic Vinaigrette

Ingredients

½ cup extra-virgin olive oil
¼ cup balsamic vinegar
1 tsp. honey
1 tsp. Dijon mustard
Salt and freshly ground pepper, to taste

Directions

Combine all ingredients in a jar with a tight-fitting lid and shake until well combined.

Air Fryer Baked Potatoes

Prep Time: 5 minutes
Cook Time: 40 minutes
Yield: 4 servings

Ingredients

4 baking potatoes
Olive oil
Sea salt
Pepper

Directions

1. Preheat your air fryer to 400°F.

2. Pierce your potatoes with a fork several times. Rub the outsides with olive oil, salt, and pepper. Place the potatoes on the trivet and air fry for 20 minutes.

3. With a pair of tongs, flip the potatoes over and continue to air fry for another 20 minutes. Remove from the air fryer and let sit for 5 minutes before serving.

4. Serve with your choice of toppings.

Note: I use sea salt for almost everything because it has larger particle sizes and gives a richer flavor.

Green Chile Enchilada Casserole

This Green Chile Enchilada Casserole is hearty and comforting, perfect for a weeknight dinner. The addition of cilantro gives a fresh, herby twist to this delicious, cheesy casserole. Enjoy!

Prep Time: 15 minutes
Cook Time: 30 minutes
Yield: 4 servings

Ingredients

1 (10.5 oz.) can cream of chicken soup
½ cup sour cream
1 (15 oz.) can green chili enchilada sauce, divided
Salt and pepper, to taste
2 cups cooked shredded chicken
¼ cup chopped fresh cilantro
8 (7 or 8-inch) flour tortillas (or 12 6-inch corn tortillas for a more traditional twist)
2 cups Mexican blend shredded cheese, divided
Optional toppings: chopped black olives, extra sour cream, salsa, shredded lettuce, diced tomatoes

Directions

1. Preheat your oven to 350°F and lightly grease an 8 × 8-inch baking dish.
2. In a large bowl, mix together the cream of chicken soup, sour cream, ⅓ cup of the enchilada sauce, and season with ¼ teaspoon each of salt and pepper. Add the shredded chicken and cilantro, and stir until evenly combined.
3. Pour ¼ cup of the remaining enchilada sauce into the bottom of the prepared baking dish, spreading it out to ensure the whole bottom is covered. Tear up 3 of the tortillas and evenly distribute them over the sauce.
4. Spread a third of the chicken mixture over the torn tortillas. Repeat with another layer of torn tortillas, chicken mixture, ⅓ cup of enchilada sauce, and half of the cheese.
5. For the final layer, distribute the remaining torn tortillas, chicken mixture, enchilada sauce, and top with the remaining cheese.
6. Bake in the preheated oven for 25 to 30 minutes, or until the cheese is beautifully melted and bubbling.
7. Remove the casserole from the oven and let it rest for 5 minutes before serving. This allows the flavors to meld and the cheese to set slightly.
8. Serve the Green Chile Enchilada Casserole warm with your choice of toppings.

Queso Dip with Corn Chips

This easy dish is a favorite when I have friends over. I like to use Kraft American cheese, shredded Mexican blend cheese, and Ro*Tel tomatoes (found in the Hispanic or international food aisle). For a shortcut for mincing garlic, I love the frozen squares of garlic by Dorot.

Prep Time: 5 minutes
Cook Time: 18 minutes
Yield: 12 servings

Ingredients

1 cup water
¾ lb. American cheese
8 oz. cream cheese, softened
1 cup shredded cheese
1 cup salsa or 1 (10 oz.) can Ro*Tel diced tomatoes and green chilies
1 T. butter
1 T. milk
1 T. minced garlic
1 T. dried oregano
Corn chips, to serve

Directions

1. Add the water to your Instant Pot and place the trivet in the bottom.
2. Add all ingredients to an Instant Pot–safe bowl (such as stainless steel, CorningWare, or Pyrex bakeware) and wrap the whole bowl, top and bottom, with foil.
3. Place the lid on the Instant Pot, make sure the valve is sealed, and set the machine for 18 minutes on manual high pressure.
4. After the timer goes off, release the pressure immediately.
5. Remove the lid once all pressure has been released.
6. Remove the aluminum foil and whisk the dip until smooth.
7. Serve with corn chips and other dippers of choice.

Cucumber, Tomato, and Avocado Salad

Prep Time: 15 minutes
Yield: 4 main servings or 8 side servings

Ingredients

2 cucumbers, diced
2 tomatoes, diced
2 avocados, diced
¼ red onion, thinly sliced
¼ cup chopped fresh cilantro
¼ cup olive oil
2 T. fresh lime juice
1 tsp. honey
Salt and pepper, to taste

Directions

1. In a large salad bowl, combine the cucumbers, tomatoes, avocados, red onion, and cilantro.
2. In a small bowl, whisk together the olive oil, lime juice, and honey.
3. Drizzle the dressing over the salad, season with a dash of salt and pepper, and gently toss to combine. Serve immediately.

Note: This salad is best consumed the day it is made to prevent the avocados from browning.

Remixed Meatloaf Spaghetti

This Remixed Meatloaf Spaghetti is a fun twist on traditional spaghetti and meat sauce, and a clever way to transform leftover meatloaf into a whole new meal. Enjoy!

Prep Time: 10 minutes
Cook Time: 20 minutes
Yield: 4 servings

Ingredients

4 cups cooked spaghetti (or 8 oz. uncooked)
1 T. olive oil
1 small onion, finely chopped
2 to 3 cloves garlic, minced
2 cups crumbled or diced leftover meatloaf
3 cups pasta sauce
Salt and pepper, to taste
Optional: grated Parmesan cheese and fresh basil leaves

Directions

1. If using dry pasta, prepare it according to package instructions.
2. Meanwhile, in a large skillet or saucepan, heat olive oil over medium heat. Add the onion and garlic. Sauté until the onion becomes translucent and the garlic is fragrant, about 2 to 3 minutes.
3. Incorporate the meatloaf chunks into the skillet. Stir to combine and cook for about 2 to 3 minutes to reheat the meatloaf.
4. Add pasta sauce.
5. Season with salt and pepper. Stir well.
6. Reduce heat to low, cover, and let the sauce simmer for about 10 to 15 minutes to allow the flavors to meld together.
7. Either add the spaghetti directly to the saucepan and toss to combine, or serve the meat sauce over individual portions of spaghetti.
8. If desired, garnish with Parmesan cheese and basil leaves before serving.

Cheesy Garlic Bread

Prep Time: 10 minutes
Cook Time: 15 minutes
Yield: 8 servings

Ingredients

½ cup unsalted butter, softened
3 cloves garlic, minced
1 loaf French bread, halved lengthwise
2 cups shredded mozzarella cheese
¼ cup chopped fresh parsley

Directions

1. Preheat the oven to 375°F.
2. In a small bowl, mix together the butter and garlic.
3. Spread the garlic butter evenly over the cut sides of the bread.
4. Sprinkle the shredded mozzarella over the butter.
5. Place the bread on a baking sheet and bake for 10 minutes, or until the cheese is melted.
6. Switch the oven to broil and cook for another 2 to 3 minutes, until the cheese is bubbly and golden.
7. Sprinkle with parsley before serving.

Italian Chopped Salad

Prep Time: 20 minutes
Yield: 4 main servings or 8 side servings

Ingredients

1 head iceberg lettuce, chopped
1 red onion, thinly sliced
1 cup cherry tomatoes, halved
1 (15 oz.) can chickpeas, drained and rinsed
1 cup pearl mozzarella balls
1 cup cubed provolone cheese
½ cup sliced pepperoncini
½ cup cubed genoa salami
½ cup chopped sun-dried tomatoes
½ cup Italian dressing
Salt and pepper, to taste

Directions

1. In a large salad bowl, combine the lettuce, red onion, cherry tomatoes, chickpeas, pearl mozzarella, provolone cheese, pepperoncini, salami, and sun-dried tomatoes.
2. Drizzle the dressing over the salad, season with a dash of salt and pepper, and gently toss to combine. Serve immediately.

Italian Dressing

Ingredients

½ cup extra-virgin olive oil
¼ cup red wine vinegar
1 tsp. honey
1 tsp. dried oregano
1 tsp. dried basil
½ tsp. garlic powder
Salt and freshly ground pepper, to taste

Directions

Shake all ingredients together in a jar until well combined.

Homemade Pizza

We love a pizza night for big crowds, and this recipe for pizza dough never disappoints. A couple of things we've learned: Go lightly on the sauce and toppings so that the crust doesn't become soggy (think of a pizza that you would get on the streets of Italy. Excellent ingredients, but used sparingly). We use Tipo 00 flour, which is more heat resistant than a regular flour. This will keep your crust from burning while making sure it gets cooked all the way through.

Prep Time: 15 minutes, plus 2½ hours to rise
Cook Time: 10 minutes
Yield: 2 or 3 small pizzas

Ingredients

2 tsp. active dry yeast
1 tsp. sugar
1⅓ cups plus 1½ T. lukewarm water
3½ cups Tipo 00 flour
2 tsp. sea salt
1 T. olive oil
Cornmeal for work surface when rolling dough
Toppings: Prepared marinara sauce, cheese of choice (shredded or in small chunks), small pieces of cooked or cured meat, vegetables, and any other favorite toppings.

Directions

1. In a small bowl, dissolve the yeast and sugar in the lukewarm water. Allow it to sit for about 10 minutes until it starts to bubble slightly.
2. In the bowl of your stand mixer, combine the flour and salt.

Those who harvest it
will eat it and praise the LORD.

ISAIAH 62:9

3. Make a well in the center of the flour and pour in the yeast mixture and olive oil.
4. Using the dough hook attachment, mix on a low speed until the dough starts to come together.
5. Once the dough has formed, increase the speed to medium and knead the dough with the mixer for about 5 minutes, or until the dough is smooth and elastic. The dough should be a little sticky, but if it's too sticky, you can add a bit more flour.
6. Transfer the dough to a clean, lightly oiled large bowl and cover it with a damp cloth. Allow it to rise in a warm, draft-free place for about 1½ to 2 hours, or until it has doubled in size. (I like to stick it in the oven with the oven light turned on.)
7. After the dough has risen, gently punch it down to remove any air bubbles and divide it into 2 or 3 pieces. Shape each piece into a ball, place the dough on a greased cookie sheet, cover it with a damp cloth, and let the dough rest for another 20 to 30 minutes.
8. Preheat your oven to its highest temperature (usually around 500 to 550°F). If you're using a pizza stone, place it in the oven now to preheat as well.
9. Roll out each dough ball on a floured surface to your desired thickness. (We like to cover the surface with cornmeal so that the dough doesn't stick to the surface.)
Add your pizza sauce and toppings (don't use too many, or it will be hard for the dough to cook all the way through), then transfer the pizza onto the heated stone or onto a baking sheet.
10. Bake for about 10 to 12 minutes, or until the crust is golden and the cheese is bubbly and slightly browned.

Note: If you are fortunate enough to have a pizza oven, bake the pizzas at the maximum temperature on the pizza oven (often around 900°F) for about 90 seconds.

A Prayer Over the Rhythm of Sabbath and Seasons

Lord, Your rhythms of Sabbath
and seasons, gratefulness and sustenance,
savor and service, are how I honor You.
Help me embrace and embody
Your rhythms so that I may know
peace and wholeness.

As I follow Your rhythms,
may my table lead others to You,
to peace and wholeness.

Lord, may I see bountiful food
and my vibrant community
as the gifts You made them to be.

Please, help me to begin from where
I am in the kitchen. I don't want to
be hindered by intimidation.

May grace cover mistakes, make laughter
bubble from the kitchen,
and lead to full tables and full hearts.

Please strengthen me to accept
the invitation to Sabbath;
it is one of Your kindest gifts to me.

Lord, may Your rhythms
be my guide
to experience life to the full.

May it be so.

Week Two
Apple Picking

I s there anything more quintessentially fall than apple picking? Okay, maybe visiting a pumpkin patch, but just go with me here.

There are a lot of abandoned orchards near our house where we can bring a couple of Home Depot buckets and telescoping fruit picker poles, and then come home with dozens of apples. I grab my electric apple/potato peeler and get down to work. Then we eat apple everything for a few weeks. What we can't eat, we freeze: Dip the apple slices into lemon water (about a tablespoon of lemon per gallon of water), place slices on a baking sheet without the sides touching, and then freeze. Put the frozen apples into a freezer bag and use for months to come.

I adore apples and love to feature them in as many dishes as possible.

Week 2 Menu

Saturday

Oven-Roasted Chicken

Stuffing (no recipe)

Air Fryer Zucchini with Herbs
  and Parmesan

Dessert:

Apple Cake

Sunday

Breakfast:

Overnight Oatmeal with
  Apples and Apricots

Lunch:

Chicken Chipotle Black
  Bean Soup

Taco Salad

Tortillas (no recipe)

Dinner:

Chicken and Vegetable Stuffed
  Twice-Baked Potatoes

Monday

Greek Yogurt Chicken Salad with
  Apples and Almonds

Crackers (no recipe)

Tuesday

Pulled Pork Quesadillas

Chicken Chipotle Black Bean
  Soup

Taco Salad

Wednesday

Leftovers or frozen meal of choice

Thursday

Dinner out

Friday

Pizza night!

Sabbath Soup

Chicken Chipotle Black Bean Soup

Prep Time: 10 minutes • Cook Time: 30 minutes • Yield: 4 bowls or 8 cups

Ingredients

2 (15 oz.) cans black beans, drained and rinsed, divided

1 (7 oz.) can chipotle peppers in adobo sauce, divided

2 cups low-sodium chicken broth, divided

1 T. avocado or olive oil

½ medium yellow onion, finely chopped

5 cloves garlic, minced

1 (15 oz.) can fire-roasted corn, drained

1 cup chunky salsa

1 tsp. ground cumin

½ tsp. smoked paprika

Salt and freshly ground black pepper, to taste

2 cups cooked, shredded chicken

½ cup Greek yogurt or sour cream

1 large heirloom tomato, diced

Fresh cilantro leaves, roughly chopped

Lime wedges, tortilla chips, and shredded cheese, to serve

Directions

1. In a food processor, combine 1 can of black beans, 2 chipotle peppers with their sauce, and 1 cup of chicken broth. Process until smooth, then set aside.

2. Heat the oil in a large Dutch oven or heavy-bottomed pot over medium heat. Add the onion and sauté until soft and translucent, about 7 minutes.

3. Stir in the minced garlic and cook until fragrant, about 1 minute. Pour in the pureed black bean mixture, the remaining can of black beans, remaining chicken broth, salsa, corn, cumin, and smoked paprika. Stir to combine and bring the mixture to a gentle boil.

4. Reduce the heat to low and simmer the soup for 15 minutes, stirring occasionally. Taste and season with salt and freshly ground black pepper as needed.

5. Finely chop the remaining chipotle peppers and stir them into the soup along with the shredded chicken. Cook for an additional 5 minutes to allow the flavors to meld and the chicken to heat through.

6. Ladle the soup into bowls and top each serving with a dollop of sour cream or Greek yogurt, diced tomato, and a sprinkle of fresh cilantro leaves. Serve with lime wedges on the side to squeeze over the soup.

7. I love to serve this with some tortilla chips and shredded cheese.

Oven-Roasted Chicken

Prep Time: 10 minutes
Cook Time: 1 hour and 40 minutes
Yield: 4 to 6 servings

Ingredients

1 whole chicken, giblets removed, rinsed and patted dry
Cooking spray
Salt (1 tsp. per pound of chicken)
Pepper (⅓ tsp. per pound of chicken)
6 garlic cloves, cut in half
4 T. butter
Garlic salt and pepper

Directions

1. Preheat your oven to 425°F.
2. Place the chicken in a roasting pan covered in cooking spray, breast side up. Season the chicken cavity with salt and pepper, then place the garlic inside. Adjust the suggested levels if you like a more seasoned chicken. Chop the butter into pats and place them all over the top of the chicken. Sprinkle the skin with garlic salt and pepper.
3. Roast until the chicken's internal temperature reaches 165°F. Let it roast for an hour and then keep checking the internal temperature until it reaches 165°F. Let it sit for 20 minutes before serving.

Air Fryer Zucchini with Herbs and Parmesan

Prep Time: 10 minutes
Cook Time: 10 minutes
Yield: 4 servings

Ingredients

2 medium zucchinis, sliced into rounds or half-moons
2 T. olive oil
1 tsp. dried oregano
1 tsp. dried basil
Salt and pepper, to taste
¼ cup grated Parmesan cheese
Optional: Fresh parsley, for garnish
Optional: Lemon wedges, for serving

Directions

1. Preheat air fryer to 375°F.
2. In a mixing bowl, combine the zucchini, olive oil, oregano, basil, and salt and pepper. Toss well to coat the zucchini evenly.
3. Sprinkle the Parmesan cheese over the zucchini and toss again to make sure the slices are evenly coated.
4. Lay the seasoned zucchini slices in a single layer in the air fryer basket. You may need to cook them in batches, depending on the size of your air fryer.
5. Cook the zucchini at 375°F for 7 to 10 minutes, or until they are tender and slightly golden on the edges. Give the basket a shake halfway through to ensure even cooking.
6. Once cooked, you can garnish the zucchini with parsley and serve with lemon wedges if desired.

Apple Cake

This cake is amazing both on its own or served with ice cream (or any kind of cream) and strong coffee. If you are serving this to guests, time it to finish baking right while they are coming through the door. Half the delight of this cake is the smell wafting through your house.

Prep Time: 15 minutes
Cook Time: 60 minutes
Yield: 16 servings

Ingredients

2 cups sugar
½ cup oil
2 eggs
4 cups peeled and diced apples
2 cups flour
2 tsp. baking soda
1 tsp. nutmeg
2 tsp. cinnamon
1 tsp. salt

Directions

1. Preheat your oven to 350°F. Grease a 9 × 13-inch pan.
2. Combine sugar, oil, and eggs in a large bowl, stirring until well mixed.

3. Stir in apples. Sift together flour, baking soda, nutmeg, cinnamon, and salt, then add to the bowl.
4. Stir all ingredients together to form a batter until the flour mixture is thoroughly mixed into the wet ingredients. Pour into greased pan. Bake one hour, or until golden and cake is set.

Overnight Oatmeal with Apples and Apricots

Some days I need my breakfast to be waiting for me—amazing, hot, and ready to go. What I don't eat on the first day I just refrigerate and then reheat throughout the week. I also like to put a little sweetener in the oatmeal. Dealer's choice! You can add it into the slow cooker with the raw oats, or add it as a topping once the oats are cooked.

Prep Time: 5 minutes
Cook Time: 8 hours
Yield: 6 servings

Ingredients

1½ cups steel-cut oats
4 cups water
2 cups milk, any kind you like (I use nonfat)
1 large tart apple, peeled and chopped
1 cup chopped dried apricots
2 tsp. pure vanilla extract
1½ tsp. ground cinnamon
½ tsp. ground nutmeg
½ tsp. kosher salt
Sweetener of your choice: brown sugar, white sugar, honey, or agave.
Toppings of your choice: blueberries, raspberries, blackberries, granola, shredded coconut, sliced almonds, chopped pecans, Greek yogurt

Directions

1. Place all the ingredients except the toppings in the bottom of a 4- to 6-quart slow cooker, then stir to combine. Cover and cook on low for 8 hours. Remove the cover and stir. Taste and see if you need to add anything else, like more vanilla or cinnamon.
2. I like to keep oatmeal in the fridge for up to a week. Place it in a big tub, and reheat individual servings in the microwave for 2 minutes and 30 seconds.

Taco Salad

Prep Time: 30 minutes
Cook Time: 10 minutes
Yield: 4 main servings or 8 side servings

Ingredients

1 lb. ground beef
1 packet taco seasoning (about 1 oz. or 3 T.)
6 cups chopped romaine lettuce
1 (15 oz.) can black beans, drained and rinsed
1 cup corn kernels
1 cup cherry tomatoes, halved
1 cup shredded cheddar cheese
¼ cup sliced black olives (optional)
1 avocado, diced
½ cup sour cream
½ cup salsa
Salt and pepper, to taste

Directions

1. In a large skillet, cook the ground beef over medium heat until browned. Drain off any excess fat.
2. Stir in the taco seasoning, following the package directions.
3. In a large salad bowl, arrange the romaine lettuce. Top with the cooked beef, black beans, corn, cherry tomatoes, cheddar cheese, black olives, and avocado.
4. In a small bowl, combine the sour cream and salsa to create a dressing. Drizzle the dressing over the salad, sprinkle with a dash of salt and pepper, and gently toss to combine. Serve immediately.

But when you give a banquet, invite the poor, the crippled, the lame, the blind.
LUKE 14:13

Chicken and Vegetable Stuffed Twice-Baked Potatoes

Prep Time: 10 minutes
Cook Time: 30 minutes
Yield: 6 servings

Ingredients

6 baked potatoes
1 T. cooking oil or butter
1 cup diced onion
1 cup diced mushrooms
2 cups leftover cooked chicken
2 cups leftover air-fried zucchini
2 cups shredded cheddar cheese
Salt and pepper, to taste
Sour cream, to taste

Directions

1. Preheat your oven to 375°F.
2. Cut the baked potatoes in half lengthwise and scoop out and set aside the flesh, leaving a thin layer of potato in the skin.
3. Heat the butter or oil in a deep skillet or Dutch oven. Add the onion, and sauté over medium heat for 4 minutes. Add in the mushrooms and sauté for another 4 minutes, or until the onion is golden brown. Shred the chicken and chop the zucchini into small pieces. Add the chicken, zucchini, and scooped-out potato flesh to the onion and mushroom mixture, and mix well.
4. Add some shredded cheese to the mix, along with a sprinkling of salt and pepper. Mix well, then turn off the heat for the skillet.
5. Spoon the mixture back into the potato skins and top with more cheese.
6. Bake until the cheese is melted and bubbly, about 15 to 20 minutes.
7. Serve hot with a dollop of sour cream.

Greek Yogurt Chicken Salad with Apples and Almonds

This dish is versatile and can be enjoyed in several ways. It's a great way to use up leftover chicken and perfect for those warmer days when you want something light and satisfying. You can serve it on crackers or warm pita bread for a quick and easy lunch. For a lighter option, you could serve it atop a bed of mixed greens. Pair the chicken salad with some fresh grapes on the side for a refreshing and balanced meal!

Prep Time: 15 minutes
Yield: 4 servings

Ingredients

2 cups leftover chicken, shredded
Juice of 1 lemon
1½ cups nonfat Greek yogurt
1 T. honey
½ tart apple, chopped
½ cup slivered almonds
½ cup dried cranberries
Salt and pepper, to taste
Optional: Crackers, warm pita bread, and grapes for serving

Directions

1. Place the shredded chicken in a large mixing bowl.
2. Squeeze the juice of the lemon over the chicken. This will not only add a tangy freshness to the salad but will also keep the chicken moist.
3. Add the Greek yogurt and honey to the bowl. Stir until the chicken is evenly coated.
4. Next, add the apple, almonds, and dried cranberries to the bowl. Stir to combine all the ingredients well.
5. Season with salt and pepper, to taste. Your chicken salad is now ready to serve with crackers, pita, grapes, or however you like it!

Pulled Pork Quesadillas

Enjoy these Pulled Pork Quesadillas as a delicious and satisfying way to use up leftover pulled pork.

Prep Time: 10 minutes
Yield: 4 servings

Ingredients

1 yellow onion, chopped
8 flour tortillas
2 cups leftover pulled pork
2 cups Mexican blend shredded cheese
Sour cream and salsa, for serving

Directions

1. Heat a nonstick pan over medium heat and add a little bit of cooking spray or olive oil. Sauté the onion until it becomes translucent and slightly caramelized, about 5 to 7 minutes. Remove the onion from the pan and set aside.
2. Place one tortilla in the same pan and top it evenly with a quarter of the pork.
3. Sprinkle a quarter of the onion over the pork.
4. Spread a quarter of the cheese over the onion.
5. Place another tortilla on top and press it down gently.
6. Cook the quesadilla on medium heat until the bottom tortilla is golden brown and crispy, about 3 to 4 minutes.
7. Carefully flip the quesadilla over and cook on the other side until it is also golden brown and the cheese is melted, about 3 to 4 minutes more.
8. Remove the quesadilla from the pan and let it cool for a couple of minutes before cutting it into quarters.
9. Repeat the process with the remaining tortillas, pork, onion, and cheese.
10. Serve the pulled pork quesadillas with sour cream and salsa on the side for dipping.

*"Bear in mind that the L*ORD *has given you the Sabbath;
that is why on the sixth day he gives you bread for two days.
Everyone is to stay where he is on the seventh day; no one is to go out."
So the people rested on the seventh day.
The people of Israel called the bread manna.*

EXODUS 16:29-31

A Prayer for the Fall Season

Lord, I welcome fall
to my home and to my table.
I open my heart and
my hands to
the rhythms
You have created.

Lord, help me to
see the gifts
of this season.

I ask that fall brings
a fresh creative
spark through
pumpkins,
soups, and
spice.

May my home
be a place of
warmth and joy—
because You
are with me
and go before me.

May all who
eat at this table
be reminded
of Your constant provision
in this season
and the seasons to follow.

Week Three
Comfort Food

Do you ever just need a week of guaranteed winners? Sometimes, when I'm especially busy, I just need to know that everything I make or buy is going to be a crowd pleaser and work. This is that menu. Every one of these recipes is going to be a winner.

Week 3 Menu

Saturday

Slow Cooker Ham with
   Pineapple Glaze
Mac 'n' Cheese
Asparagus (no recipe)
Dessert:
Chocolate Chip Cookies

Sunday

Breakfast:
Quiche (Spinach)

Lunch:
Taco Soup
Harvest Salad
Corn Bread Muffins

Dinner:
Ravioli with Alfredo sauce
   (store-bought)
Butternut Squash

Monday

Cuban Sandwiches
Mac 'n' Cheese
Harvest Salad

Tuesday

Taco Soup
Cheese and Veggie Quesadillas

Wednesday

Leftovers or frozen meal of choice

Thursday

Dinner out

Friday

Pizza night!

Sabbath Soup

Taco Soup

Prep Time: 10 minutes • Cook Time: 8 hours • Yield: 4 bowls or 8 cups

Ingredients

1 lb. ground beef

1 onion, chopped

1 (15 oz.) can kidney beans

3 (15 oz.) cans stewed tomatoes

1 (15 oz.) can tomato sauce

2 (15 oz.) cans ranch style beans
(1 with jalapeños)

1 (10 oz.) can Ro*Tel mild diced
tomatoes and green chilies

1 packet (1 oz. or 3 T.) taco
seasoning mix

1 (1 oz.) packet ranch dressing
mix

8 flour tortillas

Oil for frying

Directions

1. In a frying pan, brown the ground beef with the onion. Put beef and onion mixture into a Crock-Pot or slow cooker. Add all other ingredients, except the flour tortillas. Cook all day, about 8 hours or so.

2. Right before serving, cut flour tortillas into fourths and fry in a thin layer of hot oil. Serve with Taco Soup.

Slow Cooker Ham with Pineapple Glaze

Prep Time: 15 minutes
Cook Time: 4 to 6 hours
Yield: 8 to 10 servings

Ingredients

- 2 cups pineapple juice
- 1 (5 to 7 lb.) fully-cooked ham
- 10 whole cloves
- 1 cup brown sugar
- 1 T. Dijon mustard
- 1 T. balsamic vinegar
- 1 T. honey
- 2 T. cornstarch

Directions

1. Using a sharp knife, score the ham in a diamond pattern, making cuts about ¼ inch deep. Insert the whole cloves into the intersections of the cuts.
2. Place the ham flat side down in the slow cooker. Pour the pineapple juice over the ham, making sure it coats all sides and gets into the cuts that you made.
3. In a small bowl, combine the brown sugar, Dijon mustard, balsamic vinegar, and honey. Using a spatula or your hands (I like to keep disposable gloves on hand—no pun intended—for just such jobs), spread the glaze evenly over the top and sides of the ham.
4. Cover the slow cooker with the lid and cook on low for 4 to 6 hours, basting the ham with the juices every 2 hours, if possible. The ham is done when it reaches an internal temperature of 140°F when measured with a meat thermometer.
5. Carefully remove the ham from the slow cooker and transfer it to a serving dish. Tent the ham loosely with aluminum foil and let it rest for 15 to 20 minutes to allow the juices to redistribute.
6. Meanwhile, pour the juices from the slow cooker into a saucepan (you can use a strainer to get all the big chunks). Bring the juices to a boil. Remove 2 tablespoons of the juice to a small bowl, and whisk in the cornstarch to create a slurry. Gradually pour it back into the boiling juices, whisking constantly to prevent lumps and form nice glaze. Once the slurry is fully incorporated, reduce the heat to low and simmer, stirring occasionally, for about 5 minutes or until it thickens to your desired consistency.
7. Discard the cloves, transfer the ham to a cutting board, and thinly slice the ham. Arrange the slices back on the serving dish, and drizzle the warm pineapple glaze over the ham, keeping a little extra on the side for guests to add as desired.

Mac 'n' Cheese

The BEST I've ever eaten.

Prep Time: 30 minutes
Cook Time: 30 minutes
Yield: 8 servings

Ingredients

- 1 (16 oz.) package penne pasta
- 2 cups shredded Gruyère cheese
- 4 cups shredded sharp cheddar cheese
- 1 T. extra-virgin olive oil
- 6 T. unsalted butter
- ⅓ cup all-purpose flour
- 3 cups whole milk
- 1 cup heavy whipping cream
- 1½ tsp. salt
- ½ tsp. black pepper
- ½ tsp. dry mustard
- ½ tsp. garlic powder
- ¼ tsp. nutmeg
- 1½ cups panko breadcrumbs
- ½ cup shredded Parmesan cheese
- ¼ tsp. smoked paprika
- 4 T. butter, melted

Directions

1. Preheat the oven to 350°F. Lightly grease a 9 × 13-inch baking dish.
2. Cook the pasta according to package directions, and drain.
3. In a large bowl, combine the Gruyère and cheddar cheese. Reserve 2 cups of the cheese mixture for later use.
4. Place the cooked pasta in a large bowl and driz-

zle it with the olive oil while still warm. Stir to coat the pasta, then set it aside to cool.

5. In a large saucepan, melt the butter over medium heat. Whisk in the flour and continue whisking for about 1 minute, until bubbly.

6. Gradually whisk in the milk and heavy cream until smooth. Continue whisking until the mixture bubbles again, then whisk for an additional 2 minutes.

7. Season the sauce with salt, pepper, dry mustard, garlic powder, and nutmeg. Stir to combine.

8. Gradually add handfuls of the cheese mixture to the sauce, whisking until smooth between each addition. (Do not stir in the 2 reserved cups of cheese.)

9. Pour the cheese sauce over the cooled pasta, stirring to fully coat the pasta in the sauce.

10. Spread half of the pasta in the prepared baking dish, sprinkle with the reserved 2 cups of cheese, then top with the remaining pasta.

11. In a small bowl, combine the panko crumbs, Parmesan cheese, melted butter, and smoked paprika. Sprinkle this mixture evenly over the pasta.

12. Bake for about 30 minutes, or until the topping is golden brown and the cheese is bubbly.

Chocolate Chip Cookies

Hint: This dough can be frozen as pre-scooped balls or ready-to-slice logs.

Prep Time: 20 minutes
Cook Time: 10 minutes
Yield: 112 cookies (recipe may be halved)

Ingredients

5 cups oatmeal
2 cups butter, room temperature
2 cups granulated sugar
2 cups brown sugar
4 eggs
2 tsp. vanilla
4 cups flour
2 tsp. baking powder
2 tsp. baking soda
1 tsp. salt

24 oz. chocolate chips
1 8 oz. Hershey bar, grated
3 cups chopped nuts (your choice)

Directions

1. Preheat the oven to 375°F.

2. Measure the oatmeal and place it in a blender to blend into a fine powder.

3. In a large mixing bowl, cream together the butter and both sugars. Add the eggs and vanilla and stir to combine with the butter mixture, then stir in the flour, blended oatmeal, baking powder, baking soda, and salt. Stir in the chocolate and nuts.

4. Scoop the dough into balls and place about 12 to a cookie sheet, evenly spaced, baking in batches. Bake for 10 minutes.

5. To freeze for later baking: Flash freeze scooped dough balls on a cookie sheet. Individually frozen dough balls are easier to handle and will keep their shape better when transferred to a freezer bag for longer-term storage. Alternately, form the dough into a log about 2 inches around and wrap in plastic wrap. Put the dough in the bag and write baking directions on the bag. I like to experiment with the cookies and find out what the baking time and temp is for frozen dough as well as thawed dough. Bake for 10 minutes, and then keep checking every 2 minutes to get them just perfect.

Do not be anxious about anything, but in every situation, by prayer and petition, with thanksgiving, present your requests to God.

PHILIPPIANS 4:6

Quiche (Spinach)

Prep Time: 20 minutes
Cook Time: 45 minutes
Yield: 8 servings

Ingredients

4 large eggs
⅔ cup whole milk
½ cup heavy cream (or heavy whipping cream)
¼ tsp. salt
¼ tsp. pepper
1 cup shredded or crumbled cheese (feta, cheddar, blue cheese, goat cheese, or Gruyère)
1 (10 oz.) package frozen, chopped spinach, thawed and squeezed dry
1 store-bought frozen pastry pie shell, defrosted overnight
¼ cup grated Parmesan cheese

Directions

1. Preheat oven to 350°F.
2. In a large bowl, beat the eggs, milk, cream, salt, and pepper on high speed, approximately 1 minute.
3. With a spoon, fold in your favorite shredded or crumbled cheese and the spinach. Pour the mixture into the crust.
4. Sprinkle the Parmesan cheese on top.
5. Cover the edges of the pie shell with aluminum foil to keep them from burning.
6. Bake quiche until the center is set and a toothpick comes out clean, about 45 minutes.
7. Let the quiche cool for 10 minutes before serving.

Harvest Salad

Prep Time: 20 minutes
Yield: 4 main servings or 8 side servings

Ingredients

6 cups mixed greens
1 apple, thinly sliced
1 pear, thinly sliced
½ cup dried cranberries
½ cup chopped walnuts
½ cup crumbled blue cheese
½ cup cubed and roasted butternut squash (optional)
¼ cup olive oil
2 T. apple cider vinegar
1 tsp. honey
Salt and pepper, to taste

Directions

1. In a large salad bowl, combine the mixed greens, apple, pear, dried cranberries, walnuts, blue cheese, and butternut squash.
2. In a small bowl, whisk together the olive oil, apple cider vinegar, and honey.
3. Drizzle the dressing over the salad, season with a dash of salt and pepper, and gently toss to combine. Serve immediately.

Corn Bread Muffins

Prep Time: 10 minutes
Cook Time: 20 minutes
Yield: 9 servings

Ingredients

1 cup cornmeal
1 cup all-purpose flour
¼ cup sugar
1 T. baking powder
½ tsp. salt
1 cup milk
¼ cup vegetable oil
2 large eggs

Directions

1. Preheat the oven to 400°F and grease a 12-cup muffin tin, or use paper liners.
2. In a large bowl, combine the cornmeal, flour, sugar, baking powder, and salt.
3. In a separate bowl, whisk together the milk, vegetable oil, and eggs.
4. Add the wet ingredients to the dry and stir until just combined.
5. Pour the batter into the prepared muffin pan and bake for 15 to 20 minutes, or until a toothpick inserted in the center comes out clean.
6. Allow to cool slightly before serving.

Butternut Squash

Prep Time: 5 minutes
Cook Time: 90 minutes
Yield: 6 servings

Ingredients

1 large butternut squash, halved lengthwise and
  seeds removed
2 cups water
1 T. salted butter, cut into pieces
Salt and freshly ground black pepper, to taste

Directions

1. Preheat the oven to 350°F.
2. Place squash, cut side down, in a 9 × 13-inch
   baking dish. Pour water into the dish around the
   squash halves.
3. Bake in the preheated oven until tender and
   easily pierced with a fork, about 90 minutes. If
   all the water evaporates while cooking, add more
   water.
4. Remove skin and cut into serving size pieces.
   Top with butter and season with salt and pepper.

Cuban Sandwiches

This is a classic Cuban dish known for its delightful
combination of flavors and textures, with the tangy
mustard and pickles, melted Swiss cheese, and tender roasted pork and ham. It's a hearty and satisfying meal that's perfect for lunch or dinner.

Prep Time: 10 minutes
Cook Time: 6 minutes
Yield: 4 servings

Ingredients

4 sandwich rolls (Cuban bread if available, or
  French rolls), split in half lengthwise
¼ cup yellow mustard
2 T. mayonnaise
1 lb. thinly sliced roast pork deli meat
½ lb. thinly sliced ham deli meat
8 slices Swiss cheese
½ cup dill pickles, sliced
2 T. unsalted butter, softened

Directions

1. Preheat a griddle or large skillet over medium
   heat.
2. Spread the yellow mustard on one half of each
   sandwich roll, and mayonnaise on the other half.
3. On the half with the mayonnaise, stack the roast
   pork, ham, Swiss cheese, and dill pickles.
4. Close the sandwiches. Spread the butter on the
   outside (both top and bottom) of each sandwich.
5. Place the sandwiches on the preheated griddle
   or skillet. Cook for 2 to 3 minutes on each side,
   or until the bread is toasted to a golden brown
   and the cheese has melted.
6. To help flatten the sandwiches and create a
   crispy crust, you can press them down with a
   spatula or place another heavy skillet on top
   while they cook.
7. Once the sandwiches are cooked, remove them
   from the griddle or skillet and let them cool for
   a minute or two.
8. Slice the sandwiches in half diagonally and serve
   hot. Enjoy!

Cheese and Veggie Quesadillas

Prep Time: 10 minutes
Cook Time: 15 minutes
Yield: 4 servings

Ingredients

4 large flour tortillas
2 cups shredded cheddar cheese
1 red bell pepper, diced
1 green bell pepper, diced
1 onion, diced

Directions

1. Preheat a large skillet over medium heat.
2. Spread ½ cup of cheese on half of each tortilla.
3. Sprinkle the peppers and onion over the cheese.
4. Fold the empty half of each tortilla over the
   filled half.
5. Cook the quesadillas in the skillet for 2 to 3
   minutes on each side, until the cheese is melted
   and the tortillas are crispy. Cook in batches, if
   needed, to keep the quesadillas in a single layer
   in your skillet.
6. Cut into triangles and serve hot.

A Prayer of Thankfulness

You create good things.
You grow good things
with the sun and the rain
and I thank You
for all the ways
that You sustain
my good body
with good food.

When I am hungry,
may I remember
You are my provider
who gives good things.

When I am full,
may I remember
to give thanks
for Your goodness to me.

Thank You for food
that is from You
and for my sustenance.

Week Four

The After-Thanksgiving-Day Plan

I have a pretty good guess what you're having for dinner on Thanksgiving Thursday (if you live in the U.S.). If you live outside of the States and want to re-create this menu plan, you can go with two or three roast chickens to equal a massive turkey. (I lived in Japan in the '90s and the person who invited me over for Thanksgiving served turkey. When I asked how they acquired the bird, they let me know that there were just some things about which I was better off left in the dark. I didn't ask any more questions. But it was delicious.)

This week looks a little different from the others, so you can make the most of your turkey leftovers. I also feature a lighter soup recipe so you can take a break from the starch fest that is the American Thanksgiving.

Week 4 Menu

Saturday

Shepherd's Pie with Turkey
Air Fryer Honey Glazed Carrots

Dessert:
Fresh Fruit Galette
   (Pear)

Sunday

Breakfast:

Breakfast Casserole

Lunch:

Five-Spoon Interpretive
   Veggie Soup

Buffalo Ranch Salad

Rolls

Dinner:

Turkey Tetrazzini
Caesar Salad

Monday

Not Turkey!*

Tuesday

Five-Spoon Interpretive
   Veggie Soup

Rolls

Wednesday

Leftovers or frozen meal of choice

Thursday

Dinner out

Friday

Pizza night!

*Go through a drive-through, order via DoorDash—just don't eat anything with turkey. You've worked hard; it's time to eat something completely different.

Sabbath Soup

Five-Spoon Interpretive Veggie Soup

Prep Time: 10 minutes • Cook Time: 45 minutes, or simmer longer if you choose
Yield: 4 bowls or 8 cups

This is the very loose recipe I prefer when I want to use up all the veggies in my crisper and any veggies left over from my Thanksgiving prep. Vegetable soup is the opposite of a soufflé; it is the most adjustable, forgiving food you will ever create. It's called Five-Spoon because you will want to keep tasting and adjusting the flavors—I pull out 5 spoons to taste and add more flavors.

Non-negotiable Ingredients

Oil or butter—olive oil and butter are the clear winners here, but I've used vegetable oil in a pinch.

Salt and pepper, to taste

Chopped vegetables—I like to chop mine into 1-inch pieces, keeping everything uniform so they cook quickly and evenly.

4 to 6 cups stock—I use a chicken or vegetable stock but have also used beef broth, and even tomato juice.

Seasoning—Some spice combinations you might consider:

Mexican: cumin, chili powder, peppers, oregano, garlic.

Italian: basil, Italian herb blend, oregano.

Indian: tandoori spices, garam masala, curry, yogurt, coconut milk, tamarind, cardamom, cumin, coriander, cilantro, fennel, garlic, saffron.

Fresh herbs: herbs give a great punch, and they're easy to grow in your kitchen windowsill.

Directions

1. Cut up the aromatics such as your onion, garlic, and some fresh herbs. If you have celery, you can throw it in at this point. Start sautéing those in the oil or butter. Let them get a little color to enhance the taste.

2. Put in the heartier veggies first. These are your carrots, potatoes, turnips, and other root veggies. Give them a few minutes. This would also be the time to add canned beans if you'd like.

3. Now, start adding in other vegetables: squash, zucchini, tomatoes, green beans, asparagus, corn, eggplant, or mushrooms. Let these get a little color as well. (I've been known to use canned vegetables when I don't have what I want.)

4. Add what remains, including things like spinach, cabbage, and any other "thin" additions.

5. Cover the vegetables with your broth, and get creative with your spice and seasoning additions, and simmer until the flavor and texture is just right.

Shepherd's Pie with Turkey

This is one of my very favorite ways to use up leftovers like turkey, chicken, or whatever meat you have, along with vegetables and mashed potatoes. (I've been known to even use up green bean casserole in this dish. I promise, it's going to be amazing no matter what combination you put together.)

Prep Time: 15 minutes
Cook Time: 45 minutes
Yield: 8 servings

Ingredients

- 1 stick (8 T.) butter, divided
- 1 medium onion, chopped (about 1½ cups)
- 2 cups cooked diced vegetables (I like carrots, corn, mushrooms, peas, and green beans)
- 1½ lbs. cooked turkey, chopped
- 1 tsp. Worcestershire sauce
- 2 T. tomato paste
- ½ cup chicken or vegetable broth
- 1 tsp. salt, plus more to taste
- ½ tsp. pepper
- 2 tsp. dried parsley
- 1 tsp. dried rosemary
- 1 tsp. dried thyme
- 4 cups mashed potatoes (leftover or made from instant)
- ¼ cup Parmesan cheese

Directions

1. Preheat the oven to 400°F.
2. Melt 4 tablespoons of the butter in a large sauté pan on medium heat. Add the onion and cook until tender, about 6 to 10 minutes. Add the cooked vegetables and heat through. (Or, if you don't have leftover cooked vegetables, now is the time to get them started. Add uncooked carrots first because they are denser and take longer to cook, then other uncooked vegetables. If you are including peas or corn, add them toward the end of the cooking time, as they cook very fast.)
3. Add the cooked turkey, then the Worcestershire sauce, tomato paste, and broth. Season with salt, pepper, and the rest of the seasonings. Cook uncovered for 10 minutes, adding more broth if necessary to keep the meat from drying out.
4. Taste and season with more salt and pepper, if desired.
5. Spread the cooked filling in an even layer in a 9 × 13-inch baking dish. (I prefer a metal or ceramic dish because it will be going under the broiler, and glass dishes have been known to shatter under the broiler. If using glass, do not put it under the broiler.)
6. Spread the mashed potatoes over the top of the meat. Use a fork to make ridges in the potatoes.
7. Bake until browned and bubbling, about 30 minutes. Remove from oven, sprinkle Parmesan cheese on top, and broil for 3 more minutes until potatoes and cheese are golden brown.

Air Fryer Honey Glazed Carrots

Prep Time: 5 minutes
Cook Time: 15 minutes
Yield: 6 servings

Ingredients

- 1 lb. baby carrots
- 2 T. olive oil
- Salt and freshly ground black pepper, to taste
- 3 T. honey (for an extra kick, you could substitute with Mike's Hot Honey)

Directions

1. Place the carrots in a mixing bowl and drizzle them with olive oil. Toss until evenly coated.
2. Sprinkle salt and pepper over the carrots, tossing again to ensure they're well-seasoned.
3. Drizzle the honey over the carrots and toss one more time to coat them evenly.
4. Place the honey-glazed carrots in a single layer in the air fryer basket. Avoid overcrowding to ensure even cooking.
5. Set the air fryer to 375°F. Air fry for 12 to 15 minutes, checking halfway through to shake the basket (or use tongs to flip the carrots) for even cooking.

Fresh Fruit Galette (Pear)

Prep Time: 20 minutes
Cook Time: 15 to 25 minutes
Yield: 8 servings

Ingredients

1 (10 × 15-inch) layer frozen puff pastry, thawed
½ cup granulated sugar
1 tsp. cornstarch
1 cup sliced fresh pears
1 T. lemon juice
1 small egg, for brushing on pastry
Turbinado sugar

Directions

1. Heat oven to 375°F.
2. Place a frozen puff pastry sheet on a baking sheet lined with parchment paper and let it defrost: either on the kitchen counter for 4 hours, or overnight in the fridge (then set out on the counter for one hour before baking).
3. In a bowl whisk together sugar and cornstarch. Add in the fruit and lemon juice and stir to coat.
4. Pour fruit mixture into the center of the puff pastry. Fold the edges of the puff pastry toward the border of the fruit mixture to form an outer crust. There should be a rustic circle of fruit visible in the center of the galette.
5. Whisk the egg in a small bowl and brush the exposed pastry with the egg using a pastry brush.
6. Sprinkle with the turbinado sugar.
7. Bake for 15 to 25 minutes or until the pastry is golden brown. (Check often after the 15-minute mark.)
8. When done, remove the galette from the oven. Let the pastry sit for at least 10 minutes, allowing the fruit juices to firm up slightly.

Note: You can make this dish with many kinds of fruit! Instead of pears, try it with fresh apples, peaches, apricots, or berries.

Breakfast Casserole

Here is a simple dish you can make in the morning, or prep the night before and keep it in the fridge overnight. Either way, your crew will love it.

Prep Time: 20 minutes
Cook Time: 1 hour
Yield: 6 to 8 servings

Ingredients

12 eggs
1 cup sour cream (regular or light)
¼ cup milk
2 cups shredded cheddar cheese
Salt and pepper, to taste
1 T. vegetable oil
1 onion, chopped
16 oz. mushrooms, chopped
2 lbs. cooked breakfast meat (ground turkey sausage, ground pork sausage, chorizo, ham, leftover steak) or 1 lb. bacon, cooked

Directions

1. Preheat the oven to 350°F. Spray a 9 × 13-inch pan with cooking spray.
2. Combine the eggs, sour cream, milk, and cheese in a large bowl with a bit of salt and pepper. Mix on low speed with electric mixer, just until combined.
3. Heat a large skillet over medium heat. Add the vegetable oil and cook the onion until soft. Add the mushrooms and cook for 4 more minutes.
4. Add vegetables and meat to the bowl with the eggs and stir to combine.
5. Pour the mixture into a greased 9 × 13-inch pan and bake for 35 to 50 minutes or until the edges are set and the center is just firm.

The LORD replied, "My Presence will go with you, and I will give you rest."

EXODUS 33:14

Buffalo Ranch Salad

Prep Time: 30 minutes
Yield: 4 main servings or 8 side servings

Ingredients

1 lb. chicken breast, grilled and diced
¼ cup buffalo sauce
6 cups mixed greens
½ cup thinly sliced celery
½ cup shredded carrots
½ cup crumbled blue cheese
¼ cup Ranch Dressing
Salt and pepper, to taste

Directions

1. Preheat your grill or stovetop grill pan over medium heat.
2. Cook the chicken breast until it's no longer pink in the center. Once cooked, allow it to cool, then dice it into bite-size pieces.
3. In a bowl, mix the diced chicken with buffalo sauce.
4. In a large salad bowl, arrange the mixed greens. Top with buffalo chicken, celery, carrots, and blue cheese.
5. Drizzle the dressing over the salad and gently toss to combine. Season with a dash of salt and pepper. Serve immediately.

Ranch Dressing

Ingredients

½ cup buttermilk
½ cup mayonnaise
½ cup sour cream
1 T. chopped fresh chives
1 T. chopped fresh parsley
1 garlic clove, minced
1 tsp. white vinegar
Salt and freshly ground pepper, to taste

Directions

Combine all ingredients in a bowl and whisk until well combined.

Rolls

The ingredients for rolls and sandwich bread dough are the same, so feel free to double the recipe to get both rolls for dinner and sliced bread for sandwiches for the week. Look at you being so clever!

Prep Time: 10 minutes, plus 2 hours to rise
Cook Time: 30 minutes
Yield: 6 Rolls

Ingredients

1 cup warm water
½ T. active dry yeast
2 T. honey
2¾ cups all-purpose flour, divided
1 tsp. salt
2 T. melted butter, divided

Directions

1. Mix the water, yeast, and honey together. Add 2 cups of flour, salt, and 1 tablespoon melted butter and mix.
2. Put dough on a surface with ¼ cup of flour and knead it for about 5 minutes, adding in the other half cup of flour to get a doughy texture.
3. Take your dough ball and put it in a bowl. Cover it with a dishcloth and stick it in the oven with the oven light on for an hour (it should approximately double in size).
4. Preheat the oven to 350°F.
5. Butter a pie tin. Cut the dough into six pieces and form the pieces into rolls.
6. Place the rolls in the pie tin and let the dough double again, covered.
7. Bake for 30 minutes.
8. Remove from oven and brush with the other tablespoon of melted butter.

Note: For sandwich bread, at step 5, butter a loaf pan instead of the pie tin and shape the dough to fit. Allow the dough to rise and bake as above. Allow just a few more minutes to bake, until the loaf is golden and sounds hollow when tapped. Brush with butter, then let it cool on a wire rack before slicing.

Turkey Tetrazzini

This is a delicious and comforting dish that makes great use of leftover turkey.

Prep Time: 15 minutes
Cook Time: 30 minutes
Yield: 6 to 8 servings

Ingredients

1 (8 oz.) package thin spaghetti, broken in thirds
2 cups cubed cooked turkey
3 T. butter
1 cup sliced fresh mushrooms
1 small onion, chopped
1 (10 oz.) can Ro*Tel diced tomatoes with chilies (choose your favorite heat level)
1 (10¾ oz.) can condensed cream of mushroom soup, undiluted
¾ cup milk
¼ cup water
½ tsp. poultry seasoning
⅛ tsp. ground mustard
¾ cup shredded cheddar cheese
¾ cup shredded part-skim mozzarella cheese
1 T. shredded Parmesan cheese
Parsley for garnish

Directions

1. Preheat your oven to 350°F and grease an 11 × 7-inch baking dish.
2. Cook the pasta according to the package directions, omitting the salt. Once cooked, drain and place the pasta in the prepared baking dish.
3. Spread the turkey over the top of the pasta.
4. Melt the butter in a large skillet over medium heat. Add the mushrooms and onion to the skillet, sautéing until tender.
5. Whisk in the tomatoes, mushroom soup, milk, water, poultry seasoning, and ground mustard until blended.
6. Add the cheddar cheese to the skillet and continue to cook and stir over medium heat until the cheese has fully melted.
7. Pour the sauce from the skillet over the turkey in the baking dish, making sure it's evenly distributed.
8. Sprinkle the mozzarella and Parmesan cheeses over the top of the dish.
9. Bake the dish, uncovered, in the preheated oven for 25 to 30 minutes, or until heated through and the cheese on top is melted and lightly browned.
10. Remove the dish from the oven and let it cool for a few minutes before serving. Sprinkle with fresh parsley for garnish. Enjoy your homemade Turkey Tetrazzini!

Caesar Salad

Prep Time: 15 minutes
Yield: 4 main servings or 8 side servings

Ingredients

1 head romaine lettuce, torn into bite-size pieces
1 cup croutons
½ cup freshly grated Parmesan cheese
½ cup Creamy Caesar Dressing

Directions

1. In a large salad bowl, combine the romaine lettuce, croutons, and Parmesan cheese.
2. Pour the dressing over the salad and toss until well coated.
3. Serve immediately, with additional Parmesan cheese on top if desired.

Creamy Caesar Dressing

Ingredients

¾ cup mayonnaise
2 T. fresh lemon juice
2 garlic cloves, minced
1 tsp. Worcestershire sauce
1 tsp. Dijon mustard
¼ cup grated Parmesan cheese
Salt and freshly ground pepper, to taste

Directions

Combine all ingredients in a blender or food processor and blend until smooth.

A Prayer
Before Cooking

Bless these hands.
Bless these ingredients.
Bless these moments and
please fill my soul
as I prepare this meal
to fuel the bodies of those I love.

As I chop, stir, taste, season, and cook,
please keep it ever before me
that this is holy work.

Please meet me here.

Make space for me
to set aside
what has transpired
in the hours prior so
I may fully savor
Your goodness and Your provision.

Thank You for the gift of
partnering with You
in the miracle that is this meal.

Week Five
A Simple Meal

T here are some weeks where I just need someone to boss me around and tell me what to make. Keep it simple. I just want to get people fed without a lot of fanfare and not making a lot of decisions—but I need everything to taste amazing. Too much to ask? No. This week's set of menus contains not one fussy element. All of these meals are simple but flavorful. And you? Will love every last recipe.

Week 5 Menu

Saturday

Slow Cooker Seasoned Pork
 Roast
Risotto with Mushrooms
Roasted Broccoli with Parmesan
 (no recipe)

Dessert:
Fruit Crisp (Apple)

Sunday

Breakfast:
Overnight Egg, Sausage, and
 Hashbrown Casserole

Lunch:
Minestrone
Spinach, Bacon, and Egg Salad
Overnight Soup Bread

Dinner:
Spaghetti with Meat Sauce
Cheesy Garlic Bread
Green Beans (no recipe)

Monday

Pulled Pork Lettuce Wraps
Tortilla chips (no recipe)

Tuesday

Minestrone
Spinach, Bacon, and Egg Salad
Overnight Soup Bread, toasted

Wednesday

Leftovers or frozen meal of choice

Thursday

Dinner out

Friday

Pizza night!

Sabbath Soup

Minestrone

Prep Time: 10 minutes • Cook Time: 30 minutes • Yield: 4 bowls or 8 cups

Ingredients

2 T. olive oil

1 large onion, chopped

2 carrots, peeled and chopped

2 celery ribs, chopped

3 cloves garlic, minced

1 zucchini, chopped (about 2 cups)

1 medium potato, peeled and chopped

1 (14.5 oz.) can diced tomatoes

1 (15 oz.) can kidney beans, drained and rinsed

4 cups vegetable broth

2 tsp. dried basil

1 tsp. dried oregano

1 tsp. salt

½ tsp. black pepper

½ cup small pasta (like ditalini or orzo)

2 cups fresh spinach, chopped

Optional: ¼ cup freshly grated Parmesan cheese

Directions

1. In a large pot, heat the olive oil over medium heat. Add the onion, carrots, celery, and garlic. Cook until the vegetables are tender, about 5 minutes.

2. Add the zucchini, potato, tomatoes, kidney beans, vegetable broth, basil, oregano, salt, and black pepper to the pot. Stir until everything is well combined.

3. Bring the soup to a boil. Once boiling, reduce the heat to low, cover the pot, and let it simmer for about 15 to 20 minutes, or until the vegetables are soft.

4. Meanwhile, in a separate pot, cook the pasta according to the package directions. Drain the pasta once it's cooked.

5. Add the cooked pasta and spinach to the soup. Stir until the spinach has wilted and everything is well combined.

6. Serve the soup hot, garnished with a sprinkle of freshly grated Parmesan cheese if you like.

Slow Cooker Seasoned Pork Roast

Prep Time: 20 minutes
Cook Time: 5 to 6 hours
Yield: 10 servings

Ingredients

1 (4 lb.) pork loin, trimmed of excess fat
Salt and pepper, to taste
1 large onion, sliced
1 T. oil
6 cloves garlic, chopped
½ cup apple juice
½ cup balsamic vinegar
2 T. soy sauce
½ cup brown sugar

Directions

1. Season all sides of the pork loin roast generously with salt and pepper.
2. Place the onion in the bottom of your slow cooker.
3. Heat a large skillet over medium-high heat. Add the oil to the pan and when it's hot, sear the pork roast on all sides. Then, place the roast on top of the onion in the slow cooker.
4. Turn off the heat to your skillet and add the garlic, apple juice, balsamic vinegar, and soy sauce. Stir these ingredients together, making sure to scrape up any brown bits that stuck to the pan.
5. Sprinkle the brown sugar on top of the pork loin and then pour the sauce mixture over the pork.
6. Cover and cook on low for 5 to 6 hours, or until the internal temperature is 145°F.
7. Once cooked, remove the pork loin to a plate and cover it with foil. Allow it to rest for 10 minutes.
8. While the pork is resting, pour the sauce and juices from the slow cooker into a saucepan. Bring this to a simmer over medium heat and allow the sauce to thicken, about 5 to 6 minutes. Stir occasionally.
9. Pour the sauce over the pork, slice it, and serve.

Risotto with Mushrooms

Prep time: 15 minutes
Cook time: 25 minutes
Yield: 8 servings

Ingredients

7 cups chicken stock
2 T. olive oil
1 large shallot, finely chopped
2 cloves garlic, minced
Salt and pepper, to taste
1 cup sliced mushrooms
1 bay leaf
5 T. unsalted butter, divided
2 cups arborio rice
1 cup white wine or 1 additional cup chicken stock
1 T. fresh herbs (I like basil, but parsley, tarragon, and chives are all wonderful)
¾ cup grated Parmesan, plus more for garnish
Lemon wedges

Directions

1. Warm the chicken stock in a large saucepan on medium-low heat. Keep it covered and warm.
2. In another saucepan or Dutch oven, heat the olive oil over medium heat. Add the shallot and garlic. Add salt and pepper to your own taste, also considering any salt and pepper that may already be in your stock. Cook for 3 to 4 minutes, stirring occasionally, until softened. Add mushrooms and sauté for 2 minutes.
3. Add bay leaf and 3 tablespoons of butter to the mixture. Stir until butter melts, around 1 minute.
4. Add rice and toast it for 3 to 4 minutes, stirring once. The rice should smell nutty and turn light golden brown.
5. Add the wine (or 1 cup of additional stock) and let it simmer until it evaporates completely, around 2 to 3 minutes.
6. Add 1 cup of warm stock to the rice, stirring gently until it's absorbed. This takes around 2 to 3 minutes.
7. Continue adding stock, 1 cup or ladleful at a time, and keep stirring until the rice is al dente. This takes around 17 to 19 minutes total. You may have some stock left over. Remove the bay

leaf and add your fresh herbs.

8. If you prefer a risotto with more sauce, add more stock in ¼ cup increments until desired consistency is reached.

9. Stir in Parmesan, 2 tablespoons of butter, 1 teaspoon salt, and more black pepper. Serve with lemon wedges and extra Parmesan.

Fruit Crisp (Apple)

You can customize this recipe to use whatever fruit you have on hand. Serve warm, and if desired, add a scoop of vanilla ice cream and a sprig of fresh mint.

Prep Time: 15 minutes
Cook Time: 35 to 40 minutes
Yield: 8 servings

Ingredients

Fruit Filling
  4 to 5 cups peeled, cored, and thinly sliced apples
  ½ cup granulated sugar
  1 T. cornstarch
  Optional: ½ tsp. cinnamon
  Pinch of salt

Crisp Topping
  1 cup old-fashioned oats
  ½ cup all-purpose flour
  ½ cup brown sugar, packed
  ½ tsp. cinnamon
  ¼ tsp. salt
  6 T. unsalted butter, cold and cut into small pieces

Directions

1. Preheat your oven to 375°F. Lightly grease an 8 × 8-inch baking dish.

2. Prepare the fruit filling: In a large bowl, combine the fruit, sugar, cornstarch, cinnamon, and a pinch of salt. Stir gently until well combined, then transfer to the prepared baking dish.

3. Prepare the crisp topping: In another bowl, combine the oats, flour, brown sugar, cinnamon, and salt. Add the butter and use your fingers or a pastry cutter to incorporate it into the oat mixture until it looks like coarse crumbs. Sprinkle the crisp topping evenly over the fruit filling.

4. Bake for 35 to 40 minutes, or until the topping is golden brown and the fruit filling is bubbling.

5. Remove the crisp from the oven and allow it to cool for about 10 minutes before serving.

Variation:

Blueberry Lemon Crisp: Use 4 to 5 cups of fresh or frozen blueberries. Add the zest and juice of one lemon to the fruit filling, and omit the cinnamon.

Overnight Egg, Sausage, and Hashbrown Casserole

Prep Time: 30 minutes the night before
Cook Time: 1 hour, plus 20 minutes to rest before and after baking
Yield: 6 to 8 servings

Ingredients

  1 lb. breakfast sausage
  ½ cup diced green bell pepper
  ½ cup diced red bell pepper
  1 small onion, diced
  8 large eggs
  1 cup whole milk
  1 tsp. salt
  ½ tsp. black pepper
  1 tsp. dried thyme
  1 tsp. smoked paprika
  ½ tsp. garlic powder
  1 (20 oz.) package refrigerated hash browns
  2 cups shredded cheddar cheese, divided
  Optional: chopped green onions or parsley for garnish

Directions

1. Brown the sausage in a large skillet over medium heat, breaking it up into small crumbles. Once cooked through, remove it from the pan and set it aside.

2. In the same skillet, add the peppers and onion. Sauté until the vegetables are tender and the onion is translucent.

3. In a large bowl, whisk together the eggs, milk, salt, pepper, thyme, smoked paprika, and garlic powder until well combined.

4. Add the cooked sausage, sautéed vegetables, hash browns, and 1½ cups of the shredded cheddar cheese to the egg mixture. Stir well to combine.

5. Grease a 9 × 13-inch baking dish, then pour the egg and sausage mixture into the dish. Sprinkle the remaining ½ cup of cheese on top.
6. Cover the dish with aluminum foil and place it in the refrigerator overnight.
7. The next morning, preheat your oven to 350°F. Remove the casserole from the refrigerator and let it sit at room temperature while the oven is preheating.
8. Bake the casserole, covered, for 45 minutes. Then remove the foil and bake for an additional 15 minutes, or until the cheese on top is bubbly and starting to brown.
9. Remove the casserole from the oven and let it rest for 10 minutes before cutting into it.
10. Serve hot, garnished with green onion or parsley if desired.

Spinach, Bacon, and Egg Salad

Prep Time: 15 minutes
Yield: 4 main servings or 8 side servings

Ingredients

6 cups fresh baby spinach
8 oz. fresh mushrooms, sliced
4 large hard-boiled eggs, sliced
6 slices bacon, cooked and crumbled
1 cup cherry tomatoes, halved
½ red onion, thinly sliced
3 T. warm bacon drippings or olive oil
2 T. red wine vinegar
1 T. sugar
Salt and freshly ground black pepper, to taste

Directions

1. Arrange the spinach in a large salad bowl. Top with the mushrooms, eggs, bacon, tomatoes, and onion.
2. In a small bowl, whisk together the warm bacon drippings (or olive oil), red wine vinegar, and sugar. Drizzle the warm dressing over the salad, sprinkle with salt and pepper, and gently toss to combine. Serve immediately.

Overnight Soup Bread

Who knew that this life-changing recipe would come from, of all places, TikTok! I have come to see it many places since, and it really is one of the simplest recipes for amazing, warm bread that complements soup perfectly.

One warning: This is not spur-of-the-moment bread. This bread, while it takes very little effort, does take a little forethought. But that's okay, because if you're prepping your soup on Saturday, just mix up this dough Saturday evening and then forget about it until about an hour before "Soup's On!" Your dough needs between 12 and 16 hours to rise, and then another hour of forming and baking. But trust me. It's easy, and it's worth it.

Prep Time: 10 minutes, plus 12 to 16 hours to rise
Cook Time: 45 minutes
Yield: 8 to 12 servings

Ingredients

1½ cups water, room temperature to warm
½ tsp. yeast
3 cups flour
1½ tsp. salt

Directions

1. Mix all ingredients together in an ovenproof bowl (not plastic). One option is to use the stand mixer to mix the dough and leave it in that bowl to rise.
2. Cover the bowl with a kitchen towel and place it in the oven with the oven light on. Let it sit undisturbed for 12 to 16 hours.
3. Remove the bowl from the oven and preheat the oven to 450°F.
4. Line a Dutch oven with parchment paper. You may find it helpful to first crinkle the parchment as this will help it stay in place inside your Dutch oven.
5. Flour a surface and place the dough on that surface. Stretch and fold the dough ball, then place it in the parchment-lined Dutch oven.
6. Use kitchen shears to make three snips on the top of the bread, allowing the bread to expand. Cover the Dutch oven with its lid.

7. Cook the bread in the covered Dutch oven for 30 minutes.
8. After 30 minutes, remove the Dutch oven lid and continue cooking for 15 more minutes.
9. Serve warm, accompanied by salted butter or a mix of oil and balsamic vinegar.

Spaghetti with Meat Sauce

Enjoy this hearty and flavorful Spaghetti with Meat Sauce. It's a satisfying meal that's perfect for any night of the week.

Prep time: 15 minutes
Cook time: 30 minutes
Yield: 4 to 6 servings

Ingredients

1 (16 oz.) package spaghetti
2 T. olive oil
1 lb. ground beef
1 onion, diced
3 cloves garlic, minced
1 (28 oz.) can crushed tomatoes
1 T. tomato paste
1 tsp. dried basil
1 tsp. dried oregano
Salt and pepper, to taste
Optional: Grated Parmesan cheese, for serving

Directions

1. Bring a large pot of salted water to a boil. Add the spaghetti and cook according to the package directions until al dente. Drain the pasta and set it aside.
2. Meanwhile, in a large skillet, heat the olive oil over medium-high heat.
3. Add the ground beef to the skillet. Break it up with a wooden spoon and cook until it's browned and cooked through, about 6 to 8 minutes.
4. Add the onion and garlic to the skillet. Sauté until the onion is translucent, about 2 to 3 minutes.
5. Stir in the crushed tomatoes, tomato paste, basil, oregano, and season with about ½ teaspoon each of salt and pepper. Bring the mixture to a simmer.

6. Reduce the heat to low and let the sauce simmer for about 10 to 15 minutes, or until it has thickened slightly.
7. Serve the cooked spaghetti on plates or in bowls. Top with the meat sauce and sprinkle with Parmesan cheese, if desired.

Cheesy Garlic Bread

Prep Time: 10 minutes
Cook Time: 15 minutes
Yield: 8 servings

Ingredients

½ cup unsalted butter, softened
3 cloves garlic, minced
1 loaf French bread, halved lengthwise
2 cups shredded mozzarella cheese
¼ cup chopped fresh parsley

Directions

1. Preheat the oven to 375°F.
2. In a small bowl, mix together the butter and garlic.
3. Spread the garlic butter evenly over the cut sides of the bread.
4. Sprinkle the shredded mozzarella over the butter.
5. Place the bread on a baking sheet and bake for 10 minutes, or until the cheese is melted.
6. Switch the oven to broil and cook for another 2 to 3 minutes, until the cheese is bubbly and golden.
7. Sprinkle with parsley before serving.

Pulled Pork Lettuce Wraps

Enjoy these refreshing and flavorful Pulled Pork Lettuce Wraps, a healthier alternative to traditional wraps and buns.

Prep time: 15 minutes
Cook time: 10 minutes
Yield: 4 servings

Ingredients

¼ cup hoisin sauce
1 T. soy sauce
1 T. rice vinegar
1 T. honey
1 T. vegetable oil
1 tsp. minced fresh ginger
2 cloves garlic, minced
2 cups leftover pulled pork (or shredded cooked pork loin)
1 head butter lettuce or iceberg lettuce, leaves separated and washed
½ cup shredded carrots
½ red bell pepper, thinly sliced
¼ cup chopped fresh cilantro
2 green onions, thinly sliced
¼ cup unsalted roasted peanuts or cashews, chopped
Optional: Lime wedges, sriracha, or other hot sauce, for serving

Directions

1. In a small bowl, whisk together the hoisin sauce, soy sauce, rice vinegar, and honey. Set it aside.
2. In a large skillet, heat the vegetable oil over medium heat. Add the ginger and garlic, and sauté until fragrant, about 1 minute.
3. Add the pork to the skillet, stirring to combine. Cook for 3 to 4 minutes, until heated through.
4. Stir in the sauce, ensuring the pork is well-coated. Cook for another 2 to 3 minutes, until the sauce has slightly thickened.
5. Remove the skillet from the heat and allow the pork mixture to cool slightly.
6. To assemble the lettuce wraps, place a spoonful of the pork mixture onto each lettuce leaf. Top with carrots, red bell pepper, cilantro, and green onion. Sprinkle with peanuts or cashews.
7. Serve the lettuce wraps with lime wedges, and sriracha or other hot sauce on the side for those who like a little extra heat.

Rejoice in the LORD your God, for he has given you the autumn rains because he is faithful. He sends you abundant showers, both autumn and spring rains, as before.

JOEL 2:23

Week Six

When There's No Time to Cook

This is a great set of recipes when you'd like to simply buy all the food and spend almost zero time in the kitchen.

I know that when life gets super busy, it's tempting to keep eating out. But what if you already had a rotisserie chicken, some twice-baked potatoes, and roasted asparagus in the house? What if you picked up some deli soup and a fun salad, or prepared a platter of charcuterie? Add some ice cream and toppings for a simple dessert, and you are set. That is a couple days' worth of meals, no cooking (except heating things up), and you don't have to be looking for parking at a busy restaurant (and while this is not the cheapest way to eat, it sure beats going out meal after meal).

Week 6 Menu

Saturday

Rotisserie Chicken (store-bought, from the deli)
Air Fryer Twice-Baked Potatoes
Asparagus (no recipe)

Dessert:
Ice Cream Sundae Bar

Sunday

Breakfast:
Amazing Mix-In Muffins (Orange and Cranberry)

Lunch:
Lemon Ginger Chicken Noodle Soup
Cucumber, Tomato, and Avocado Salad
Veggie-Stuffed Vietnamese Spring Rolls (store-bought)

Dinner:
Charcuterie Board
Baguette (no recipe)

Monday

Baked Potato Bar
Broccoli (no recipe)

Tuesday

Lemon Ginger Chicken Noodle Soup
Toasted Baguette (no recipe)

Wednesday

Leftovers or frozen meal of choice

Thursday

Dinner out

Friday

Pizza night!

Sabbath Soup

Lemon Ginger Chicken Noodle Soup

Prep Time: 10 minutes • Cook Time: 35 minutes • Yield: 4 bowls or 8 cups

Ingredients

1 lb. boneless, skinless chicken breasts

Salt and pepper, to taste

2 T. olive oil

1 medium onion, diced

2 medium carrots, peeled and chopped

2 celery ribs, chopped

3 cloves garlic, minced

2-inch piece of fresh ginger, peeled and minced

1 tsp. turmeric

8 cups chicken broth

2 bay leaves

1 cup dried noodles (use your favorite kind)

1 large lemon, zested and juiced

Fresh parsley, chopped (for garnish)

Optional: crushed red pepper flakes for some heat

Directions

1. Sprinkle the chicken breasts on both sides with salt and pepper. Heat 1 tablespoon of olive oil in a large pot or Dutch oven over medium-high heat. Add the chicken and cook until browned on both sides. Remove the chicken and set it aside (it doesn't need to be cooked through at this point).

2. In the same pot, add another tablespoon of olive oil. Add the onion, carrots, and celery. Cook until the vegetables begin to soften, about 5 minutes.

3. Add the garlic, ginger, and turmeric to the pot. Stir well and cook for another minute, until fragrant.

4. Return the chicken to the pot. Add the chicken broth and bay leaves. Bring the soup to a boil, then reduce the heat to low and cover the pot. Let it simmer for about 20 minutes, until the chicken is cooked through.

5. Remove the chicken from the pot and shred it using two forks. While you're shredding the chicken, add the dried noodles to the pot and let them cook according to the package directions.

6. Once the noodles are done, return the shredded chicken to the pot. Add the lemon zest and juice. Taste the soup and adjust the salt and pepper as needed.

7. Serve the soup hot, garnished with fresh parsley and a sprinkle of crushed red pepper flakes if you like some heat.

Air Fryer Twice-Baked Potatoes

Prep Time: 10 minutes
Cook Time: 50 minutes
Yield: 8 servings

Ingredients

    4 large russet potatoes
    1 T. olive oil
    Salt and pepper, to taste
    1 cup sour cream
    2 cups shredded cheddar cheese, divided
    4 strips bacon, cooked and crumbled
    2 green onions, sliced

Directions

1. Preheat your air fryer to 400°F.
2. Pierce your potatoes with a fork several times, and coat with the olive oil, salt, and pepper. Place the potatoes on the trivet and air fry for 20 minutes.
3. With a pair of tongs, flip the potatoes over and continue to air fry for another 20 minutes. Remove from the air fryer and let sit for 5 minutes to cool slightly.
4. Once the potatoes are cooked, cut in half lengthwise and scoop out the middle, leaving a thin layer of potato in the skin.
5. Mix the scooped potato with the sour cream, 1 cup of cheddar cheese, bacon, and green onion.
6. Stuff the potato skins with this mixture, then top with the remaining cheddar cheese.
7. Cook the potatoes in the air fryer at 375°F for 10 minutes, or until cheese is melted and bubbly. Serve hot.

*For the LORD your God
will bless you in all your
harvest and in all the work of
your hands, and your joy
will be complete.*

DEUTERONOMY 16:15

Ice Cream Sundae Bar

An ice cream sundae bar is a great option when you have a crowd with diverse preferences or dietary needs. But it's also just plain fun! For a special treat, build your sundae bar with two or three "base" options, add some "flavor" options, and go crazy with a few "toppings" to make it really sing.

Prep Time: 15 minutes
Yield: customizable

Ingredients

The base: ice cream, cones, frozen yogurt, gelato, cake, cupcakes, cookies, donuts, brownies
The flavor: any kind of fresh berry, sliced peaches cooked down with a little bit of water and sugar, macerated strawberries, marshmallows, candies
The toppings: chocolate syrup, chopped nuts, whipped cream, cookie crumbs, sprinkles

Directions

Prepare and set out all ingredients in individual containers. Don't forget serving spoons! Let each person choose their base, flavor, and topping combinations for their own one-of-a-kind ice cream sundae masterpiece.

Amazing Mix-in Muffins (Orange and Cranberry)

Here is what I love about this recipe—I usually have all these main ingredients on hand, use whatever mix-ins I currently have, and I've got muffins. To make your own combination, use about 1½ cups total of your desired mix-ins as the last step in making the batter.

Prep Time: 10 minutes
Cook Time: 25 minutes
Yield: 12 muffins

Ingredients

    2 cups all-purpose flour
    ¾ cup granulated sugar
    ½ tsp. salt
    2 tsp. baking powder
    ⅓ cup vegetable oil
    1 large egg, room temperature
    1 tsp. vanilla extract

¾ cup milk (whole, low-fat, or non-dairy options all work)

1 cup dried cranberries

¼ cup fresh orange juice

1 T. orange zest

Directions

1. Preheat your oven to 400°F. Line a 12-cup muffin tin with paper liners or grease the cups with nonstick cooking spray.

2. In a large bowl, whisk together the flour, sugar, salt, and baking powder.

3. In a separate medium bowl, combine the vegetable oil, egg, vanilla extract, and milk. Stir well.

4. Gently pour the wet ingredients into the dry ingredients and mix until just combined. Be careful not to overmix, as this can result in tough muffins.

5. Fold in the cranberries, juice, and zest until evenly distributed throughout the batter.

6. Divide the batter evenly among the 12 muffin cups, filling each about two-thirds full.

7. Bake for 20 to 25 minutes, or until a toothpick inserted into the center of a muffin comes out clean.

8. Remove the muffins from the oven and allow them to cool in the tin for 5 minutes before transferring to a wire rack to cool completely.

Cucumber, Tomato, and Avocado Salad

Prep Time: 15 minutes
Yield: 4 main servings or 8 side servings

Ingredients

2 cucumbers, diced

2 tomatoes, diced

2 avocados, diced

¼ red onion, thinly sliced

¼ cup chopped fresh cilantro

¼ cup olive oil

2 T. fresh lime juice

1 tsp. honey

Salt and pepper, to taste

Directions

1. In a large salad bowl, combine the cucumbers, tomatoes, avocados, red onion, and cilantro.

2. In a small bowl, whisk together the olive oil, lime juice, and honey.

3. Drizzle the dressing over the salad, season with a dash of salt and pepper, and gently toss to combine. Serve immediately.

Note: This salad is best consumed the day it is made to prevent the avocados from browning.

Charcuterie Board

A charcuterie board is a great option for parties, but it's also great for an easy dinner treat. Don't let the fancy reputation scare you away. Just remember to include a few items from each of the categories below.

Prep Time: 10 minutes
Yield: customizable

Ingredients

Base

Crackers, pita bread, pretzels

Slices of cucumber

Substance

Hard cheeses: cheddar, Swiss, smoked gouda

Soft cheeses: goat, brie, crema, spreadable cheeses, Havarti

Cured meats: ham, sausage, salami, prosciutto, pepperoni

Hard-boiled eggs

Flavor

Nuts, pickles, olives, sliced apples, cocktail onions

Extras

Dips, tapenades, jams

Fruit: strawberries, grapes, dried apricots

Dark chocolate

Directions

1. Get a nice tray, platter, or wooden cutting board to hold your spread. Gather serving tools: toothpicks, small tongs, a small knife for spreading soft cheese, and spoons for dips or jams.

2. Choose two or more options from each category and lay them out in bite-size slices or chunks, grouped together on your serving tray. Be sure to

offer and label gluten-free items for those with sensitivities or allergies and consider separating them from any gluten-containing items by placing them in their own bowl or tray. You may also want to separate nuts or other potential allergens into their own bowls. Enjoy!

Baked Potato Bar

Prep Time: 20 minutes
Cook Time: 40 minutes
Yield: 4 servings

Ingredients

4 baking potatoes
Olive oil
Sea salt
Pepper
Optional Toppings
Bacon Bits
Cheddar cheese, shredded
Butter
Horseradish sauce
Sour cream

Directions

1. Preheat your air fryer to 400°F.
2. Pierce your potatoes with a fork several times. Rub the outsides with olive oil, salt, and pepper. Place the potatoes on the trivet and air fry for 20 minutes.
3. With a pair of tongs, flip the potatoes over and continue to air fry for another 20 minutes. Remove from the air fryer and let sit for 5 minutes before serving.
4. Serve with your choice of toppings. I've listed our favorites!

A Prayer for the People I Love

Lord, there's a lot of love at this table.

There are a lot of other emotions
and challenges at this table
that can make me doubt love
or what it can do.

Please open my heart to
see the love and be the love.

As we sit together to eat:
may we listen,
may we hear,
may we share
our hearts in ways
that honor each other.
May we laugh
from the joy that comes
from being imperfectly known and loved.

Thank You for this time
to gather with those
I love so much.
Please help me to
be present in this moment—
I don't want to miss a thing.

Winter

Training Our Eyes
to Be Bountiful

It seems to me that our three basic needs, for food and security and love, are so mixed and mingled and entwined that we cannot straightly think of one without the others.

M.F.K. FISHER, *THE ART OF EATING*

One of the questions I've learned to ask myself when I'm preparing my soup for Sabbath is, "Is God bringing anyone to mind that can use a meal this week?"

For me this week, it was my neighbor Paul, who has helped us so many times but also is a volunteer fire-fighter and serves our community so well. We try to take him dinner once or twice a week since he often can't eat at regular times due to being on emergency calls for our neighbors.

One week, I thought of our nearby friends, Kelly and Denny. Kelly was under the weather, and she is the main chef for her large family. I added a couple more cans of tomatoes and beans, and shredded some more chicken for the chili I was already making for us and Paul (remember, soup stretches). I baked some potatoes, pulled together a salad, and reached deep into the freezer for some cheesecake I'd bought too much of and froze for a future meal. Without a lot of extra work, I was able to send Denny home with a meal that could feed their large family.

The delivery of a meal isn't just about the provision of food. It isn't just the physical act of feeding someone; it is relief from the decisions required to buy, prep, and serve food. It's the trip to the store that doesn't have to be made. It is the food, but it's so much more.

My friend Susy, a fellow writer and another mountain girl, recently dropped off some homemade enchiladas, a bagged salad, and the world's most divine peach pie. While we had food at our house, I also had a book deadline (the very book you hold in your hand). And the food was in the form of ingredients, requiring decisions and time regarding how they would be made into meals. What Susy provided was not just food, but enough food to cover:

3 meals

3 sets of decisions

3 redeemed hours (between shopping, deciding, cooking, baking, and dishes)

20 minutes of visiting at our house (and because she knew I was on a deadline, only 20 minutes)

What a gift it is to be cared for and strengthened. That's what a meal does for a body; it strengthens it. And the act of sharing a meal also strengthens the body of people, the community we are lucky to be part of. An act of Sabbath love is to extend the possibility for rest and ease to others.

When life is hard and I'm left to my own devices, a healthy, hearty meal is the last thing on my mind. But when I'm cooking for someone else, I'm trying to pay extra attention to not only making sure that the meal is well-balanced (and by well-balanced I mean vegetables, yes, but also something sweet to put a small smile on their face) but also that there is enough food so that my people can feel full.

And, in the process, we are not just feeding the people who we love, but we are ensuring that they *feel* cared for and loved. What Susy and others have done for me is described perfectly in this season's epigraph quote from M.F.K. Fisher.

A Bountiful Eye

One morning, while having some peaceful reading time, I came across the pause-worthy description of "bountiful eye" in Proverbs: "Whoever has a bountiful eye will be blessed, for he shares his bread with the poor" (22:9 ESV).

The meaning of the "bountiful eye" is to have an eye out for ways to be generous and gracious, loving, and kind toward others. When we are delivering food, we are also delivering a side of security and love. Choosing to feed someone is choosing to love and take care of them.

The people I'm sharing my food with are not who we would consider "poor" in the conventional sense of the word. But sometimes, the person I'm taking food to is doing poorly; they have run out of time, or energy, or health, and need a break, even if it's just for one meal.

If you feel unsure about your cooking skills, don't let that stop you from providing food. Here are some practical ways to live with a bountiful eye.

Keep It Simple

Most of the meals in this book are very simple to prepare. Something like spaghetti and meat sauce, a salad, and garlic bread (with some brownies) is easy and a crowd pleaser (even for tiny palates.) And the good news? It's easy to make a double portion so you can either deliver twice the food, or you can feed your friend and your own household at the same time.

Buy a Meal

My go-to meal to share when I don't have extra time to cook is a store-bought rotisserie chicken, a loaf of French bread, a bag of salad (with the croutons, dressing, and such already included), and a treat from the bakery. If the recipient needs extra support, I'll include either a coffee cake for the next morning or a Starbucks gift card.

Bring Groceries

I heard about the concept of "grief groceries" recently and I absolutely love it. Instead of saying, "Let me know how I can help," show up with some groceries to help carry the friend over for a few days. These should be comforting, low-maintenance items that don't require a lot of decision-making. Think frozen pizzas, warm-up meals from the deli, bagged salad or heat-and-serve veggies, ice cream, a gallon of milk, a rotisserie chicken, or some fried chicken with sides, etc. Don't forget to add in something you know the person favors: a box of truffles, a package of Red Vines, the bag of extra-cheesy nacho chips. Sometimes a treat isn't a treat; it's an absolute necessity for wellness, don't you think?

Send Money

When my friend who lived out of state lost her husband, I sent money to her son to provide lunch for the family after his stepdad's memorial service. I knew my friend was too overwhelmed to make decisions, and

I wasn't familiar with the dining options in the area, so this seemed like the best way to deliver love and nourishment.

"Simple" still says "Love"

Delivering a pot of soup and a loaf of bread is much better than doing nothing at all. In fact, I would consider that to be a pure gesture of comfort and care. Your recipient will appreciate the gift of nourishment, regardless of whether you make a Michelin-star meal or a simple chili.

Plan Ahead

Plan for future opportunities to share a meal. Prepare and label freezer meals with reheating or cooking directions to have on hand for times when another family needs a meal in a hurry. Maybe sometimes that means your family. (If you occasionally take meals to families with allergies, make sure to place ingredient warnings on the labels.)

Do I think a meal is going to fix everything? No. And yet...

I believe it is a gift to not have to do something. As someone who has received a well-timed delivery of culinary kindness when I didn't feel up for eating, let alone preparing food for my family, I know a ready-made meal offers relief from the burden of "having to."

I believe a meal shows someone they are seen, loved, and worthy of receiving.

And I believe extending a bowl of satisfying soup, a homemade berry cobbler, or crisp-crust pizza with extra toppings is a tangible act of God's love.

Supplies for Benevolent Eyes

Have some supplies on hand for when you decide to provide a meal. Here are some of the items I keep in my storage:

Cooler bags—I have a few cooler bags from Trader Joe's and Costco that are great for packing up a meal (or two) to bring to a friend. You can also get the "hot/cold" bags from the supermarket. These are not as insulated as the ones I normally use, but they are cheap enough that they don't need to be returned when you are dropping off food. (Sometimes, I'm just leaving food on a doorstep so that I don't bother people during a difficult time.)

Blue ice—I keep a bunch of blue ice packs in the freezer to transport food. (I have some inexpensive ones that I purchased at the Dollar Store so if I don't get them back, it's no big deal.)

Foil pans, aluminum foil, and Ziplock bags—If someone lives far away, I will pack everything in foil and plastic bags, and place the items in an inexpensive cooler bag and let them know that nothing needs to be returned. I don't want to add extra chores to someone who is having a hard time already. These are great for a casserole (covered in aluminum foil to be able to just pop into the oven when they need it).

Inexpensive plastic storage containers—These are for your liquid items—soups, sauces, etc.

Disposable picnic items—I keep an assortment of paper plates, bowls, napkins, and plastic utensils on hand for someone who is going through a rough time such that doing dishes is just too much.

Winter
Sabbath Experiences

Winter is the time for comfort, for good food and warmth, for the touch of a friendly hand and for a talk beside the fire: it is the time for home.

EDITH SITWELL

1. Make a winter Sabbath altar or centerpiece. Create it with candles, pinecones, written praises, or special objects that represent the season.

2. Give yourself the gift of a winter hibernation day. Get the soup warming in a slow cooker, then grab a favorite pillow and blanket and snuggle on the couch or the bed for a day of true physical rest.

3. Light a candle and say a prayer for a need in your life.

4. Zoom. Yes, this can be a part of a Sabbath practice. Are there kindred-spirit friends you don't see often? Plan a weekly online prayer circle or catch-up session.

5. Enjoy a personal tea or coffee ceremony. Make your beverage of choice with intention. Express gratitude or say a prayer with each step of preparation, sitting and waiting for the drink to brew, pouring the liquid into a favorite cup, and savoring each sip.

6. Set out a puzzle on the dining table and let it be a meditative offering for anyone who wants to pause. Each time a puzzle is completed, bring out a new one.

7. Select a book to read a bit of each morning or evening. Whether it is a devotional, an inspiring nonfiction, or a clever novel, commit to this quiet ritual that feeds your mind or spirit.

8. Write and mail letters of encouragement to friends. Choose a favorite paper and pen and spend a quiet half hour each week to pray for a different friend and write them a note from the heart.

9. Sabbath journaling for winter: Spend moments this season writing about the habits or activities you want to let go of. What can you prune from life now that will serve your wellness going forward?

10. In the winter, I love to dream about the coming year. Where will we travel, what do we want to plant in the garden, who will we invite to visit? Spend a little time with the people you love, planning and dreaming for the year to come. (Calendars and seed catalogs can help your imagination!)

Week Seven
Welcome to Winter

The Cream of Mushroom Soup featured this week is one of our favorite meals when we're looking for something simple but hearty. The addition of the Worcestershire sauce is what makes it hard for me to stop after one cup (or bowl).

Week 7 Menu

Saturday

Pesto Chicken
Air Fryer Smashed Baby Potatoes
Broccoli (no recipe)
Dessert:
Fruit Crisp (Pear)

Sunday

Breakfast:
Quiche (Ham and Cheese)
Lunch:
Cream of Mushroom Soup
Cobb Salad
Overnight Soup Bread
Dinner:
Italian Zucchini and Sausage
    Bake
Risotto
Air Fryer Honey Glazed Carrots

Monday

Leftovers
Air Fryer Zucchini with Herbs and
    Parmesan
Toasted Bread (no recipe)

Tuesday

Cream of Mushroom Soup
Toasted Baguette (no recipe)

Wednesday

Leftovers or frozen meal of choice

Thursday

Dinner out

Friday

Pizza night!

Sabbath Soup

Cream of Mushroom Soup

Prep Time: 5 minutes • Cook Time: 30 minutes • Yield: 4 bowls or 8 cups

Ingredients

2 T. butter

½ lb. sliced fresh mushrooms (I like cremini)

¼ cup chopped onion

6 T. all-purpose flour

½ tsp. salt

⅛ tsp. pepper

2 (14.5 oz.) cans chicken broth

1 cup half-and-half

1 to 2 tsp. Worcestershire sauce (to taste)

Directions

1. In a large saucepan, heat butter over medium heat. Add mushrooms and onion; cook and stir until tender.

2. Stir in flour, salt, and pepper until blended; gradually whisk in broth. Bring to a boil, stirring constantly; cook and stir for 2 minutes or until thickened.

3. Reduce heat; stir in half-and-half and Worcestershire sauce. Simmer, uncovered, for 15 minutes, stirring occasionally. Taste and adjust seasoning with additional salt, pepper, or more Worcestershire sauce.

Pesto Chicken

This is a simple yet flavorful dish that can be prepared in no time. The pesto provides a fresh, herby taste, while the mozzarella cheese gives it a nice, gooey finish. It's a perfect weeknight meal when you're short on time but still want something delicious and satisfying.

Prep Time: 10 minutes
Cook Time: 30 to 40 minutes
Yield: 6 servings

Ingredients

6 boneless skinless chicken breasts
½ cup prepared pesto sauce
6 slices mozzarella cheese
Cooking spray

Directions

1. Preheat your oven to 350°F. Spray a baking dish with a light coating of cooking spray.
2. Place the chicken breasts in the prepared baking dish. Pour the pesto sauce evenly over each chicken breast, making sure each piece is well coated.
3. Bake the chicken for 25 to 30 minutes, or until the chicken is almost cooked through.
4. Take the dish out of the oven and place one slice of mozzarella cheese on top of each chicken breast.
5. Return the dish to the oven and continue baking for an additional 5 to 10 minutes, or until the cheese is melted and bubbly and the chicken is no longer pink in the center.
6. Serve the Pesto Chicken hot, ideally with a side of pasta, roasted vegetables, or a fresh salad. Enjoy!

Air Fryer Smashed Baby Potatoes

Prep Time: 5 minutes
Cook Time: 45 minutes
Yield: 6 servings

Ingredients

1 lb. baby potatoes
2 T. olive oil
2 cloves garlic, minced
1 tsp. dried rosemary
Salt and black pepper, to taste
Optional: ¼ cup Parmesan cheese, for serving

Directions

1. Wash and dry the baby potatoes. Place them in a large pot and cover with water. Bring the water to a boil and cook the potatoes for 10 to 15 minutes, or until they are fork-tender.
2. Drain the potatoes and let them cool for a few minutes. Preheat the air fryer to 400°F.
3. In a small bowl, mix together the olive oil, garlic, rosemary, salt, and black pepper.
4. Place enough of the potatoes to cover the bottom of the basket of the air fryer, spaced apart, and smash them down slightly with the bottom of a glass or a fork. (Depending on the size of your air fryer, you may have to do a couple of batches. If so, place the cooked potatoes on a plate and cover with foil to keep warm.)
5. Brush the tops of the potatoes with the olive oil mixture.
6. Place the basket in the air fryer and cook for 8 minutes, flip, and then cook for another 8 minutes, or until the potatoes are golden and crispy on the outside.
7. Serve the smashed potatoes hot, garnished with grated Parmesan cheese, if desired.

Fruit Crisp (Pear)

You can customize this recipe to use whatever you
have on hand. Serve warm, and if desired, add a
scoop of vanilla ice cream and a sprig of fresh mint.

Prep Time: 15 minutes
Cook Time: 35 to 40 minutes
Yield: 8 servings

Ingredients

Fruit Filling

- 4 to 5 cups peeled, cored, and thinly sliced pears
- ½ cup granulated sugar
- 1 T. cornstarch
- Optional: ½ tsp. cinnamon or nutmeg, or lemon zest
- Pinch of salt

Crisp Topping

- 1 cup old-fashioned oats
- ½ cup all-purpose flour
- ½ cup brown sugar, packed
- ½ tsp. cinnamon
- ¼ tsp. salt
- 6 T. unsalted butter, cold and cut into small pieces

Directions

1. Preheat your oven to 375°F. Lightly grease an
   8 × 8-inch baking dish.
2. Prepare the fruit filling: In a large bowl, combine
   the pears, sugar, cornstarch, optional spices, and
   a pinch of salt. Stir gently until well combined,
   then transfer to the prepared baking dish.
3. Prepare the crisp topping: In another bowl,
   combine the oats, flour, brown sugar, cinnamon,
   and salt. Add the butter and use your fingers or
   a pastry cutter to incorporate it into the oat mixture until it looks like coarse crumbs. Sprinkle
   the crisp topping evenly over the fruit filling.
4. Bake for 35 to 40 minutes, or until the topping
   is golden brown and the fruit filling is bubbling.
5. Remove the crisp from the oven and allow it to
   cool for about 10 minutes before serving.

Quiche (Ham and Cheese)

Prep Time: 20 minutes
Cook Time: 45 minutes
Yield: 8 servings

Ingredients

- 1 store-bought frozen pastry pie shell, defrosted
  overnight
- 4 large eggs
- ⅔ cup whole milk
- ½ cup heavy cream (or heavy whipping cream)
- ¼ tsp. salt
- ¼ tsp. pepper
- 1 cup diced ham
- 1 cup shredded or crumbled cheese (feta,
  cheddar, blue cheese, goat cheese, or Gruyère)
- 1 cup diced cooked vegetables
- ¼ cup grated Parmesan cheese

Directions

1. Preheat oven to 350°F.
2. In a large bowl, beat the eggs, milk, cream, salt,
   and pepper on high speed, approximately 1
   minute.
3. Fold in the ham, along with your cheese and
   vegetables of choice. Use whatever you have
   on hand. Use whatever vegetables you have on
   hand. I love cooked asparagus, broccoli, onion,
   and mushrooms. Pour mixture into the crust.
4. Sprinkle the Parmesan cheese on top.
5. Cover the edges of the pie shell with aluminum
   foil to keep them from burning.
6. Bake quiche until the center is set and a toothpick comes out clean, about 45 minutes.
7. Let the quiche cool for 10 minutes before serving.

Cobb Salad

Prep Time: 30 minutes
Yield: 4 main servings or 8 side servings

Ingredients

6 cups mixed greens
2 grilled chicken breasts, sliced
8 strips bacon, cooked and crumbled
2 avocados, sliced
4 hard-boiled eggs, sliced
1 cup crumbled blue cheese
⅓ cup olive oil
3 T. apple cider vinegar
Salt and pepper, to taste

Directions

1. Arrange the mixed greens in a large salad bowl.
2. Arrange the chicken, bacon, avocado, eggs, and blue cheese on top of the greens in rows.
3. In a small bowl, whisk together the olive oil and apple cider vinegar.
4. Drizzle the dressing over the salad and add a sprinkle of salt and pepper.
5. Serve immediately, tossing the salad at the table just before serving.

Overnight Soup Bread

Who knew that this life-changing recipe would come from, of all places, TikTok! I have come to see it many places since, and it really is one of the simplest recipes for amazing, warm bread that complements soup perfectly.

One warning: This is not spur-of-the-moment bread. This bread, while it takes very little effort, does take a little forethought. But that's okay, because if you're prepping your soup on Saturday, just mix up this dough Saturday evening and then forget about it until about an hour before "Soup's On!" Your dough needs between 12 and 16 hours to rise, and then another hour of forming and baking. But trust me. It's easy, and it's worth it.

Prep Time: 10 minutes, plus 12 to 16 hours to rise
Cook Time: 45 minutes
Yield: 8 to 12 servings

Ingredients

1½ cups water, room temperature to warm
½ tsp. yeast
3 cups flour
1½ tsp. salt

Directions

1. Mix all ingredients together in an ovenproof bowl (not plastic). One option is to use the stand mixer to mix the dough and leave it in that bowl to rise.
2. Cover the bowl with a kitchen towel and place it in the oven with the oven light on. Let it sit undisturbed for 12 to 16 hours.
3. Remove the bowl from the oven and preheat the oven to 450°F.
4. Line a Dutch oven with parchment paper. You may find it helpful to first crinkle the parchment as this will help it stay in place inside your Dutch oven.
5. Flour a surface and place the dough on that surface. Stretch and fold the dough ball, then place it in the parchment-lined Dutch oven.
6. Use kitchen shears to make three snips on the top of the bread, allowing the bread to expand. Cover the Dutch oven with its lid.
7. Cook the bread in the covered Dutch oven for 30 minutes.
8. After 30 minutes, remove the Dutch oven lid and continue cooking for 15 more minutes.
9. Serve warm, accompanied by salted butter or a mix of oil and balsamic vinegar.

Like a snow-cooled drink at harvest time is a trustworthy messenger to the one who sends him; he refreshes the spirit of his master.

PROVERBS 25:13

Italian Zucchini and Sausage Bake

Prep Time: 20 minutes
Cook Time: 35 minutes
Yield: 8 servings

Ingredients

4 medium zucchini
2 T. olive oil
1 lb. Italian sausage
1 large onion, chopped
3 cloves garlic, minced
1 (15 oz.) can diced tomatoes
1 tsp. dried basil
1 tsp. dried oregano
Salt and pepper, to taste
2 cups shredded mozzarella cheese
¼ cup grated Parmesan cheese

Directions

1. Preheat your oven to 375°F and lightly grease a baking sheet or dish.
2. Cut each zucchini in half lengthwise and use a spoon or melon baller to hollow out the centers, making a "boat" with sides that are about ¼ inch thick. Place the zucchini on the baking sheet.
3. In a large skillet, heat the olive oil over medium-high heat. Add the Italian sausage (removing any skin) and cook until browned, breaking it up with a wooden spoon as it cooks. Remove the sausage from the skillet and set it aside.
4. In the same skillet, add the onion and minced garlic, cooking until the onion is translucent.
5. Add the tomatoes, basil, oregano, and a pinch of salt and pepper. Stir well and cook for a few more minutes.
6. Add back the sausage and cook for another 2 to 3 minutes until everything is well combined.
7. Spoon the sausage mixture into each zucchini boat, pressing it down and filling to the top.
8. Top each zucchini boat with a generous amount of mozzarella and Parmesan cheese.
9. Bake in the preheated oven for 25 to 30 minutes, or until the cheese is melted and bubbly and the zucchini is tender.
10. Remove from the oven and allow to cool for a few minutes before serving.

Risotto

Prep time: 15 minutes
Cook time: 25 minutes
Yield: 8 servings

Ingredients

7 cups chicken stock
2 T. olive oil
1 large shallot, finely chopped
2 cloves garlic, minced
Salt and pepper, to taste
1 cup sliced mushrooms
1 bay leaf
5 T. unsalted butter, divided
2 cups arborio rice
1 cup white wine or 1 additional cup chicken stock
1 T. fresh herbs (I like basil, but parsley, tarragon and chives are all wonderful)
¾ cup grated Parmesan, plus more for garnish
Lemon wedges

Directions

1. Warm the chicken stock in a large saucepan on medium-low heat. Keep it covered and warm.
2. In another saucepan or Dutch oven, heat the olive oil over medium heat. Add the shallot and garlic. Add salt and pepper to your own taste, also considering any salt and pepper that may already be in your stock. Cook for 3 to 4 minutes, stirring occasionally, until softened. Add mushrooms and sauté for 2 minutes.
3. Add bay leaf and 3 tablespoons of butter to the mixture. Stir until butter melts, around 1 minute.
4. Add rice and toast it for 3 to 4 minutes, stirring once. The rice should smell nutty and turn light golden brown.
5. Add the wine (or 1 cup of additional stock) and let it simmer until it evaporates completely, around 2 to 3 minutes.
6. Add 1 cup of warm stock to the rice, stirring gently until it's absorbed. This takes around 2 to 3 minutes.
7. Continue adding stock, 1 cup or ladleful at a time, and keep stirring until the rice is al dente. This takes around 17 to 19 minutes total. You may have some stock left over. Remove the bay leaf and add your fresh herbs.

8. If you prefer a risotto with more sauce, add more stock in ¼ cup increments until desired consistency is reached.

9. Stir in Parmesan, 2 tablespoons of butter, 1 teaspoon salt, and more black pepper. Serve with lemon wedges and extra Parmesan.

Air Fryer Honey Glazed Carrots

Prep Time: 5 minutes
Cook Time: 15 minutes
Yield: 6 servings

Ingredients

1 lb. baby carrots
2 T. olive oil
Salt and freshly ground black pepper, to taste
3 T. honey (for an extra kick, you could substitute with Mike's Hot Honey)

Directions

1. Place the carrots in a mixing bowl and drizzle them with olive oil. Toss until evenly coated.

2. Sprinkle salt and pepper over the carrots, tossing again to ensure they're well-seasoned.

3. Drizzle the honey over the carrots and toss one more time to coat them evenly.

4. Place the honey-glazed carrots in a single layer in the air fryer basket. Avoid overcrowding to ensure even cooking.

5. Set the air fryer to 375°F. Air fry for 12 to 15 minutes, checking halfway through to shake the basket (or use tongs to flip the carrots) for even cooking.

*This will bring health
to your body and nourishment
to your bones.*

Proverbs 3:8

Air Fryer Zucchini with Herbs and Parmesan

Prep Time: 10 minutes
Cook Time: 10 minutes
Yield: 4 servings

Ingredients

2 medium zucchinis, sliced into rounds or half-moons
2 T. olive oil
1 tsp. dried oregano
1 tsp. dried basil
Salt and pepper, to taste
¼ cup grated Parmesan cheese
Optional: Fresh parsley, for garnish
Optional: Lemon wedges, for serving

Directions

1. Preheat air fryer to 375°F.

2. In a mixing bowl, combine the zucchini, olive oil, oregano, basil, and salt and pepper. Toss well to coat the zucchini evenly.

3. Sprinkle the Parmesan cheese over the zucchini and toss again to make sure the slices are evenly coated.

4. Lay the seasoned zucchini slices in a single layer in the air fryer basket. You may need to cook them in batches, depending on the size of your air fryer.

5. Cook the zucchini at 375°F for 7 to 10 minutes, or until they are tender and slightly golden on the edges. Give the basket a shake halfway through to ensure even cooking.

6. Once cooked, you can garnish the zucchini with parsley and serve with lemon wedges if desired.

Week Eight

Christmas Week Classics

✦

As Christmas is a holiday that lands on a different day of the week each year, feel free to adjust what days you're serving which meals. And know that these are *for sure* classic meals that will be loved by friends and family alike.

Week 8 Menu

Saturday

Slow Cooker Ham with Pineapple Glaze
Air Fryer Twice-Baked Potatoes
Asparagus (no recipe)

Dessert:
Apple Cake

Sunday

Breakfast:
Overnight French Toast

Lunch:
Roasted Butternut Squash Soup
BLT Salad
Toasted Crostini (no recipe)

Dinner:
Chicken à la King
Garlic Green Beans

Monday

Cuban Sandwiches
Asparagus (no recipe)

Tuesday

Roasted Butternut Squash Soup
BLT Salad
Toasted Crostini (no recipe)

Wednesday

Leftovers or frozen meal of choice

Thursday

Dinner out

Friday

Pizza night!

Sabbath Soup

Roasted Butternut Squash Soup

Prep Time: 15 minutes • Cook Time: 75 minutes • Yield: 4 bowls or 8 cups

Ingredients

1 large butternut squash (3 lbs.)

2 T. olive oil, plus more for drizzling

1¼ tsp. salt, divided (more to taste)

½ tsp. freshly ground black pepper, divided

⅓ cup chopped shallot

4 garlic cloves, minced

1 tsp. maple syrup

⅛ tsp. ground nutmeg

4 cups vegetable or chicken broth, divided

1 to 2 T. butter, to taste

¼ cup heavy cream

Fresh herbs (optional)

Directions

1. Preheat the oven to 425°F and line a large baking sheet with parchment paper.

2. Cut the squash in half lengthwise and scoop out the seeds with a spoon. Drizzle the cut sides of the squash with about a tablespoon of the olive oil and use your hands to rub it in, ensuring even coverage. Sprinkle with ¼ teaspoon each salt and pepper.

3. Place the butternut squash halves cut-side down on the prepared baking sheet. Roast for 40 to 50 minutes, or until the squash is tender and easily pierced with a fork. Once done, remove the squash from the oven and allow it to cool until it can be handled safely.

4. Meanwhile, heat the remaining olive oil in a large pot over medium heat. Sauté the shallot with the remaining salt and pepper, stirring frequently until it becomes translucent, about 3 to 4 minutes.

5. Add the garlic and cook for an additional minute, stirring constantly. Remove from heat.

6. Remove and discard the squash skin, and add scoops of the squash flesh to a blender. Add the shallot and garlic mixture, along with the maple syrup, nutmeg, and about a cup of the broth.

7. With the blender lid slightly ajar to allow steam to escape, start blending the soup on low speed. Gradually increase the speed to high and slowly pour in the remaining broth through the opening in the lid. If your blender has a small capacity, you may need to work in batches to avoid overflowing.

8. Continue blending the soup until it reaches a smooth and creamy consistency. Add 1 to 2 tablespoons of butter to the blender and blend again until the butter is fully incorporated. Taste the soup and adjust the seasoning with additional salt and pepper, if needed.

9. Return the soup to the pot and place it over medium heat, stirring occasionally until warmed through.

10. Ladle the soup into bowls. Slowly pour up to 1 tablespoon cream in a swirl pattern directly into each bowl. Garnish with a sprinkle of freshly ground black pepper and fresh herbs.

Slow Cooker Ham with Pineapple Glaze

Prep Time: 15 minutes
Cook Time: 4 to 6 hours
Yield: 8 to 10 servings

Ingredients

2 cups pineapple juice
1 (5 to 7 lb.) fully-cooked ham
10 whole cloves
1 cup brown sugar
1 T. Dijon mustard
1 T. balsamic vinegar
1 T. honey
2 T. cornstarch

Directions

1. Using a sharp knife, score the ham in a diamond pattern, making cuts about ¼ inch deep. Insert the whole cloves into the intersections of the cuts.
2. Place the ham flat side down in the slow cooker. Pour the pineapple juice over the ham, making sure it coats all sides and gets into the cuts that you made.
3. In a small bowl, combine the brown sugar, Dijon mustard, balsamic vinegar, and honey. Using a spatula or your hands (I like to keep disposable gloves on hand—no pun intended—for just such jobs), spread the glaze evenly over the top and sides of the ham.
4. Cover the slow cooker with the lid and cook on low for 4 to 6 hours, basting the ham with the juices every 2 hours, if possible. The ham is done when it reaches an internal temperature of 140°F when measured with a meat thermometer.
5. Carefully remove the ham from the slow cooker and transfer it to a serving dish. Tent the ham loosely with aluminum foil and let it rest for 15 to 20 minutes to allow the juices to redistribute.
6. Meanwhile, pour the juices from the slow cooker into a saucepan (you can use a strainer to get all the big chunks). Bring the juices to a boil. Remove 2 tablespoons of the juice to a small bowl, and whisk in the cornstarch to create a slurry. Gradually pour it back into the boiling juices, whisking constantly to prevent lumps and form nice glaze. Once the slurry is fully incorporated, reduce the heat to low and simmer, stirring occasionally, for about 5 minutes or until it thickens to your desired consistency.
7. Discard the cloves, transfer the ham to a cutting board, and thinly slice the ham. Arrange the slices back on the serving dish, and drizzle the warm pineapple glaze over the ham, keeping a little extra on the side for guests to add as desired.

Air Fryer Twice-Baked Potatoes

Prep Time: 10 minutes
Cook Time: 50 minutes
Yield: 8 servings

Ingredients

4 large russet potatoes
1 T. olive oil
Salt and pepper, to taste
1 cup sour cream
2 cups shredded cheddar cheese, divided
4 strips bacon, cooked and crumbled
2 green onions, sliced

Directions

1. Preheat your air fryer to 400°F.
2. Pierce your potatoes with a fork several times, and coat with the olive oil, salt, and pepper. Place the potatoes on the trivet and air fry for 20 minutes.
3. With a pair of tongs, flip the potatoes over and continue to air fry for another 20 minutes. Remove from the air fryer and let sit for 5 minutes to cool slightly.
4. Once potatoes are cooked, cut in half lengthwise and scoop out the middle, leaving a thin layer of potato in the skin.
5. Mix the scooped potato with the sour cream, 1 cup of cheddar cheese, bacon, and green onion.
6. Stuff the potato skins with this mixture, then top with the remaining cheddar cheese.
7. Cook the potatoes in the air fryer at 375°F for 10 minutes, or until cheese is melted and bubbly. Serve hot.

Apple Cake

This cake is amazing both on its own or served with ice cream (or any kind of cream) and strong coffee. If you are serving this to guests, time it to finish baking right while they are coming through the door. Half the delight of this cake is the smell wafting through your house.

Prep Time: 15 minutes
Cook Time: 60 minutes
Yield: 16 servings

Ingredients

2 cups sugar
½ cup oil
2 eggs
4 cups peeled and diced apples
2 cups flour
2 tsp. baking soda
1 tsp. nutmeg
2 tsp. cinnamon
1 tsp. salt

Directions

1. Preheat your oven to 350°F. Grease a 9 × 13-inch pan.
2. Combine sugar, oil, and eggs in a large bowl, stirring until well mixed.
3. Stir in apples. Sift together flour, baking soda, nutmeg, cinnamon, and salt, then add to the bowl.
4. Stir all ingredients together to form a batter until the flour mixture is thoroughly mixed into the wet ingredients. Pour into greased pan. Bake one hour, or until golden and cake is set.

Overnight French Toast

This recipe is great to make with a crusty bread. Sourdough or French breads are great, but my favorite is brioche. For an extra special treat, serve this French toast with fresh berries and a side of bacon.

Prep Time: 10 minutes, plus 4 hours or overnight in the fridge
Cook Time: 45 to 60 minutes
Yield: 8 servings

Ingredients

1 loaf crusty bread
8 large eggs
2 cups whole milk
½ cup heavy cream
2 T. vanilla extract
1 tsp. cinnamon
½ tsp. nutmeg
½ tsp. salt
¼ cup sugar
½ cup brown sugar

Topping
½ cup all-purpose flour
½ cup packed light brown sugar
1 tsp. ground cinnamon
¼ tsp. salt
½ cup cold unsalted butter, diced
Warm maple syrup and butter, for serving

Directions

1. Grease a 9 × 13-inch pan with cooking spray. Cut bread into 1-inch chunks and spread evenly in pan.
2. In a medium bowl, mix together eggs, milk, cream, vanilla, cinnamon, nutmeg, salt, and sugars. Pour evenly over bread. Gently squish down the bread (using a food prep glove if you like) so that it's completely soaked in the mixture.
3. Cover the pan with plastic wrap and place in the fridge overnight (or for at least 4 hours).
4. Combine all the topping ingredients except butter in a medium bowl. Using a pastry blender or a large fork, cut the butter into the mixture until it resembles small pebbles. Cover and refrigerate overnight.
5. The next day, preheat the oven to 350°F.
6. Uncover the baking dish and place the topping evenly over the bread.
7. Bake for 45 to 60 minutes or until a clean toothpick comes out.

BLT Salad

Prep Time: 20 minutes
Yield: 4 main servings or 8 side servings

Ingredients

8 slices bacon, cooked and crumbled
4 cups chopped romaine lettuce
2 tomatoes, diced
½ cup bread croutons
¼ cup mayonnaise
1 T. lemon juice
Salt and pepper, to taste

Directions

1. In a large salad bowl, combine the bacon, romaine lettuce, tomatoes, and bread croutons.
2. In a small bowl, whisk together the mayonnaise and lemon juice.
3. Drizzle the dressing over the salad, season with a dash of salt and pepper, and gently toss to combine. Serve immediately.

*You make known to
me the path of life;
you will fill me
with joy
in your presence.*

PSALM 16:11

Chicken à la King

This classic recipe for Chicken à la King is a delicious and comforting meal that's perfect for dinner on a chilly night. The creamy sauce is packed with chicken and vegetables, making it a hearty dish that's sure to satisfy.

Prep Time: 15 minutes
Cook Time: 30 minutes
Yield: 8 servings

Ingredients

2 T. unsalted butter
1 small onion, finely diced
1 bell pepper, finely diced
1 cup sliced mushrooms
2 cloves garlic, minced
2 cups diced cooked chicken
¼ cup all-purpose flour
2 cups chicken broth
1 cup heavy cream
½ cup frozen peas
Salt and pepper, to taste
2 T. chopped fresh parsley
Toasted bread or biscuits, to serve

Directions

1. Melt butter in a large skillet over medium heat. Add the onion, bell pepper, and mushrooms. Cook until vegetables are tender, about 5 minutes.
2. Stir in the minced garlic and cook for an additional minute.
3. Add the diced chicken to the skillet.
4. Sprinkle the flour over the chicken and vegetables. Stir to coat.
5. Gradually add the chicken broth to the skillet, stirring constantly to prevent lumps from forming.
6. Add the heavy cream and frozen peas. Season with salt and pepper. Stir well to combine.
7. Reduce heat to low and simmer for about 15 minutes or until the sauce has thickened.
8. Stir in the parsley.
9. Serve the Chicken à la King over toasted bread or biscuits.

Garlic Green Beans

This recipe is very easy to do without precise measurements, and you can easily add more for any number of people you want to feed. As a general rule, 1 pound of fresh green beans will serve about 6 people.

Prep Time: 5 minutes
Cook Time: 9 minutes
Yield: customizable

Ingredients

Fresh green beans
Olive oil
Garlic powder
Salt
Pepper

Directions

1. Start by washing the green beans and trimming the ends.
2. Place the cleaned green beans in a mixing bowl. Drizzle olive oil over them, making sure they are evenly coated.
3. Season the green beans with garlic powder, salt, and pepper. Toss the beans to ensure even seasoning.
4. Lay out the seasoned green beans in a single layer in the air fryer basket. Try to avoid overcrowding for even cooking.
5. Set the air fryer to 370°F. Air fry the green beans for 7 to 9 minutes. Check halfway through and shake the basket or use tongs to flip the green beans for even cooking.
6. Serve and enjoy!

Come to me, all you who are weary and burdened, and I will give you rest.

MATTHEW 11:28

Cuban Sandwiches

This is a classic Cuban dish known for its delightful combination of flavors and textures, with the tangy mustard and pickles, melted Swiss cheese, and tender roasted pork and ham. It's a hearty and satisfying meal that's perfect for lunch or dinner.

Prep Time: 10 minutes
Cook Time: 6 minutes
Yield: 4 servings

Ingredients

4 sandwich rolls (Cuban bread if available, or French rolls), split in half lengthwise
¼ cup yellow mustard
2 T. mayonnaise
1 lb. thinly sliced roast pork deli meat
½ lb. thinly sliced ham deli meat
8 slices Swiss cheese
½ cup dill pickles, sliced
2 T. unsalted butter, softened

Directions

1. Preheat a griddle or large skillet over medium heat.
2. Spread the yellow mustard on one half of each sandwich roll, and mayonnaise on the other half.
3. On the half with the mayonnaise, stack the roast pork, ham, Swiss cheese, and dill pickles.
4. Close the sandwiches. Spread the butter on the outside (both top and bottom) of each sandwich.
5. Place the sandwiches on the preheated griddle or skillet. Cook for 2 to 3 minutes on each side, or until the bread is toasted to a golden brown and the cheese has melted.
6. To help flatten the sandwiches and create a crispy crust, you can press them down with a spatula or place another heavy skillet on top while they cook.
7. Once the sandwiches are cooked, remove them from the griddle or skillet and let them cool for a minute or two.
8. Slice the sandwiches in half diagonally and serve hot. Enjoy!

A Prayer for the Winter Season

Lord, I welcome winter
to my home and to my table.
I open my heart and
my hands to
the rhythms
You have created.

Lord, help me to
see the gifts
of this season.

I ask that winter brings
a fresh creative spark
through stews, cookies,
and casseroles.

May my home
be filled with joy
and cheer
that outlasts
the season.

In the long stretch
of cold and dark,
I ask for strength
and endurance.

May all who eat at this table
be reminded
of Your constant provision,
in this season
and the seasons to follow.

Week Nine
New Year's Joys

Whether it's your New Year's celebration or just another gathering of friends and family to honor the season, here is a menu that pulls out all the stops for your main meal, but will let you take it easy for the rest of the week.

Week 9 Menu

Saturday

Air Fryer Honey Soy Beef Kebabs
Risotto
Broccoli (no recipe)

Dessert:
Chocolate Bûche
de Noël (Yule Log)

Sunday

Breakfast:
Air Fryer Sugar and Cinnamon
Donuts

Lunch:
Wonton Soup
Asian Sesame Salad
(with Chicken)

Dinner:
Air Fryer Buffalo Chicken Wings
Leafy Green Salad (no recipe)

Monday

Taco Salad
Corn Bread

Tuesday

Wonton Soup
Asian Sesame Salad
(with Chicken)
Veggie-Stuffed Vietnamese
Spring Rolls (store-bought)

Wednesday

Leftovers or frozen meal of choice

Thursday

Dinner out

Friday

Pizza night!

Sabbath Soup

Wonton Soup

Prep Time: 5 minutes • Cook Time: 20 minutes • Yield: 4 bowls or 8 cups

Ingredients

2 cups chicken stock

2 T. soy sauce

1-inch fresh ginger, thinly sliced

3 cloves garlic, minced

2 cups thinly sliced shitake or
baby bella mushrooms

Salt and pepper, to taste

48 mini wontons (I use the
Bibigo Chicken and Cilantro
Mini Wontons from the freezer
section at Costco)

1 scallion, thinly sliced

Directions

1. In your stockpot, bring the chicken stock, soy sauce, ginger, and garlic to a boil. Add mushrooms and cook for 5 minutes. Start with ¼ teaspoon each of salt and pepper, and adjust if necessary.

2. Add mini wontons and cook for another 2 to 3 minutes (until wontons start to float to the top). Serve with scallions on top.

Air Fryer Honey Soy Beef Kebabs

Prep Time: 15 minutes, plus 30 minutes or up to 24 hours to marinate
Cook Time: 10 minutes
Yield: 4 servings

Ingredients

¼ cup low-sodium soy sauce
2 T. honey
2 T. olive oil
2 cloves garlic, minced
1 tsp. grated fresh ginger
1 T. sesame seeds
Salt and pepper, to taste
1 lb. beef sirloin, cut into 1-inch cubes
Bamboo skewers, soaked in water for 30 minutes

Directions

1. In a large bowl, combine soy sauce, honey, olive oil, garlic, ginger, sesame seeds, salt, and pepper. Stir well to combine.
2. Add the beef cubes to the bowl and toss them in the marinade until well coated. Let it marinate for at least 30 minutes or refrigerate overnight for best results.
3. Preheat your air fryer to 400°F for 5 minutes.
4. Thread the marinated beef onto the soaked bamboo skewers, leaving a small space between each piece.
5. Place the beef skewers in a single layer inside the air fryer basket. You may need to cook them in batches depending on the size of your air fryer.
6. Cook the beef kebabs in the air fryer for 8 to 10 minutes, flipping them halfway through the cooking time. The exact cooking time may vary based on the thickness of the beef and the desired level of doneness.
7. Once the beef is cooked to your liking, remove the kebabs from the air fryer and let them rest for a few minutes before serving.

Risotto

Prep time: 15 minutes
Cook time: 25 minutes
Yield: 8 servings

Ingredients

7 cups chicken stock
2 T. olive oil
1 large shallot, finely chopped
2 cloves garlic, minced
Salt and pepper, to taste
1 cup sliced mushrooms
1 bay leaf
5 T. unsalted butter, divided
2 cups arborio rice
1 cup white wine or 1 additional cup chicken stock
1 T. fresh herbs (I like basil, but parsley, tarragon, and chives are all wonderful)
¾ cup grated Parmesan, plus more for garnish
Lemon wedges

Directions

1. Warm the chicken stock in a large saucepan on medium-low heat. Keep it covered and warm.
2. In another saucepan or Dutch oven, heat the olive oil over medium heat. Add the shallot and garlic. Add salt and pepper to your own taste, also considering any salt and pepper that may already be in your stock. Cook for 3 to 4 minutes, stirring occasionally, until softened. Add mushrooms and sauté for 2 minutes.
3. Add bay leaf and 3 tablespoons of butter to the mixture. Stir until butter melts, around 1 minute.
4. Add rice and toast it for 3 to 4 minutes, stirring once. The rice should smell nutty and turn light golden brown.
5. Add the wine (or 1 cup of additional stock) and let it simmer until it evaporates completely, around 2 to 3 minutes.
6. Add 1 cup of warm stock to the rice, stirring gently until it's absorbed. This takes around 2 to 3 minutes.
7. Continue adding stock, 1 cup or ladleful at a time, and keep stirring until the rice is al dente. This takes around 17 to 19 minutes total. You may have some stock left over. Remove the bay leaf and add your fresh herbs.

8 If you prefer a risotto with more sauce, add more stock in ¼ cup increments until desired consistency is reached.

9. Stir in Parmesan, 2 tablespoons of butter, 1 teaspoon salt, and more black pepper. Serve with lemon wedges and extra Parmesan.

Chocolate Bûche de Noël (Yule Log)

Prep Time: 25 minutes
Cook Time: 15 minutes
Yield: 8 servings

Ingredients

Cake

    4 large eggs, separated
    ¾ cup granulated sugar, divided
    1 tsp. pure vanilla extract
    ½ cup all-purpose flour
    ¼ cup unsweetened cocoa powder
    ½ tsp. baking powder
    ¼ tsp. salt
    Powdered sugar, for dusting

Filling

    1 cup heavy cream
    2 T. powdered sugar
    1 tsp. pure vanilla extract

Ganache

    1 cup heavy cream
    8 oz. semi-sweet chocolate, chopped

Directions

For the Cake:

1. Preheat your oven to 350°F. Line a 15 × 10-inch jelly roll pan with parchment paper, then grease and lightly flour the paper.

2. In a large bowl, beat egg yolks until thickened. Gradually add ½ cup sugar, beating until thick and lemon-colored. Stir in vanilla.

3. In another bowl, combine flour, cocoa, baking powder, and salt; gradually add to yolk mixture until well blended.

4. In a separate bowl, beat egg whites until soft peaks form. Gradually add remaining ¼ cup sugar, beating on high until stiff peaks form. Gently fold into chocolate mixture.

5. Spread batter evenly into prepared pan. Bake for 12 to 15 minutes or until cake springs back when lightly touched.

6. Dust a clean kitchen towel with powdered sugar. Once the cake is done, immediately invert onto a smooth kitchen towel, such as a flour-sack towel. Gently peel off the paper. Starting at one short side, roll up the cake in the towel jelly-roll style. Cool completely on a wire rack.

For the Filling:

7. Beat the cream until it begins to thicken. Add powdered sugar and vanilla; beat until stiff peaks form.

8. Unroll the cooled cake; spread cream filling to within half an inch of the edges. Roll up the cake again without the towel; place seam side down on a serving platter.

For the Ganache:

9. Heat cream over medium heat until hot but not boiling. Remove from heat and stir in chocolate until smooth. Let cool until it reaches a spreadable consistency.

10. Frost cake with chocolate ganache. If desired, make shallow cuts in the frosting with a fork to resemble bark. Refrigerate until serving.

Air Fryer Sugar and Cinnamon Donuts

Prep Time: 5 minutes
Cook Time: 10 minutes
Yield: 6 servings

Ingredients

    1 (16.3 oz) can Pillsbury Grands! Flaky Layers Original Biscuits (from the refrigerated section of the supermarket)
    Cooking spray (preferably butter-flavored)
    ½ cup granulated sugar
    2 tsp. ground cinnamon
    ¼ cup unsalted butter, melted

Directions

1. Open the can of biscuits and separate each biscuit.

2. Use a very small round biscuit cutter (or the cap from a plastic water bottle) to cut out the center of each biscuit to create a donut shape. Save the cutouts to make donut holes.

3. Fully preheat your air fryer to 350°F (if your air fryer requires preheating).

4. Lightly spray the air fryer basket with the cooking spray to prevent sticking. Place the donuts and donut holes into the basket, ensuring they are not touching. You may need to do this in batches depending on the size of your air fryer.

5. Cook for about 5 minutes or until they're golden brown and cooked through. Repeat this process until all the donuts and donut holes have been cooked.

6. While the donuts are cooking, mix together the sugar and cinnamon in a shallow bowl or plate.

7. Once the donuts are cooked, allow them to cool slightly and then lightly brush each one with the melted butter. Immediately dip each buttered donut into the cinnamon sugar mixture, turning to coat evenly.

8. Serve the donuts warm for best flavor.

Asian Sesame Salad (with Chicken)

This is a great side salad, or you can turn it into a main dish with the addition of cooked, shredded chicken. The addition of sesame seeds, mandarin oranges, and wonton strips takes it to the next level.

Prep Time: 15 minutes
Yield: 4 main servings or 8 side servings

Ingredients

6 cups mixed greens
1 cup shredded carrots
1 cucumber, sliced
¼ cup Asian Salad Dressing
Optional additions:
2 cups cooked, shredded chicken
2 cups wonton strips
Sesame seeds for garnish
Canned mandarin oranges

Directions

1. In a large salad bowl, combine the mixed greens, carrots, and cucumber.

2. Toss with the Asian Salad Dressing and serve immediately.

3. If desired, add chicken, wonton strips, sesame seeds, and mandarin oranges in desired amounts per plate. You may want a little extra dressing if you include a lot of additions.

Asian Salad Dressing

Ingredients

¼ cup soy sauce
2 T. sesame oil
2 T. rice vinegar
1 tsp. sugar
1 garlic clove, minced
1 tsp. finely grated fresh ginger
1 T. lime juice
Optional: 1 tsp. sesame seeds for garnish

Directions

1. In a bowl, whisk together soy sauce, sesame oil, rice vinegar, and sugar until the sugar is completely dissolved.

2. Add the garlic and ginger and whisk again to combine everything.

3. Squeeze in the lime juice—this will add a tangy freshness to the dressing.

4. Once everything is well mixed, taste and adjust as needed. For example, if it's too salty, you can add more vinegar or lime juice. If it's too tangy, add a bit more sugar.

Air Fryer Buffalo Chicken Wings

Prep Time: 10 minutes
Cook Time: 24 minutes
Yield: 4 to 5 servings

Ingredients

2½ lbs. chicken wings
½ cup hot sauce
⅓ cup butter, melted
Blue Cheese Dressing, to serve

Directions

1. Preheat the air fryer to 400°F.

2. Place the chicken wings in a large colander and rinse them under cold running water. After draining, press dry with a paper towel. This will help the wings crisp up nicely in the air fryer.

3. Lightly spray the air fryer basket with oil to prevent sticking. Place the wings in the basket

in a single layer, cooking in multiple batches if needed to avoid overcrowding.

4. Air fry the wings for 22 to 24 minutes, flipping at the halfway point. The wings should reach an internal temperature of 165°F and be crispy and golden brown.

5. While the wings are cooking, prepare the sauce. Melt the butter in a small saucepan over low heat, then whisk in your favorite hot sauce (we like Frank's Red Hot or Sriracha). Simmer the sauce for 2 to 3 minutes, stirring occasionally.

6. Once the wings are cooked, transfer them to a large mixing bowl. Pour the sauce over the wings and toss to coat evenly. Serve immediately with Blue Cheese Dressing.

Blue Cheese Dressing

Prep Time: 5 minutes
Yield: 8 servings

Ingredients

½ cup mayonnaise
¼ cup sour cream
1 T. white vinegar
½ cup crumbled blue cheese
Salt and freshly ground pepper, to taste

Directions

Mix all ingredients in a bowl until well combined.

Taco Salad

Prep Time: 30 minutes
Cook Time: 10 minutes
Yield: 4 main servings or 8 side servings

Ingredients

1 lb. ground beef
1 packet taco seasoning (about 1 oz. or 3 T.)
6 cups chopped romaine lettuce
1 (15 oz.) can black beans, drained and rinsed
1 cup corn kernels
1 cup cherry tomatoes, halved
1 cup shredded cheddar cheese
¼ cup sliced black olives (optional)
1 avocado, diced
½ cup sour cream

½ cup salsa
Salt and pepper, to taste

Directions

1. In a large skillet, cook the ground beef over medium heat until browned. Drain off any excess fat.

2. Stir in the taco seasoning, following the package directions.

3. In a large salad bowl, arrange the romaine lettuce. Top with the cooked beef, black beans, corn, cherry tomatoes, cheddar cheese, black olives, and avocado.

4. In a small bowl, combine the sour cream and salsa to create a dressing. Drizzle the dressing over the salad, sprinkle with a dash of salt and pepper, and gently toss to combine. Serve immediately.

Corn Bread

Prep Time: 10 minutes
Cook Time: 20 minutes
Yield: 9 servings

Ingredients

1 cup cornmeal
1 cup all-purpose flour
¼ cup sugar
1 T. baking powder
½ tsp. salt
1 cup milk
¼ cup vegetable oil
2 large eggs

Directions

1. Preheat the oven to 400°F and grease a 9 × 9-inch baking pan.

2. In a large bowl, combine the cornmeal, flour, sugar, baking powder, and salt.

3. In a separate bowl, whisk together the milk, vegetable oil, and eggs.

4. Add the wet ingredients to the dry and stir until just combined.

5. Pour the batter into the prepared pan and bake for 20 minutes, or until a toothpick inserted in the center comes out clean.

6. Allow to cool slightly before cutting into squares to serve.

A Prayer for a Busy Week

Lord, this week is full
and I'm struggling to find
moments of peace.

I feel the crunch of
time and responsibilities.
I often find myself frustrated
and overwhelmed.

I don't want to live this way.

Lord, meet me
in the fullness of my days.
I humbly ask that the moments
I spend creating meals
would be moments
of connection with You.

May the time spent cooking be a
pause for peace.

As I prepare for meals:
may my breath slow,
my nerves release,
my heart center
on who You are
and not what
needs to be done.

Please show me how to
work and live
out of Your abundance of
provision and love.

Week Ten
Family Favorites

Winter shifts most any human into a Sabbath-rest mode. The cozy factor and more days spent indoors will create a sense of cocooning. Comfort is necessary, and serving up the foods your family loves most will please their palates and their spirits.

Almost any family favorite can be turned into a soup; this week's menu is proof of that. Your family (kids included) will love this twist on a traditional lasagna by making it into a soup.

Week 10 Menu

Saturday
Orange-Glazed Pork Chops
Broccoli and Cheddar Rice
  Casserole
Dessert:
Gingerbread Cake with
  Cinnamon Cream
  Cheese Frosting

Sunday
Breakfast:
Amazing Mix-In Muffins
  (Blueberry and Raspberry)
Lunch:
Lasagna Soup
Caesar Salad
Overnight Soup Bread
Dinner:
Air Fryer Yakitori Chicken
Mixed Vegetable Stir-Fry
Rice (no recipe)

Monday
Slow Cooker Pulled Pork
Mixed Vegetable Stir-Fry
Rice (no recipe)

Tuesday
Lasagna Soup
Bagged Salad (no recipe)
Toasted Bread (no recipe)

Wednesday
Leftovers or frozen meal of choice

Thursday
Dinner out

Friday
Pizza night!

Sabbath Soup

Lasagna Soup

Prep Time: 20 minutes • Cook Time: 40 minutes • Yield: 4 bowls or 8 cups

Ingredients

½ lb. ground beef

½ lb. ground Italian sausage

2 T. olive oil

2 yellow onions, chopped

5 garlic cloves, minced

2 T. tomato paste

1 (24 oz.) can crushed tomatoes

1½ T. dried Italian herbs

8 cups chicken or vegetable broth

9 lasagna noodles

10 oz. ricotta cheese

1 cup shredded mozzarella cheese

½ cup grated Parmesan cheese

Fresh basil for serving

Directions

1. In a large skillet, brown the meat over medium-high heat, breaking it up with a wooden spoon as it cooks. Drain the cooked meat on a plate lined with paper towels to absorb excess grease.

2. Meanwhile, in a large Dutch oven or heavy-bottomed pot, heat the olive oil over medium heat. Sauté the onion until just starting to brown, about 7 to 8 minutes. Stir in the garlic.

3. After cooking for another 1 to 2 minutes, push the vegetables to one side of the pot and add the tomato paste to the empty space. Allow the tomato paste to caramelize for 1 to 2 minutes before stirring it into the onion mixture.

4. Stir in the crushed tomatoes, herbs, and broth. Bring the mixture to a boil, then reduce the heat to medium-low. Break the noodles into pieces and add them to the pot. Stirring occasionally, simmer the soup for 10 to 12 minutes or until the noodles are tender and cooked through.

5. Meanwhile, combine the three cheeses in a medium bowl.

6. When the noodles are al dente, stir the browned meat into the soup and heat through for an additional 2 to 3 minutes.

7. Ladle the hot soup into individual bowls. Place a generous dollop of the cheese mixture on top of each serving and garnish with basil. Serve immediately.

Orange-Glazed Pork Chops

Prep Time: 5 minutes
Cook Time: 30 minutes
Yield: 4 servings

Ingredients

4 pork chops
Salt and pepper, to taste
2 T. olive oil
½ cup orange marmalade
¼ cup orange juice
2 cloves garlic, minced
1 T. soy sauce
1 tsp. dried rosemary

Directions

1. Season the pork chops with salt and pepper on both sides.
2. Heat the olive oil in a skillet over medium-high heat. Add the pork chops and cook until browned on both sides, about 5 to 7 minutes each side. Remove the chops and set them aside.
3. In the same skillet, add the orange marmalade, orange juice, garlic, soy sauce, and rosemary. Stir well to combine and heat until bubbling.
4. Return the pork chops to the skillet, coating them in the glaze. Reduce the heat to medium-low and simmer for another 5 minutes, or until the pork chops are cooked through.
5. Serve the pork chops with the remaining glaze from the pan.

Broccoli and Cheddar Rice Casserole

Prep Time: 15 minutes
Cook Time: 45 minutes
Yield: 8 servings

Ingredients

1 T. olive oil
1 small onion, finely chopped
2 cups long-grain white rice
4 cups chicken broth
½ tsp. dry mustard
½ tsp. smoked paprika
Salt and pepper, to taste
2 cups broccoli florets
2 cups shredded cheddar cheese

Directions

1. Preheat the oven to 375°F.
2. In a large oven-safe skillet or Dutch oven, heat the olive oil over medium heat. Add the onion and cook until it is soft and translucent, about 5 minutes.
3. Add the rice to the skillet and stir to coat with the oil and onion. Cook for another 2 minutes.
4. Pour in the chicken broth, dry mustard, and smoked paprika and bring the mixture to a simmer. Season with salt and pepper.
5. Stir in the broccoli florets, then sprinkle the cheddar cheese on top. Cover the skillet with a lid or aluminum foil and transfer it to the preheated oven.
6. Bake for 35 to 40 minutes, until the rice is tender and the cheese is bubbly and slightly golden.
7. Let the dish stand for a few minutes before fluffing the rice with a fork. Serve hot.

Gingerbread Cake with Cinnamon Cream Cheese Frosting

Prep Time: 20 minutes
Cook Time: 35 to 40 minutes
Yield: 8 servings

Ingredients

Gingerbread Cake
2 cups all-purpose flour
½ cup dark brown sugar, packed
1 tsp. baking soda
1½ tsp. ground ginger
1 tsp. ground cinnamon
¼ tsp. ground cloves
¼ tsp. ground nutmeg
½ tsp. salt
¾ cup unsalted butter, melted
¾ cup molasses
¼ cup honey
2 large eggs, room temperature
1 cup buttermilk
1 tsp. vanilla extract

Cinnamon Cream Cheese Frosting
½ cup unsalted butter, room temperature
8 oz. cream cheese, room temperature
3 to 4 cups powdered sugar, sifted

1 tsp. vanilla extract

2 tsp. ground cinnamon

Directions

1. Preheat your oven to 350°F. Grease and flour a 9-inch cake pan.

2. In a large bowl, whisk together the flour, brown sugar, baking soda, ginger, cinnamon, cloves, nutmeg, and salt.

3. In another bowl, combine the melted butter, molasses, honey, eggs, buttermilk, and vanilla extract.

4. Gradually add the wet ingredients to the dry ingredients, stirring until just combined.

5. Pour the batter into the prepared cake pan and smooth the top with a spatula.

6. Bake for 35 to 40 minutes, or until a toothpick inserted into the center comes out clean.

7. Allow the cake to cool in the pan for 10 minutes, then transfer it to a wire rack to cool completely.

8. While the cake is cooling, prepare the frosting: In a large bowl, beat together the butter and cream cheese until smooth and creamy. Gradually add the powdered sugar, 1 cup at a time, beating well after each addition. Finally, beat in the vanilla extract and cinnamon.

9. Once the cake has cooled completely, spread the frosting evenly over the top.

He wrote them to observe
the days as days of
feasting and joy
and giving presents of food
to one another and
gifts to the poor.

ESTHER 9:22

Amazing Mix-In Muffins (Blueberry and Raspberry)

Prep Time: 10 minutes

Cook Time: 25 minutes

Yield: 12 muffins

Ingredients

2 cups all-purpose flour

¾ cup granulated sugar

½ tsp. salt

2 tsp. baking powder

⅓ cup vegetable oil

1 large egg, room temperature

1 tsp. vanilla extract

¾ cup milk

¾ cup fresh or frozen blueberries

¾ cup fresh or frozen raspberries

Directions

1. Preheat your oven to 400°F. Line a 12-cup muffin tin with paper liners or grease the cups with nonstick cooking spray.

2. In a large bowl, whisk together the flour, sugar, salt, and baking powder.

3. In a separate medium bowl, combine the vegetable oil, egg, vanilla extract, and milk. Stir well.

4. Gently pour the wet ingredients into the dry ingredients and mix until just combined. Be careful not to overmix, as this can result in tough muffins.

5. Fold in the berries until evenly distributed throughout the batter.

6. Divide the batter evenly among the 12 muffin cups, filling each about two-thirds full.

7. Bake for 20 to 25 minutes, or until a toothpick inserted into the center of a muffin comes out clean.

8. Remove the muffins from the oven and allow them to cool in the tin for 5 minutes before transferring to a wire rack to cool completely.

Caesar Salad

Prep Time: 15 minutes
Yield: 4 main servings or 8 side servings

Ingredients

1 head romaine lettuce, torn into bite-size pieces
1 cup croutons
½ cup freshly grated Parmesan cheese
½ cup Creamy Caesar Dressing

Directions

1. In a large salad bowl, combine the romaine lettuce, croutons, and Parmesan cheese.
2. Pour the dressing over the salad and toss until well coated.
3. Serve immediately, with additional Parmesan cheese on top if desired.

Creamy Caesar Dressing

Ingredients

¾ cup mayonnaise
2 T. fresh lemon juice
2 garlic cloves, minced
1 tsp. Worcestershire sauce
1 tsp. Dijon mustard
¼ cup grated Parmesan cheese
Salt and freshly ground pepper, to taste

Directions

Combine all ingredients in a blender or food processor and blend until smooth.

Sing to the LORD *a new song,*
for he has done marvelous things.

PSALM 98:1

Overnight Soup Bread

Who knew that this life-changing recipe would come from, of all places, TikTok! I have come to see it many places since, and it really is one of the simplest recipes for amazing, warm bread that complements soup perfectly.

One warning: This is not spur-of-the-moment bread. This bread, while it takes very little effort, does take a little forethought. But that's okay, because if you're prepping your soup on Saturday, just mix up this dough Saturday evening and then forget about it until about an hour before "Soup's On!" Your dough needs between 12 and 16 hours to rise, and then another hour of forming and baking. But trust me. It's easy, and it's worth it.

Prep Time: 10 minutes, plus 12 to 16 hours to rise
Cook Time: 45 minutes
Yield: 8 to 12 servings

Ingredients

1 ½ cups water, room temperature to warm
½ tsp. yeast
3 cups flour
1 ½ tsp. salt

Directions

1. Mix all ingredients together in an ovenproof bowl (not plastic). One option is to use the stand mixer to mix the dough and leave it in that bowl to rise.
2. Cover the bowl with a kitchen towel and place it in the oven with the oven light on. Let it sit undisturbed for 12 to 16 hours.
3. Remove the bowl from the oven and preheat the oven to 450°F.
4. Line a Dutch oven with parchment paper. You may find it helpful to first crinkle the parchment as this will help it stay in place inside your Dutch oven.
5. Flour a surface and place the dough on that surface. Stretch and fold the dough ball, then place it in the parchment-lined Dutch oven.
6. Use kitchen shears to make three snips on the top of the bread, allowing the bread to expand. Cover the Dutch oven with its lid.

7. Cook the bread in the covered Dutch oven for 30 minutes.

8. After 30 minutes, remove the Dutch oven lid and continue cooking for 15 more minutes.

9. Serve warm, accompanied by salted butter or a mix of oil and balsamic vinegar.

Air Fryer Yakitori Chicken

Prep Time: 10 minutes, plus 30 minutes to marinate
Cook Time: 15 minutes
Yield: 4 servings

Ingredients

¼ cup soy sauce
2 T. mirin (or substitute with 1 tablespoon of sugar)
2 T. sake (or substitute with dry white wine)
1 T. brown sugar
1 T. minced fresh ginger
1 lb. boneless skinless chicken thighs, cut into bite-size pieces
2 green onions, chopped into 1-inch lengths
Bamboo skewers (soaked in water for at least 30 minutes to prevent burning)

Directions

1. In a medium bowl, mix together the soy sauce, mirin, sake, brown sugar, and ginger to create the yakitori marinade.

2. Add the chicken pieces to the bowl and let them marinate for at least 30 minutes (or up to 24 hours in the refrigerator for a deeper flavor).

3. Preheat the air fryer to 375°F.

4. Thread the chicken pieces and green onions onto the soaked bamboo skewers, alternating between the two. Try to end with a piece of chicken to prevent the onions from burning.

5. Place the skewers in the air fryer basket, ensuring they don't overlap.

6. Cook for about 12 to 15 minutes, turning halfway through, or until the chicken is thoroughly cooked and slightly charred.

7. Serve your Air Fryer Yakitori Chicken immediately, garnished with sesame seeds or chopped spring onions, if desired. Enjoy this classic Japanese dish at home with minimal effort!

Note: Please remember that cooking times may vary depending on the model and size of your air fryer.

Mixed Vegetable Stir-Fry

Prep Time: 10 minutes
Cook Time: 12 minutes
Yield: 4 servings

Ingredients

1 small onion, thinly sliced
1 medium carrot, julienned or thinly sliced
1 bell pepper, thinly sliced
1 medium zucchini, sliced into half-moons
1 cup sliced mushrooms
2 T. vegetable oil or olive oil
3 cloves garlic, minced
Salt and freshly ground black pepper, to taste
1 T. soy sauce
1 T. oyster sauce (optional)
Dash of sesame oil (optional)

Directions

1. Prepare the onion, carrot, bell pepper, zucchini, and mushrooms so they are sliced into uniformly thin slices not more than 1½ to 2 inches long.

2. Place a large skillet or wok over medium-high heat. Add the vegetable oil and let it heat up.

3. Add the garlic and onion to the pan. Stir-fry for about 1 to 2 minutes, until the onion starts to soften and the garlic is fragrant.

4. Add the carrot and bell pepper to the pan. Stir-fry for about 2 to 3 minutes to soften them slightly.

5. Incorporate the zucchini and mushrooms into the pan. Stir-fry for another 4 to 5 minutes, or until all the vegetables are tender but still crisp.

6. Season with salt and black pepper. Add the soy sauce and oyster sauce. Stir well to combine.

7. If you're using sesame oil, add it at this point for added flavor. Continue to stir-fry for an additional 1 to 2 minutes to make sure all the vegetables are well coated with the sauce.

8. Remove from heat and transfer to a serving dish. Serve immediately as a side dish or over rice or noodles for a main course.

Slow Cooker Pulled Pork

Enjoy this slow-cooked pulled pork perfection—it's worth the wait! The delicious combination of sweet, tangy, and spicy flavors will make this a hit at any gathering. Plus, the aroma of it cooking all day will make your home smell absolutely mouthwatering! Serve the pulled pork on Hawaiian rolls, topped with extra BBQ sauce if desired. Coleslaw and dill pickles make excellent sides for this dish.

Prep Time: 15 minutes
Cook Time: 6 hours on high (or 10 to 12 hours on low)
Yield: 6 to 8 servings

Ingredients

1 (4 lb.) pork shoulder roast
Salt and pepper, to taste
1½ cups BBQ sauce, plus extra for serving
½ cup apple cider vinegar
½ cup chicken broth
¼ cup light brown sugar
1 T. yellow mustard
1 T. Worcestershire sauce
1 T. chili powder
½ tsp. cinnamon
1 large onion, finely chopped
2 cloves garlic, crushed
1½ tsp. dried thyme
Optional: Hawaiian rolls, coleslaw, and dill pickles for serving

Directions

1. Rub your pork shoulder roast with a generous amount of salt and pepper. Then place it in the bottom of your slow cooker.
2. In a medium bowl, combine the BBQ sauce, apple cider vinegar, chicken broth, brown sugar, yellow mustard, Worcestershire sauce, chili powder, and cinnamon. Stir until all ingredients are well mixed.
3. Scatter the onion, garlic, and thyme into the slow cooker and pour the sauce mixture over the top of the roast, ensuring it's well coated.
4. Place the lid on the slow cooker and cook on high for 5 to 6 hours or on low for 10 to 12 hours. The pork is done when it easily shreds with a fork.
5. Once the pork is ready, carefully remove it from the slow cooker into a large bowl. Use two forks to shred the meat. If you prefer, you can also use a hand mixer for this task.
6. After shredding the pork, return it to the slow cooker and use a wooden spoon to stir the meat into the juices to ensure every piece is succulent and flavorful.

Create in me a pure heart,
O God, and renew a steadfast
spirit within me.
Psalm 51:10

Week Eleven
The Hearty Table

This week's meals are all easy to make but will leave you and your people feeling fulfilled. These are warm, hearty, and satisfying meals that are great to serve to your family, or to use as a seasonal go-to when guests gather around your table and you want to spend less time in the kitchen and more time lingering over a comforting meal and good conversation.

Week 11 Menu

Saturday

Oven Brisket
Creamy Yukon Gold Mashed
   Potatoes
Broccoli (no recipe)

Dessert:
S'mores Brownies

Sunday

Breakfast:

Overnight Oatmeal
   with Apples and Apricots

Lunch:

Black Bean Soup
Harvest Salad
Corn Bread

Dinner:

Charcuterie Board
Caesar Salad
Cracker Assortment (no recipe)

Monday

Taco Salad with leftover brisket
Roasted Corn Salad

Tuesday

Black Bean Soup
Taco Salad

Wednesday

Leftovers or frozen meal of choice

Thursday

Dinner out

Friday

Pizza night!

Sabbath Soup

Black Bean Soup

Prep Time: 5 minutes • Cook Time: 5 hours in a slow cooker
Yield: 4 bowls or 8 cups

Ingredients

2 (15 oz.) cans black beans, (drained & rinsed)

1 (15 oz.) can chicken broth

1 (15 oz.) can cream of chicken soup

1 (15 oz.) can Mexican corn

1 (16 oz.) jar salsa, any heat level

Toppings

Mexican blend shredded cheese

Sour cream

Tortilla chips

Directions

1. Mix together all the ingredients except for the toppings. Cook for 5 hours on the low setting of a slow cooker without using the lid.

2. Garnish with cheese, a dollop of sour cream, and crumbled tortilla chips.

3. Serve with corn bread or chips (whatever you have on hand).

Oven Brisket

Prep Time: 10 minutes
Cook Time: 6 hours, plus 10 minutes to rest
Yield: 10 servings

Ingredients

3 cups water
⅓ cup liquid smoke
1 (5 to 6 lb.) boneless beef brisket
For the Rub:
3 T. sea salt
¼ cup brown sugar
1 tsp. nutmeg
¼ cup chili powder
2 T. paprika
2 T. dried mustard
2 T. garlic powder
2 T. onion powder
3 tsp. dried thyme

Directions

1. Preheat the oven to 250°F. In a large roasting pan, combine the water and liquid smoke. Place a wire rack in the pan to hold the meat above the liquid.
2. Place the brisket on a cutting board and trim any excess fat. Whisk together the rub ingredients and generously coat the brisket on all sides, using your hands to really massage the spices into the meat. Transfer the brisket to the wire rack in the roasting pan.
3. Tightly cover the roasting pan with aluminum foil, making sure to seal the edges well.
4. Roast the meat for 4 to 5 hours, or until a meat thermometer registers 175°F when inserted in the thickest part of the brisket.
5. Remove the foil and continue cooking, uncovered, for another 1 to 2 hours or until the internal temperature reaches 195°F. This will help develop a nice crust on the exterior of the brisket. (Which is kind of magical and tastes delicious.)
6. Remove the brisket from the oven and allow it to rest, loosely covered with more foil, to allow the juices to redistribute throughout the meat, ensuring a more tender and flavorful result. (It's hard to wait, but so worth it.)
7. After about 10 minutes, transfer the brisket to a cutting board and slice it thinly across the grain. Arrange the slices on a serving platter and spoon some of the pan juices over the top, if desired.

Creamy Yukon Gold Mashed Potatoes

Prep Time: 15 minutes
Cook Time: 20 minutes
Yield: 8 servings

Ingredients

3 lbs. Yukon Gold potatoes
1 cup whole milk (or half-and-half for a richer texture)
½ cup unsalted butter
Salt and freshly ground black pepper, to taste
Optional: minced garlic, fresh herbs (like chives or parsley) for garnish

Directions

1. Start by washing and peeling the potatoes. Cut them into uniform chunks, about 2 inches in size.
2. Place the potato chunks in a large pot and fill with enough water to cover them. Add a generous pinch of salt to the water. Bring the water to a boil over high heat, then reduce to a simmer. Cook the potatoes until they are fork-tender, usually around 15 to 20 minutes.
3. While the potatoes are boiling, gently heat the milk and butter in a small saucepan over low heat. Stir occasionally until the butter is melted. Keep this mixture warm.
4. Once the potatoes are cooked, drain the water and return the potatoes to the pot.
5. Slowly add the warm milk and butter mixture to the potatoes while mashing. Use a potato masher or ricer for best results.
6. Season with salt and pepper, to taste. If you're using minced garlic, you can add it here.
7. Gently mix all the ingredients until you achieve a creamy texture. If the mixture seems too dry, you can add a little more milk.
8. Transfer the mashed potatoes to a serving bowl. If desired, garnish with freshly chopped herbs.

S'mores Brownies

Prep Time: 10 minutes
Cook Time: depends on your mix
Yield: 9 brownies

Ingredients

1 box (16 oz.) classic brownie mix and ingredients to make brownies (usually eggs, oil, and water)
2 cups mini marshmallows
4 graham crackers, broken into small pieces
2 chocolate bars (I use Hershey because they melt so well), broken into 1-inch pieces

Directions

1. Line a 9 × 9-inch nonstick pan with parchment paper, both vertically and horizontally, letting the paper drape over the sides so that the brownies are easy to lift out of the pan.
2. Mix and bake brownies according to package directions.
3. As soon as you remove the brownies from the oven, set the oven to broil.
4. Sprinkle the hot brownies, fresh from the oven, with marshmallows and graham cracker bits. Return the pan to the oven and broil the brownies approximately 5 inches from the heat for 30 to 60 seconds, watching the whole time so you can remove them as soon as the marshmallows start to turn golden.
5. Immediately after removing the pan from the oven, sprinkle the chocolate pieces on top of the marshmallows and graham cracker bits.
6. Pull the brownies from the pan with the parchment paper and put on cooling rack for a couple of hours until completely cooled and chocolate is firm.

Overnight Oatmeal with Apples and Apricots

Some days I need my breakfast to be waiting for me—amazing, hot, and ready to go. What I don't eat on the first day I just refrigerate and then reheat throughout the week. I also like to put a little sweetener in the oatmeal. Dealer's choice! You can add it into the slow cooker with the raw oats, or add it as a topping once the oats are cooked.

Prep Time: 5 minutes
Cook Time: 8 hours in a slow cooker
Yield: 6 servings

Ingredients

1 ½ cups steel-cut oats
4 cups water
2 cups milk, any kind you like (I use nonfat)
1 large tart apple, peeled and chopped
1 cup chopped dried apricots
2 tsp. pure vanilla extract
1 ½ tsp. ground cinnamon
½ tsp. ground nutmeg
½ tsp. kosher salt
Sweetener of your choice: brown sugar, white sugar, honey, or agave
Toppings of your choice: blueberries, raspberries, blackberries, granola, shredded coconut, sliced almonds, chopped pecans, Greek yogurt

Directions

1. Place all the ingredients except the toppings in the bottom of a 4- to 6-quart slow cooker, then stir to combine. Cover and cook on low for 8 hours. Remove the cover and stir. Taste and see if you need to add anything else, like more vanilla or cinnamon.
2. I like to keep oatmeal in the fridge for up to a week. Place it in a big tub, and reheat individual servings in the microwave for 2 minutes and 30 seconds.

Harvest Salad

Prep Time: 20 minutes
Yield: 4 main servings or 8 side servings

Ingredients

6 cups mixed greens
1 apple, thinly sliced
1 pear, thinly sliced
½ cup dried cranberries
½ cup chopped walnuts
½ cup crumbled blue cheese

½ cup cubed and roasted butternut squash
(optional)
¼ cup olive oil
2 T. apple cider vinegar
1 tsp. honey
Salt and pepper, to taste

Directions

1. In a large salad bowl, combine the mixed greens, apple, pear, dried cranberries, walnuts, blue cheese, and butternut squash.
2. In a small bowl, whisk together the olive oil, apple cider vinegar, and honey.
3. Drizzle the dressing over the salad, season with a dash of salt and pepper, and gently toss to combine. Serve immediately.

Corn Bread

Prep Time: 10 minutes
Cook Time: 20 minutes
Yield: 9 servings

Ingredients

1 cup cornmeal
1 cup all-purpose flour
¼ cup sugar
1 T. baking powder
½ tsp. salt
1 cup milk
¼ cup vegetable oil
2 large eggs

Directions

1. Preheat the oven to 400°F and grease a 9 × 9-inch baking pan.
2. In a large bowl, combine the cornmeal, flour, sugar, baking powder, and salt.
3. In a separate bowl, whisk together the milk, vegetable oil, and eggs.
4. Add the wet ingredients to the dry ingredients and stir until just combined.
5. Pour the batter into the prepared pan and bake for 20 minutes, or until a toothpick inserted in the center comes out clean.
6. Allow to cool slightly before cutting into squares to serve.

Charcuterie Board

A charcuterie board is a great option for parties, but it's also great for an easy dinner treat. Don't let the fancy reputation scare you away. Just remember to include a few items from each of the categories below.

Prep Time: 10 minutes
Yield: customizable

Ingredients

Base
  Crackers, pita bread, pretzels
  Slices of cucumber
Substance
  Hard cheeses: cheddar, Swiss, smoked gouda
  Soft cheeses: goat, brie, crema, spreadable cheeses, Havarti
  Cured meats: ham, sausage, salami, prosciutto, pepperoni
  Hard-boiled eggs
Flavor
  Nuts, pickles, olives, sliced apples, cocktail onions
Extras
  Dips, tapenades, jams
  Fruit: strawberries, grapes, dried apricots
  Dark chocolate

Directions

1. Get a nice tray, platter, or wooden cutting board to hold your spread. Gather serving tools: toothpicks, small tongs, a small knife for spreading soft cheese, and spoons for dips or jams.
2. Choose two or more options from each category and lay them out in bite-size slices or chunks, grouped together on your serving tray. Be sure to offer and label gluten-free items for those with sensitivities or allergies and consider separating them from any gluten-containing items by placing them in their own bowl or tray. You may also want to separate nuts or other potential allergens into their own bowls. Enjoy!

Caesar Salad

Prep Time: 15 minutes
Yield: 4 main servings or 8 side servings

Ingredients

1 head romaine lettuce, torn into bite-size pieces
1 cup croutons
½ cup freshly grated Parmesan cheese
½ cup Creamy Caesar Dressing

Directions

1. In a large salad bowl, combine the romaine lettuce, croutons, and Parmesan cheese.
2. Pour the dressing over the salad and toss until well coated.
3. Serve immediately, with additional Parmesan cheese on top if desired.

Creamy Caesar Dressing

Ingredients

¾ cup mayonnaise
2 T. fresh lemon juice
2 garlic cloves, minced
1 tsp. Worcestershire sauce
1 tsp. Dijon mustard
¼ cup grated Parmesan cheese
Salt and freshly ground pepper, to taste

Directions

Combine all ingredients in a blender or food processor and blend until smooth.

Taco Salad

Prep Time: 30 minutes
Cook Time: 10 minutes
Yield: 4 main servings or 8 side servings

Ingredients

1 lb. ground beef
1 packet taco seasoning (about 1 oz. or 3 T.)
6 cups chopped romaine lettuce
1 (15 oz.) can black beans, drained and rinsed
1 cup corn kernels
1 cup cherry tomatoes, halved
1 cup shredded cheddar cheese
¼ cup sliced black olives (optional)
1 avocado, diced
½ cup sour cream
½ cup salsa
Salt and pepper, to taste

Directions

1. In a large skillet, cook the ground beef over medium heat until browned. Drain off any excess fat.
2. Stir in the taco seasoning, following the package directions.
3. In a large salad bowl, arrange the romaine lettuce. Top with the cooked beef, black beans, corn, cherry tomatoes, cheddar cheese, black olives, and avocado.
4. In a small bowl, combine the sour cream and salsa to create a dressing. Drizzle the dressing over the salad, sprinkle with a dash of salt and pepper, and gently toss to combine. Serve immediately.

Roasted Corn Salad

Prep time: 10 minutes
Cook time: 25 minutes
Yield: 8 servings

Ingredients

4 ears corn, husks removed
½ cup mayonnaise
¼ cup fresh lime juice
½ tsp. chili powder
½ cup crumbled cotija cheese
¼ cup chopped fresh cilantro
Salt and pepper, to taste

Directions

1. Heat a grill or grill pan over medium heat. Cook the corn until it is charred on all sides. Remove from the grill and allow it to cool. Once cooled, cut the kernels off the cob and place them in a large bowl.
2. In a separate bowl, mix together the mayonnaise, lime juice, and chili powder.
3. Pour the dressing over the grilled corn kernels and mix until they are well coated.
4. Add the cotija cheese and cilantro to the bowl. Mix well.
5. Season the salad with salt and pepper, to taste.
6. Serve the salad immediately or refrigerate it for an hour to allow the flavors to meld.

A Prayer for Bravery

I admit the vulnerability
I feel in the kitchen.
When I mess up
it is obvious to all.
I tend to stick with
what I know
and I know there's more
beyond what I currently know—
I feel this tension.

I want to be
brave in the kitchen;
I want to grow.
There's so much to learn.

Lord, direct me to
the resources I need to grow
as a cook,
not so that I can
prepare a four-course meal
but so that I may
embrace the posture
of a learner.

Intimidation is not
an ingredient
in any recipe;
may it be absent
from my kitchen.

Week Twelve
Go-To Dinners

W e do a lot of entertaining here at the Red House (and if you're coming all the way here, you're probably staying for a day or two). This is one of my favorite meal plans when we're having company and just need some surefire, crowd-pleasing food.

Week 12 Menu

Saturday

Slow Cooker Seasoned Pork
   Roast
Stuffing (no recipe)
Green Beans (no recipe)

Dessert:
Fruit Crisp
   (Triple Berry)

Sunday

Breakfast:
Overnight Banana Bread
   Oatmeal

Lunch:
Potato Soup
Bacon and Broccoli Salad
Rolls

Dinner:
Chicken Curry
Rice Pilaf with Toasted Almonds

Monday

Pork Sandwiches (no recipe)
Coleslaw (no recipe)

Tuesday

Potato Soup
Rolls
Side Salad (no recipe)

Wednesday

Leftovers or frozen meal of choice

Thursday

Dinner out

Friday

Pizza night!

Sabbath Soup

Potato Soup

Prep Time: 30 minutes • Cook Time: 50 minutes • Yield: 4 bowls or 8 cups

Ingredients

½ lb. bacon, diced (you may use the remaining ½ lb. of bacon to cook and crumble as a topper)

½ cup chopped yellow onion

2 cloves garlic, minced

3 lbs. gold potatoes, peeled and cubed

4 cups chicken stock (or enough to cover potatoes)

Salt and pepper, to taste

1 tsp. dried tarragon or 2 T. chopped fresh dill weed

2 T. butter

¼ cup all-purpose flour

1 cup heavy cream

½ cup chopped green onion

2 T. sour cream

½ cup shredded cheddar cheese, plus more for serving

Directions

1. Heat a Dutch oven over medium heat.
2. Add the diced bacon and cook until halfway done. Add the onion and continue to cook until the bacon is fully cooked and the onion is soft and translucent. Stir in the garlic and sauté until fragrant.
3. Add the potatoes and cook for about 5 minutes.
4. Pour in the chicken stock, making sure it just covers the potatoes. Stir well and bring to a simmer. Reduce heat to medium-low.
5. Season with salt and pepper. Add the tarragon (or dill weed). Cover and cook until the potatoes are mostly tender.
6. In a separate pan, melt additional butter over medium heat. Whisk in flour and cook, stirring constantly, for 1 to 2 minutes. Whisk in heavy cream. Bring this mixture to a boil and cook, stirring constantly, until thickened, about 5 minutes.
7. Add the cream mixture to the potato soup. Stir to combine.
8. Transfer about half of the soup to a blender and purée. Return the purée to the Dutch oven.
9. Stir in the green onion, sour cream, and cheddar cheese. Mix well and cook for a few more minutes. Taste, and add seasoning if desired.
10. Garnish with green onion, and additional crumbled bacon and cheddar cheese.

Slow Cooker Seasoned Pork Roast

Prep Time: 20 minutes
Cook Time: 5 to 6 hours on low
Yield: 10 servings

Ingredients

1 (4 lb.) pork loin, trimmed of excess fat
Salt and pepper, to taste
1 large onion, sliced
1 T. oil
6 cloves garlic, chopped
½ cup apple juice
½ cup balsamic vinegar
2 T. soy sauce
½ cup brown sugar

Directions

1. Season all sides of the pork loin generously with salt and pepper.
2. Place the onion in the bottom of your slow cooker.
3. Heat a large skillet over medium-high heat. Add the oil to the pan and when it's hot, sear the pork roast on all sides. Then, place the roast on top of the onion in the slow cooker.
4. Turn off the heat to your skillet and add the garlic, apple juice, balsamic vinegar, and soy sauce. Stir these ingredients together, making sure to scrape up any brown bits that stuck to the pan.
5. Sprinkle the brown sugar on top of the pork loin and then pour the sauce mixture over the pork.
6. Cover and cook on low for 5 to 6 hours, or until the internal temperature is 145°F.
7. Once cooked, remove the pork loin to a plate and cover it with foil. Allow it to rest for 10 minutes.
8. While the pork is resting, pour the sauce and juices from the slow cooker into a saucepan. Bring this to a simmer over medium heat and allow the sauce to thicken, about 5 to 6 minutes. Stir occasionally.
9. Pour the sauce over the pork, slice it, and serve.

Fruit Crisp (Triple Berry)

You can customize this recipe to use whatever you have on hand. Serve warm, and if desired, add a scoop of vanilla ice cream and a sprig of fresh mint.

Prep Time: 15 minutes
Cook Time: 35 to 40 minutes
Yield: 8 servings

Ingredients

Fruit Filling
4½ cups fresh or frozen berries
½ cup granulated sugar
1 T. cornstarch
Optional: ½ tsp. spice (I use cinnamon, nutmeg, or lemon zest, depending on the berry)
Pinch of salt

Crisp Topping
1 cup old-fashioned oats
½ cup all-purpose flour
½ cup brown sugar, packed
½ tsp. cinnamon
¼ tsp. salt
6 T. unsalted butter, cold and cut into small pieces

Directions

1. Preheat your oven to 375°F. Lightly grease an 8 × 8-inch baking dish.
2. Prepare the fruit filling: Use 1½ cups each of raspberries, blueberries, and blackberries, or your own favorite combination. In a large bowl, combine the berries, sugar, cornstarch, optional spices, and a pinch of salt. Stir gently until well combined, then transfer to the prepared baking dish.
3. Prepare the crisp topping: In another bowl, combine the oats, flour, brown sugar, cinnamon, and salt. Add the butter and use your fingers or a pastry cutter to incorporate it into the oat mixture until it looks like coarse crumbs. Sprinkle the crisp topping evenly over the fruit filling.
4. Bake for 35 to 40 minutes, or until the topping is golden brown and the fruit filling is bubbling.
5. Remove the crisp from the oven and allow it to cool for about 10 minutes before serving.

Overnight Banana Bread Oatmeal

This hearty Banana Bread Oatmeal is a wonderful, nutritious breakfast that can be ready for you when you wake up in the morning!

Please note: Cooking times may vary depending on your specific slow cooker model. Start checking your oatmeal a bit early to ensure it does not overcook.

Prep Time: 10 minutes
Cook Time: 8 hours
Yield: 8 servings

Ingredients

2 cups steel-cut oats
2 ripe bananas, mashed
¼ cup brown sugar
½ tsp. salt
1 tsp. cinnamon
½ tsp. nutmeg
¼ cup chopped walnuts or pecans (optional)
4 cups water
2 cups milk
2 tsp. vanilla extract
Optional toppings: Sliced bananas, additional chopped walnuts or pecans, a drizzle of honey or maple syrup, or a sprinkle of cinnamon or chia seeds

Directions

1. In the slow cooker, add the steel-cut oats, bananas, brown sugar, salt, cinnamon, nutmeg, and nuts. Stir to combine.
2. Add the water, milk, and vanilla extract to the slow cooker, stirring to combine with the oat mixture.
3. Cover the slow cooker and cook on low for 7 to 8 hours (or overnight) until the oats are tender and the liquid has been absorbed.
4. Stir the oatmeal well before serving. The bananas will have broken down completely, infusing the oatmeal with their flavor.
5. Serve the oatmeal hot with your choice of toppings.

Bacon and Broccoli Salad

Prep Time: 20 minutes
Yield: 4 main servings or 8 side servings

Ingredients

4 cups broccoli florets, cut into bite-size pieces
8 slices bacon, cooked and crumbled
½ cup finely chopped red onion
½ cup shredded cheddar cheese
¼ cup sunflower seeds (optional)
½ cup mayonnaise
2 T. apple cider vinegar
1 T. sugar
Salt and pepper, to taste

Directions

1. In a large salad bowl, combine the broccoli, bacon, onion, cheddar, and sunflower seeds.
2. In a small bowl, whisk together the mayonnaise, apple cider vinegar, and sugar.
3. Drizzle the dressing over the salad, season with a dash of salt and pepper, and gently toss to combine.
4. Refrigerate the salad for at least one hour before serving to allow the flavors to meld.
5. Serve chilled.

Restore us, God Almighty;
make your face shine on us,
that we may be saved.
PSALM 80:7-8

Rolls

The ingredients for rolls and sandwich bread dough are the same, so feel free to double the recipe to get both rolls for dinner and sliced bread for sandwiches for the week. Look at you being so clever!

Prep Time: 10 minutes, plus 2 hours to rise
Cook Time: 30 minutes
Yield: 6 Rolls

Ingredients

- 1 cup warm water
- ½ T. active dry yeast
- 2 T. honey
- 2¾ cups all-purpose flour, divided
- 1 tsp. salt
- 2 T. melted butter, divided

Directions

1. Mix the water, yeast, and honey together. Add 2 cups of flour, salt, and 1 tablespoon melted butter and mix.
2. Put dough on a surface with ¼ cup of flour and knead it for about 5 minutes, adding in the other half cup of flour to get a doughy texture.
3. Take your dough ball and put it in a bowl. Cover it with a dishcloth and stick it in the oven with the oven light on for an hour (it should approximately double in size).
4. Preheat the oven to 350°F.
5. Butter a pie tin. Cut the dough into six pieces and form the pieces into rolls.
6. Place the rolls in the pie tin and let the dough double again, covered.
7. Bake for 30 minutes.
8. Remove from oven and brush with the other tablespoon of melted butter.

Note: For sandwich bread, at step 5, butter a loaf pan instead of the pie tin and shape the dough to fit. Allow the dough to rise and bake as above. Allow just a few more minutes to bake, until the loaf is golden and sounds hollow when tapped. Brush with butter, then let it cool on a wire rack before slicing.

Chicken Curry

This quick and easy Chicken Curry is a great way to use up leftover chicken. The sour cream gives the curry a creamy texture, while the curry powder provides a warm and fragrant flavor. Enjoy this satisfying meal for your weeknight dinner!

Prep Time: 10 minutes
Cook Time: 20 minutes
Yield: 4 servings

Ingredients

- 1 T. extra-virgin olive oil
- 1 medium onion, sliced
- ¼ cup raisins (optional)
- Salt and pepper, to taste
- 1 lb. cooked chicken meat, shredded
- 1½ tsp. yellow curry powder
- 1 cup sour cream
- Fresh cilantro or parsley, chopped for garnish
- Steamed rice, for serving

Directions

1. Heat the oil in a large skillet over medium-high heat, then add the onion and raisins. Sprinkle with salt and pepper.
2. Cook, stirring occasionally, until the onion is translucent. This should take about 5 minutes.
3. Turn the heat down to medium. Add the chicken to the skillet and stir it into the onion.
4. Sprinkle the mixture with the curry powder and continue to cook for another 1 to 2 minutes, stirring frequently.
5. Add the sour cream to the skillet. Stir constantly over medium-low heat until the mixture is nice and thick. This should take another 5 minutes.
6. Remove the skillet from the heat. Taste the chicken curry and adjust the seasoning if necessary.
7. Garnish the curry with chopped cilantro or parsley and serve warm. This chicken curry goes well with steamed rice.

Rice Pilaf with Toasted Almonds

Prep time: 10 minutes
Cook time: 25 minutes
Yield: 8 servings

Ingredients

2 cups basmati rice
3 T. olive oil
1 onion, finely chopped
2 garlic cloves, minced
1 tsp. ground cumin
½ tsp. ground turmeric
½ tsp. ground coriander
4 cups chicken or vegetable broth
Salt and pepper, to taste
½ cup sliced almonds, toasted
2 T. chopped fresh parsley

*I have calmed and
quieted myself,
I am like a weaned child
with its mother;
like a weaned child
I am content.*

PSALM 131:2

Directions

1. Rinse the basmati rice under cold water until the water runs clear. Set aside to drain.
2. Heat the olive oil in a large saucepan over medium heat. Add the onion and cook until it starts to soften and become translucent, about 5 minutes.
3. Add the garlic, cumin, turmeric, and coriander. Stir and cook for another minute until fragrant.
4. Add the rice to the saucepan. Stir until the rice is well coated in the oil and spices.
5. Pour in the chicken or vegetable broth. Season with salt and pepper, to taste.
6. Bring the mixture to a boil, then reduce the heat to low, cover, and simmer for 15 to 20 minutes, or until the rice is tender and the liquid is absorbed.
7. Remove from heat and let the rice sit, covered, for 5 minutes.
8. Fluff the rice with a fork and mix in the toasted almonds and parsley. Serve the rice pilaf warm.

A Prayer Over a Gathering

Lord, we gather not for a
miracle, message,
or a measure of grace.

However, I know that
as this home fills
with the rise and fall
of conversations
and the pleasing smells of food,
we will receive
miracles, messages,
and a measure of grace.

I don't understand
what happens
when people sit
to break bread together,
but there's connection and electricity
and I thank You for it.

Bless this food.
Bless these connections.

May we leave this meal
more aware of who
You are.

May the impact we have
on each other
be a balm to our hearts
and our world.

May it be so.

Spring

Be Present to the Season You're In

*We must learn to live each day, each hour, yes, each minute as a new beginning,
as a unique opportunity to make everything new.*

HENRY NOUWEN

In winter, I swing wildly between one extreme of hibernating under several layers of quilts and only eating soup that has simmered on the stove for a minimum of six hours with homemade buttered bread, to another extreme of longing to be elbow deep in some potting soil with a basket full of seeds and my wagon full of starter plants.

On our homestead, spring doubles our work because while all winter we are concentrating on the inside of the house, spring is the season to get everything started outdoors so that we can have cut flowers and fresh strawberries in the summer.

Of course, in my fantasy dream life, I'm wearing a long skirt with a sun hat, lovingly planting seeds in the ground, and tending to the greenhouse with the air and care of a farmer Mary Poppins.

What it actually looks like is me popping Tylenol, because weeding and planting are backbreaking work. And we won't even talk about all the other chores that pop up after the snow melts: fence repair, chicken coop repairs, repainting, weed abatement for fire prevention, and so much more.

So, I find it very helpful, especially in the busyness of the spring, to find every way possible to lighten my load. A lightened load means more time to be present and envision the tasks before me with fresh eyes. It's so very easy to spend our time missing the last season or dreaming about the next one, but there is so much wisdom in the Old Testament that says be in the season you are in.

> *"For everything there is a season, and a time for every matter under heaven: a time to be born, and a time to die; a time to plant, and a time to pluck up what is planted." ECCLESIASTES 3:1-2*

Each season has its gifts and its challenges, but when we are present to the season we are in, physically and spiritually, we receive the gifts and rise to the challenges.

When we work hard in the spring to prep and prepare, whether it's planting our vegetable garden or cleaning out our pantry, we reap the rewards for seasons to come.

When I deep clean in the spring, I receive the gift of an organized pantry every time I go to cook, for months going forward.

But having those extra chores in the spring means that I need to give myself the gift of letting go of some of the other rituals I love from other seasons.

In the spring, I'm buying more prepared food than in other seasons (because after a long Saturday of weeding, the last thing I want to do is prep a bunch of meals. I want my food ready and waiting, thank you very much). In the spring, I'm baking less. Desserts aren't coming from the oven, they are coming from our favorite bakery.

We all are allotted a set number of hours. When life is at its busiest, we can either work ourselves into a panic, or we can assess and adjust what really needs to be done and how to make that happen.

And sometimes? That's buying the chocolate chip cookies for Saturday dessert instead of whipping up a batch myself.

In this season of newness, we can experience a shift toward having had *enough* of the burdens of past seasons, like: effort, striving, hustle, stress.

Yes, in the winter, I force myself to surface in a Willy Wonka–like state and not only cook, but cook enough to freeze and put away for the busy spring to come.

And in the fall, we will cut wood and stack it in the shed so we are prepared for winter.

And in the summer, I will make the wild blackberry jam so that in the fall, when the weather has cooled enough to make bread without running an air conditioner, I will pull a loaf fresh from the oven, slather heaps of jam on it, and be grateful for the blackberry picking we did in the hottest month of the year.

But enough is enough! In the spring, when the season demands so much from us, I will take all the shortcuts, dig up all the life hacks, and know that I don't have to prove anything to anyone. Spring is in charge and must be obeyed.

Save Your Sanity in Spring

My motto when it comes to cooking (and much in life) is: When freedom is outlawed, only the outlaws are free. In other words, there are no rules when it comes to getting a dinner on the table that you and your people will love. Feeding people every night is a sheer act of will. Any tactic that will make that process easier should be employed.

I'm a big believer that not everything has to be made from scratch. When most people can't tell the difference between instant and homemade mashed potatoes, that's a cheat I'm willing to make. Feel free to cheat by buying the following items premade.

Mashed Potatoes

Today, I want to give you permission to make instant mashed potatoes when the need arises. I keep a container of Idahoan Real Premium Mashed Potatoes in my cupboard and make them according to package directions. But I always fancy them up just a little bit. I might add a dollop of sour cream, some chives, and a little bit of shredded Parmesan to the potatoes to make them extra delish. Or, sometimes, I'll substitute heavy cream for the milk and whip in a little smashed garlic. Super easy.

I've heard that Julia Child once served instant mashed potatoes to her foodie husband Paul and that he couldn't tell the difference. Since hearing that story, I've never looked back.

Stuffing

Okay, I'm putting all my confessions out in the world at the same time.

There is almost no food I love as much as Stovetop Stuffing. There. I said it.

You may want to try and tell me that I just haven't had the right stuffing before and if I would only try your mom's stuffing with oysters and cranberries, I would change my mind. You can get out of here with that foolishness. I mean, why mess with perfection?

And, I've had someone tell me about a Stovetop Stuffing copycat recipe. But…why? Just…why?

Just get the Stovetop, add a little butter and water, and use your time in more productive ways. If you feel like you're cheating because it's coming out of a box (First, don't. When perfection is contained within a box, you use the box…), here is one thing I do, if I'm feeling fancy, to put it over the top:

Chop up half a yellow onion, two ribs of celery, and about six mushrooms.

Sauté the onion for 5 minutes, then add the celery and mushrooms, and continue cooking until softened.

When you are ready to add the dried breadcrumbs from the Stovetop package into the buttered water, add the vegetables at the same time, and mix together.

Marinara Sauce

It can be fun to make something special with simmer-all-day-on-the-stove pasta sauce, but generally, I use a good-quality jarred sauce (Rao's is our favorite) and call it a day. Feel free to add onion and mushrooms and anything else that will make you happy. There is no marinara-sauce law when it comes to what makes you happy.

Ravioli

While we're at it, I have not mastered homemade ravioli. The store-bought version is *so* good. Unless you have a burning desire to learn or you have prior experience, leave ravioli to the professionals.

Pie Crust

You are either born with the potential (and patience) to make homemade pie crust or not. I fall into the "not" category. While I appreciate the efforts of others who are so gifted, I'm a roll-out-the-frozen-dough kinda gal. (That goes for phyllo, puff pastry, and any crust-like substance.)

Rotisserie Chicken

This one is a half recommendation, because I love my hot-out-of-the-oven roasted chicken recipe. It is the best. But there are times you want the chicken to be amazing *and* you want it to magically appear for dinner.

Thank you, Costco chicken. On my busiest weeks, this is my go-to protein. It's wonderful.

Frozen French Fries

Frozen French fries made in the air fryer are the best fries you can make at home without a deep vat of grease (and I'll fight anyone who says differently).

Veggie-stuffed Vietnamese Spring Rolls

I've made homemade spring rolls before. They cost three times as much and tasted half as good as store-bought.

French Bread

I've included several recipes for homemade breads in this book, but not French bread. Also, my son was a baker for a grocery store, and there was no better act of love than him bringing home a fresh loaf of bread.

Tortillas

I do have a tortilla press, and yes, homemade tortillas are far superior when you're doing something like street tacos. But when I'm trying to get dinner on the table, store-bought tortillas are the best thing ever.

Tortilla Chips

Nope. Not gonna do it. Buy the chips and go take a nap. That is a better use of your time.

Tamales

Unless someone in your family makes these from scratch (and if you are part of such a family, can you please adopt me?), there are excellent ones at Costco and at most grocery stores.

* * *

Enter this spring season ready to embrace all it is, all it offers, all it stirs in you. Sabbath in spring is filled with shifting light, sprouts of green, renewed energy, permission to stay sane, and so many opportunities to savor both the season of life and the season of the year you are in.

Spring
Sabbath Experiences

I am going to try to pay attention to the spring. I am going to look around at all the flowers, and look up at the hectic trees. I am going to close my eyes and listen.

ANNE LAMOTT, *PLAN B*

1. Make a spring Sabbath altar or centerpiece. Create it with blooms, tapers, written verses of God's promises, and treasures from your yard.

2. Savor the rain or changing clouds this season often brings. Sit on the porch with a lap blanket and a mug of coffee and watch God's magic unfold.

3. Play with your pet and experience the bliss of unconditional love. Don't have a pet? Go to a cat café, walk a friend's dog, attend a goat yoga class, or visit an animal shelter and love on the animals waiting for a home.

4. Light a candle and say a prayer for a family member or someone you miss.

5. Do gentle stretching from a seated or standing position. Give thanks for your body, even the parts that ache. Our pains can remind us to slow down and care for what God has made.

6. Turn on the music! Express joy by swaying with a spouse, dancing by yourself, or being silly with the kids.

7. Get your hands dirty. Plant some seeds. Pluck some fruit. Dig in the soil and interact with creation. It is such a healing way to spend an afternoon.

8. Go on a prayer walk. Choose a verse, a line from a poem, or an encouraging phrase to think on as you walk. (If you have a happy lyric stuck in your brain, you can even use that!)

9. Sabbath journaling for spring: Spend moments this season writing about what gives you a sense of new life, resurrection, and hope.

10. Have a little adventure. In the spring, we love to take a drive to a smaller town, a patch of nature, or to a friend's house. Pack a few snacks and cold water. Our outing may only take four hours, but it varies the day enough to make it extra special.

Week Thirteen
St. Patrick's Day

Our main meal this week is a great celebration of all things Irish. (And this Irish Stew recipe is easy and was a hit with everyone around our table.) Maybe you've never been one to make a to-do about smaller holidays, but with a few simple recipes, this week's offerings may turn you into someone who scours the calendar for any and every opportunity to stir up a themed meal. And definitely, when you see the smiles around the table, you'll know you've been blessed with the luck of the Irish!

Week 13 Menu

Saturday
Slow Cooker Seasoned Pork
  Roast
Broccoli and Cheddar Rice
  Casserole
Dessert:
Ice Cream Sundae Bar

Sunday
Breakfast:
Amazing Mix-In Muffins
  (Apple and Cranberry)
Lunch:
Irish Stew
Caesar Salad
Irish Soda Bread
Dinner:
Creamy Skillet Chicken
  Cacciatore
Cheesy Garlic Bread
Garlic Green Beans

Monday
Shepherd's Pie with Pork
Bagged Salad (no recipe)

Tuesday
Irish Stew
Irish Soda Bread

Wednesday
Leftovers or frozen meal of choice

Thursday
Dinner out

Friday
Pizza night!

Sabbath Soup

Irish Stew

Prep Time: 30 minutes • Cook Time: 3 hours and 20 minutes • Yield: 4 bowls or 8 cups

Ingredients

3 T. olive oil, divided

3 lbs. beef chuck stew meat, cubed into 1-inch pieces

Kosher salt

Freshly ground black pepper

2 medium onions, coarsely chopped

3 cloves garlic, minced

6 oz. (180 g.) bacon or pancetta, diced

¼ cup all-purpose flour

1 (16 oz.) bottle Guinness Stout Beer* (alternatives on page 133)

4 cups low-sodium beef broth

¼ cup tomato paste

2 lbs. small yellow potatoes, halved

3 medium carrots, peeled and cut into 1-inch pieces

2 large celery ribs, chopped

2 dried bay leaves

3 sprigs fresh thyme (or 1 tsp. dried thyme leaves)

2 T. freshly chopped parsley, for serving

Directions

1. Preheat your oven to 350°F.
2. Heat 2 tablespoons of the olive oil in a large Dutch oven or oven-safe pot over medium-high heat. Season the beef generously with salt and pepper.
3. Add the beef to the pot in batches, being careful not to overcrowd. Brown the beef on all sides, then remove and set aside.
4. In the same pot, add the remaining 1 tablespoon of oil. Add the onions and cook for 5 to 6 minutes or until they begin to soften.
5. Add the garlic and the bacon or pancetta to the pot. Cook until the bacon is browned.
6. Stir in the flour, ensuring the onion and bacon are well coated.
7. Gradually add the Guinness, stirring as you do so to loosen any browned bits from the bottom of the pot.
8. Stir in the beef broth and tomato paste, followed by the potatoes, carrots, celery, bay leaves, and thyme. Return the beef to the pot and stir to combine everything.
9. Cover the pot and place it in the preheated oven. Cook for about 2½ to 3 hours, or until the beef and vegetables are tender.
10. Once the stew is done, remove it from the oven and discard the bay leaves and thyme sprigs. Adjust the seasoning with additional salt and pepper if needed.
11. Garnish with parsley before serving.

Slow Cooker Seasoned Pork Roast

Prep Time: 20 minutes
Cook Time: 5 to 6 hours on low
Yield: 10 servings

Ingredients

1 (4 lb.) pork loin, trimmed of excess fat
Salt and pepper, to taste
1 large onion, sliced
1 T. oil
6 cloves garlic, chopped
½ cup apple juice
½ cup balsamic vinegar
2 T. soy sauce
½ cup brown sugar

Directions

1. Season all sides of the pork loin roast generously with salt and pepper.
2. Place the onion in the bottom of your slow cooker.
3. Heat a large skillet over medium-high heat. Add the oil to the pan and when it's hot, sear the pork roast on all sides. Then, place the roast on top of the onion in the slow cooker.

Alternatives to beer in Irish Stew

*If you don't want to use beer in this soup, here are two alternatives that provide a similar depth of flavor:

Beef Broth with Molasses—To mimic the malty flavor of Guinness, mix 1 cup of beef broth with 1 to 2 tablespoons of molasses. This will provide a rich, sweet depth of flavor that's somewhat similar to Guinness.

Mushroom Broth with Soy Sauce—Mushroom broth has an umami depth of flavor, and soy sauce gives a bit of fermented flavor. Mix about 1 cup of mushroom broth with 1 tablespoon of soy sauce for this substitute.

4. Turn off the heat to your skillet and add the garlic, apple juice, balsamic vinegar, and soy sauce. Stir these ingredients together, making sure to scrape up any brown bits that stuck to the pan.
5. Sprinkle the brown sugar on top of the pork loin and then pour the sauce mixture over the pork.
6. Cover and cook on low for 5 to 6 hours, or until the internal temperature is 145°F.
7. Once cooked, remove the pork loin to a plate and cover it with foil. Allow it to rest for 10 minutes.
8. While the pork is resting, pour the sauce and juices from the slow cooker into a saucepan. Bring this to a simmer over medium heat and allow the sauce to thicken, about 5 to 6 minutes. Stir occasionally.
9. Pour the sauce over the pork, slice it, and serve.

Broccoli and Cheddar Rice Casserole

Prep Time: 15 minutes
Cook Time: 45 minutes
Yield: 8 servings

Ingredients

1 T. olive oil
1 small onion, finely chopped
2 cups long-grain white rice
4 cups chicken broth
½ tsp. dry mustard
½ tsp. smoked paprika
Salt and pepper, to taste
2 cups broccoli florets
2 cups shredded cheddar cheese

Directions

1. Preheat the oven to 375°F.
2. In a large oven-safe skillet or Dutch oven, heat the olive oil over medium heat. Add the onion and cook until it is soft and translucent, about 5 minutes.
3. Add the rice to the skillet and stir to coat with the oil and onion. Cook for another 2 minutes.
4. Pour in the chicken broth, dry mustard, and smoked paprika and bring the mixture to a simmer. Season with salt and pepper.
5. Stir in the broccoli florets, then sprinkle the cheddar cheese on top. Cover the skillet with

a lid or aluminum foil and transfer it to the preheated oven.

6. Bake for 35 to 40 minutes, until the rice is tender and the cheese is bubbly and slightly golden.

7. Let the dish stand for a few minutes before fluffing the rice with a fork. Serve hot.

Ice Cream Sundae Bar

An ice cream sundae bar is a great option when you have a crowd with diverse preferences or dietary needs. But it's also just plain fun! For a special treat, build your sundae bar with two or three "base" options, add some "flavor" options, and go crazy with a few "toppings" to make it really sing. For a festive twist this week, add green mint chips or Irish toffee to topping choices.

Prep Time: 15 minutes
Yield: customizable

Ingredients

The base: ice cream, cones, frozen yogurt, gelato, cake, cupcakes, cookies, donuts, brownies
The flavor: any kind of fresh berry, sliced peaches cooked down with a little bit of water and sugar, macerated strawberries, marshmallows, candies
The toppings: chocolate syrup, chopped nuts, whipped cream, cookie crumbs, sprinkles

Directions

Prepare and set out all ingredients in individual containers. Don't forget serving spoons! Let each person choose their base, flavor, and topping combinations for their own one-of-a-kind ice cream sundae masterpiece.

Amazing Mix-In Muffins (Apple and Cranberry)

Prep Time: 10 minutes
Cook Time: 25 minutes
Yield: 12 muffins

Ingredients

2 cups all-purpose flour
¾ cup granulated sugar
½ tsp. salt
2 tsp. baking powder
⅓ cup vegetable oil
1 large egg, room temperature
1 tsp. vanilla extract
¾ cup milk
1 cup peeled, cored and diced apple
½ cup dried cranberries
½ tsp. ground cinnamon

Directions

1. Preheat your oven to 400°F. Line a 12-cup muffin tin with paper liners or grease the cups with nonstick cooking spray.

2. In a large bowl, whisk together the flour, sugar, salt, and baking powder.

3. In a separate medium bowl, combine the vegetable oil, egg, vanilla extract, and milk. Stir well.

4. Gently pour the wet ingredients into the dry ingredients and mix until just combined. Be careful not to overmix, as this can result in tough muffins.

5. Fold in the apple, cranberry, and cinnamon until evenly distributed throughout the batter.

6. Divide the batter evenly among the 12 muffin cups, filling each about two-thirds full.

7. Bake for 20 to 25 minutes, or until a toothpick inserted into the center of a muffin comes out clean.

8. Remove the muffins from the oven and allow them to cool in the tin for 5 minutes before transferring to a wire rack to cool completely.

See! The winter is past;
the rains are over and gone.
SONG OF SONGS 2:11

Caesar Salad

Prep Time: 15 minutes
Yield: 4 main servings or 8 side servings

Ingredients

1 head romaine lettuce, torn into bite-size pieces
1 cup croutons
½ cup freshly grated Parmesan cheese
½ cup Creamy Caesar Dressing

Directions

1. In a large salad bowl, combine the romaine lettuce, croutons, and Parmesan cheese.
2. Pour the dressing over the salad and toss until well coated.
3. Serve immediately, with additional Parmesan cheese on top if desired.

Creamy Caesar Dressing

Ingredients

¾ cup mayonnaise
2 T. fresh lemon juice
2 garlic cloves, minced
1 tsp. Worcestershire sauce
1 tsp. Dijon mustard
¼ cup grated Parmesan cheese
Salt and freshly ground pepper, to taste

Directions

Combine all ingredients in a blender or food processor and blend until smooth.

Irish Soda Bread

Prep Time: 15 minutes
Cook Time: 40 minutes
Yield: 8 servings

Ingredients

4¼ cups all-purpose flour, divided
4 T. sugar
1 tsp. baking soda
1 T. baking powder
½ tsp. salt
½ cup unsalted butter, softened
1¼ cups buttermilk, divided
1 large egg
1 cup raisins

Directions

1. Preheat the oven to 375°F. Line a Dutch oven with parchment paper, ensuring that the paper extends over the sides for easy removal later. (You'll use the paper as handles to lift out the baked bread.)
2. In a food processor, pulse together 4 cups flour, sugar, baking soda, baking powder, and salt. Add the butter and pulse until the mixture resembles coarse crumbs. Place the mixture in a large bowl.
3. In a smaller bowl, whisk 1 cup of the buttermilk with the egg, then stir the buttermilk mixture into the flour mixture, and then gently fold in the raisins.
4. Turn the dough out onto a floured surface and knead slightly.
5. Form the dough into a mounded loaf and place it in the Dutch oven. Use a sharp knife to slice a shallow X into the top of the mound.
6. In a small bowl, combine the remaining buttermilk with a little additional flour to make a paste, and brush this atop the loaf.
7. Bake for 40 to 45 minutes, or until a toothpick inserted into the loaf comes out clean. Cool on a wire rack before serving.

Creamy Skillet Chicken Cacciatore

Enjoy this hearty and flavorful Creamy Skillet Chicken Cacciatore with a side of crusty bread or a green salad for a complete meal. This dish is a perfect way to use up leftover chicken, and it's sure to be a hit with your family!

Prep Time: 10 minutes
Cook Time: 25 minutes
Yield: 4 servings

Ingredients

1 T. olive oil
2 cloves garlic, minced
1 medium onion, coarsely chopped
8 oz. mushrooms, sliced
5 fresh tomatoes, diced, or 1 (14.5 oz.) can diced tomatoes
¼ cup heavy cream
½ cup chicken broth

1 T. Italian seasoning

Salt and pepper, to taste

2 cups leftover chicken, chopped

Hot pasta, for serving

Parmesan cheese

½ cup fresh basil leaves, roughly chopped

Directions

1. Heat olive oil in a large skillet over medium heat. Add garlic and onion and sauté for about 3 minutes until they start to soften.
2. Add mushrooms to the skillet and continue sautéing until onion is fully softened and mushrooms are browned.
3. Stir in the tomatoes, heavy cream, chicken broth, and Italian seasoning. Add salt and pepper, to taste.
4. Reduce heat to low and let the mixture simmer for about 10 to 15 minutes, or until the sauce has thickened to your desired consistency.
5. Add the chicken to the skillet, stirring to mix it into the sauce. Let it cook for a few more minutes until the chicken is heated through.
6. Serve the creamy chicken cacciatore over hot pasta. Top with grated Parmesan cheese and fresh basil before serving.

Cheesy Garlic Bread

Prep Time: 10 minutes

Cook Time: 15 minutes

Yield: 8 servings

Ingredients

½ cup unsalted butter, softened

3 cloves garlic, minced

1 loaf French bread, halved lengthwise

2 cups shredded mozzarella cheese

¼ cup chopped fresh parsley

Directions

1. Preheat the oven to 375°F.
2. In a small bowl, mix together the butter and garlic.
3. Spread the garlic butter evenly over the cut sides of the bread.
4. Sprinkle the shredded mozzarella over the butter.

5. Place the bread on a baking sheet and bake for 10 minutes, or until the cheese is melted.
6. Switch the oven to broil and cook for another 2 to 3 minutes, until the cheese is bubbly and golden.
7. Sprinkle with parsley before serving.

Garlic Green Beans

This recipe is very easy to do without precise measurements, and you can easily add more for any number of people you want to feed. As a general rule, 1 pound of fresh green beans will serve about 6 people.

Prep Time: 5 minutes

Cook Time: 9 minutes

Yield: customizable

Ingredients

Fresh green beans

Olive oil

Garlic powder

Salt

Pepper

Directions

1. Start by washing the green beans and trimming the ends.
2. Place the cleaned green beans in a mixing bowl. Drizzle olive oil over them, making sure they are evenly coated.
3. Season the green beans with garlic powder, salt, and pepper. Toss the beans to ensure even seasoning.
4. Lay out the seasoned green beans in a single layer in the air fryer basket. Try to avoid overcrowding for even cooking.
5. Set the air fryer to 370°F. Air fry the green beans for 7 to 9 minutes. Check halfway through and shake the basket or use tongs to flip the green beans for even cooking.
6. Serve and enjoy!

Shepherd's Pie with Pork

This is one of my very favorite ways to use up leftover meat, along with vegetables and mashed potatoes. (I've been known to even use up green bean casserole in this dish. I promise, it's going to be amazing no matter what combination you put together.)

Prep Time: 15 minutes
Cook Time: 45 minutes
Yield: 8 servings

Ingredients

8 T. butter, divided
1½ medium chopped onion
2 cups cooked diced vegetables (I like carrots, corn, mushrooms, peas, and green beans)
1½ lbs. leftover pork, chopped
1 tsp. Worcestershire sauce
2 T. tomato paste
½ cup broth (any type)
1 tsp. salt
½ tsp. pepper
2 tsp. dried parsley
1 tsp. dried rosemary
1 tsp. dried thyme
4 cups mashed potatoes (leftover or made from instant)
¼ cup Parmesan cheese

Refresh yourself
with something to eat;
then you can go.
JUDGES 19:5

Directions

1. Preheat the oven to 400°F.
2. In a deep skillet over medium heat, melt one tablespoon of the butter and sauté the chopped onion until transparent and tender.
3. In a large mixing bowl, combine the chopped onion, cooked vegetables, leftover pork, Worcestershire sauce, tomato paste, broth, salt, pepper, parsley, rosemary, and thyme. Mix well until all ingredients are evenly distributed.
4. Melt the remaining 7 tablespoons of butter in a microwave-safe bowl. Pour the melted butter into the bottom of the prepared 9 x 13-inch baking dish, making sure to coat the entire surface.
5. Spoon the meat and vegetable mixture into the dish, spreading it out evenly. Use the back of a spoon to create small wells or pockets in the mixture.
6. Carefully dollop the mashed potatoes over the meat and vegetable mixture, making sure to fill in the wells and cover the entire surface. Use a fork to create decorative ridges and peaks in the mashed potatoes.
7. Place the dish in the preheated oven and bake for 30 to 35 minutes, until the filling is bubbling and the potatoes are lightly golden.
8. Remove the skillet from the oven and sprinkle the Parmesan cheese evenly over the top of the mashed potatoes.
9. Switch the oven to broil and return the dish to the oven. Broil for 3 to 5 minutes, or until the cheese is melted and the potatoes are crispy and golden brown. Keep a close eye on the dish to prevent burning.
10. Remove the dish from the oven and let it cool for 5 to 10 minutes before serving. This will allow the filling to set and make serving easier.
11. Garnish with fresh herbs, if desired, and serve the Shepherd's Pie directly from the pan, family style.

Week Fourteen
Early-Spring Simmers

֍

Depending on where you live, spring can be quite chilly and unpredictable. Before the sun commits to warming your patch of earth, it's soothing to have meals that welcome you back after a brisk walk around the neighborhood or a trip to the local nursery to plan your upcoming garden.

Every recipe this week is one I'd want to eat after coming in from the cold. Warm, hearty, and soul satisfying. Think of dishes that simmer long on the stove or come from the oven piping hot to feed your crowd.

Week 14 Menu

Saturday

Chicken Manicotti
Risotto
Bacon and Broccoli Salad
Dessert:
Ice Cream Sundae Bar

Sunday

Breakfast:
Overnight French Toast (with Brioche)

Lunch:
Italian Chicken Stew
Cobb Salad
French Bread (no recipe)

Dinner:
Green Chile Enchilada Casserole
Mexican Rice (no recipe)
Roasted Corn Salad

Monday

Greek Yogurt Chicken Salad with Apples and Almonds
Crackers (no recipe)

Tuesday

Italian Chicken Stew
French Bread (no recipe)
Cobb Salad

Wednesday

Leftovers or frozen meal of choice

Thursday

Dinner out

Friday

Pizza night!

Sabbath Soup

Italian Chicken Stew

Prep Time: 15 minutes • Cook Time: 5 to 6 hours in a slow cooker
Yield: 4 bowls or 8 cups

Ingredients

1 medium onion, chopped

1 medium zucchini, chopped

4 medium carrots, sliced

4½ cups chicken broth

2 (14 oz.) cans diced tomatoes, undrained

1 cup sliced fresh mushrooms

2 cloves whole garlic

½ tsp. salt

¼ tsp. pepper

1 lb. boneless skinless chicken breast

French baguette, for serving

Shredded Parmesan cheese, if desired

Directions

1. In a slow cooker, mix the onion, zucchini, carrots, broth, tomatoes, mushrooms, garlic, salt, and pepper. Add the chicken. Cover and cook on low heat for 5 to 6 hours.

2. Remove the chicken and garlic from the slow cooker and place them on a large plate. Mash garlic with a fork. Shred chicken. Return garlic and chicken to slow cooker to keep warm.

3. Slice and toast the baguette.

4. To serve, place the soup in bowls and top with a slice of toast and a sprinkle of Parmesan cheese.

Chicken Manicotti

This Chicken Manicotti is a delicious and satisfying dish, perfect for a weekend family dinner. The creamy cheese and savory chicken are a wonderful combination. Enjoy this special treat!

Prep Time: 30 minutes
Cook Time: 1 hour
Yield: 6 servings

Ingredients

- 14 manicotti shells
- 3 cups cooked, shredded chicken breasts (or 1 lb. raw chicken breasts, with 1 T. butter)
- 2 cups low-fat ricotta cheese
- ½ cup shredded mozzarella or Parmesan cheese
- 1 tsp. dried parsley
- 2 eggs, lightly beaten
- 4 cups marinara sauce

Directions

1. Preheat your oven to 350°F.
2. Set a pot of water on the stove over high heat. Bring the water to a boil and then drop in the manicotti noodles for just 1 to 2 minutes to parboil them. You want them only slightly softened and still holding a firm shape. Drain and set the noodles aside.
3. If using raw chicken: Melt the butter in a large skillet over medium heat. Brown the chicken in the butter for about 5 to 7 minutes per side, until it is no longer pink in the center. Set it aside to cool, then shred the meat.
4. In a large bowl, mix together the chicken, ricotta cheese, mozzarella or Parmesan cheese, parsley, and eggs until well combined.
5. Spread about 1 cup of marinara sauce in the bottom of a 9 × 13-inch baking dish.
6. Fill each parboiled manicotti shell with the chicken and cheese mixture. Arrange the filled shells in a single layer in the baking dish.
7. Pour the remaining sauce over the manicotti, making sure all the pasta is covered.
8. Cover the dish with aluminum foil and bake in the preheated oven for 45 minutes.
9. Remove the foil and bake for an additional 10 to 15 minutes, or until the cheese is bubbly and golden.
10. Allow the manicotti to cool for a few minutes before serving.

Risotto

Prep time: 15 minutes
Cook time: 25 minutes
Yield: 8 servings

Ingredients

- 7 cups chicken stock
- 2 T. olive oil
- 1 large shallot, finely chopped
- 2 cloves garlic, minced
- Salt and pepper, to taste
- 1 cup sliced mushrooms
- 1 bay leaf
- 5 T. unsalted butter, divided
- 2 cups arborio rice
- 1 cup white wine or 1 additional cup chicken stock
- 1 T. fresh herbs (I like basil, but parsley, tarragon, and chives are all wonderful)
- ¾ cup grated Parmesan, plus more for garnish
- Lemon wedges, for serving

Directions

1. Warm the chicken stock in a large saucepan on medium-low heat. Keep it covered and warm.
2. In another saucepan or Dutch oven, heat the olive oil over medium heat. Add the shallot and garlic. Add salt and pepper to your own taste, also considering any salt and pepper that may already be in your stock. Cook for 3 to 4 minutes, stirring occasionally, until softened. Add mushrooms and sauté for 2 minutes.
3. Add bay leaf and 3 tablespoons of butter to the mixture. Stir until butter melts, around 1 minute.
4. Add rice and toast it for 3 to 4 minutes, stirring once. The rice should smell nutty and turn light golden brown.
5. Add the wine (or 1 cup of additional stock) and let it simmer until it evaporates completely, around 2 to 3 minutes.
6. Add 1 cup of warm stock to the rice, stirring gently until it's absorbed. This takes around 2 to 3 minutes.

7. Continue adding stock, 1 cup or ladleful at a time, and keep stirring until the rice is al dente. This takes around 17 to 19 minutes total. You may have some stock left over. Remove the bay leaf and add your fresh herbs.
8. If you prefer a risotto with more sauce, add more stock in ¼ cup increments until desired consistency is reached.
9. Stir in Parmesan, 2 tablespoons of butter, 1 teaspoon salt, and more black pepper. Serve with lemon wedges and extra Parmesan.

Bacon and Broccoli Salad

Prep Time: 20 minutes
Yield: 4 main servings or 8 side servings

Ingredients

4 cups broccoli florets, cut into bite-size pieces
8 slices bacon, cooked and crumbled
½ cup finely chopped red onion
½ cup shredded cheddar cheese
¼ cup sunflower seeds (optional)
½ cup mayonnaise
2 T. apple cider vinegar
1 T. sugar
Salt and pepper, to taste

Directions

1. In a large salad bowl, combine the broccoli, bacon, onion, cheddar, and sunflower seeds.
2. In a small bowl, whisk together the mayonnaise, apple cider vinegar, and sugar.
3. Drizzle the dressing over the salad, season with a dash of salt and pepper, and gently toss to combine.
4. Refrigerate the salad for at least one hour before serving to allow the flavors to meld.
5. Serve chilled.

Ice Cream Sundae Bar

An ice cream sundae bar is a great option when you have a crowd with diverse preferences or dietary needs. But it's also just plain fun! For a special treat, build your sundae bar with two or three "base" options, add some "flavor" options, and go crazy with a few "toppings" to make it really sing.

Prep Time: 15 minutes
Yield: customizable

Ingredients

The base: ice cream, cones, frozen yogurt, gelato, cake, cupcakes, cookies, donuts, brownies
The flavor: any kind of fresh berry, sliced peaches cooked down with a little bit of water and sugar, macerated strawberries, marshmallows, candies
The toppings: chocolate syrup, chopped nuts, whipped cream, cookie crumbs, sprinkles

Directions

Prepare and set out all ingredients in individual containers. Don't forget serving spoons! Let each person choose their base, flavor, and topping combinations for their own one-of-a-kind ice cream sundae masterpiece.

Overnight French Toast

This recipe is great to make with a crusty bread. Sourdough or French breads are great, but my favorite is brioche. For an extra special treat, serve this French toast with fresh berries and a side of bacon.

Prep Time: 10 minutes, plus 4 hours or overnight
Cook Time: 45 to 60 minutes
Yield: 8 servings

Ingredients

1 loaf crusty bread
8 large eggs
2 cups whole milk
½ cup heavy cream
2 T. vanilla extract
1 tsp. cinnamon
½ tsp. nutmeg
½ tsp. salt
¼ cup sugar
½ cup brown sugar

Topping

    ½ cup all-purpose flour
    ½ cup packed light brown sugar
    1 tsp. ground cinnamon
    ¼ tsp. salt
    ½ cup cold unsalted butter, diced
    Warm maple syrup and butter, for serving

Directions

1. Grease a 9 × 13-inch pan with cooking spray. Cut bread into 1-inch chunks and spread evenly in pan.
2. In a medium bowl, mix together eggs, milk, cream, vanilla, cinnamon, nutmeg, salt, and sugars. Pour evenly over bread. Gently squish down the bread (using a food prep glove if you like) so that it's completely soaked in the mixture.
3. Cover the pan with plastic wrap and place in the fridge overnight (or for at least 4 hours).
4. Combine all the topping ingredients except butter in a medium bowl. Using a pastry blender or a large fork, cut the butter into the mixture until it resembles small pebbles. Cover and refrigerate overnight.
5. The next day, preheat the oven to 350°F.
6. Uncover the baking dish and place the topping evenly over the bread.
7. Bake for 45 to 60 minutes or until a clean toothpick comes out.

Cobb Salad

Prep Time: 30 minutes
Yield: 4 main servings or 8 side servings

Ingredients

    6 cups mixed greens
    2 grilled chicken breasts, sliced
    8 strips bacon, cooked and crumbled
    2 avocados, sliced
    4 hard-boiled eggs, sliced
    1 cup crumbled blue cheese
    ⅓ cup olive oil
    3 T. apple cider vinegar
    Salt and pepper, to taste

Directions

1. Arrange the mixed greens in a large salad bowl.
2. Arrange the chicken, bacon, avocado, eggs, and blue cheese on top of the greens in rows.
3. In a small bowl, whisk together the olive oil and apple cider vinegar.
4. Drizzle the dressing over the salad and add a sprinkle of salt and pepper.
5. Serve immediately, tossing the salad at the table just before serving.

Green Chile Enchilada Casserole

This Green Chile Enchilada Casserole is hearty and comforting, perfect for a weeknight dinner. The addition of cilantro gives a fresh, herby twist to this delicious, cheesy casserole. Enjoy!

Prep Time: 15 minutes
Cook Time: 30 minutes
Yield: 4 servings

Ingredients

    1 (10.5 oz.) can cream of chicken soup
    ½ cup sour cream
    1 (15 oz.) can green chili enchilada sauce, divided
    Salt and pepper, to taste
    2 cups cooked shredded chicken
    ¼ cup chopped fresh cilantro
    8 (7-or 8-inch) flour tortillas (or 12 6-inch corn tortillas for a more traditional twist)
    2 cups Mexican blend shredded cheese, divided
    Optional toppings: chopped black olives, extra sour cream, salsa, shredded lettuce, diced tomatoes

Directions

1. Preheat your oven to 350°F and lightly grease an 8 × 8-inch baking dish.
2. In a large bowl, mix together the cream of chicken soup, sour cream, ⅓ cup of the enchilada sauce, and season with ¼ teaspoon each of salt and pepper. Add the shredded chicken and cilantro, and stir until evenly combined.
3. Pour ¼ cup of the remaining enchilada sauce into the bottom of the prepared baking dish, spreading it out to ensure the whole bottom is covered. Tear up 3 of the tortillas and evenly

distribute them over the sauce.

4. Spread a third of the chicken mixture over the torn tortillas. Repeat with another layer of torn tortillas, chicken mixture, ⅓ cup of enchilada sauce, and half of the cheese.

5. For the final layer, distribute the remaining torn tortillas, chicken mixture, enchilada sauce, and top with the remaining cheese.

6. Bake in the preheated oven for 25 to 30 minutes, or until the cheese is beautifully melted and bubbling.

7. Remove the casserole from the oven and let it rest for 5 minutes before serving. This allows the flavors to meld and the cheese to set slightly.

8. Serve the Green Chile Enchilada Casserole warm with your choice of toppings.

Roasted Corn Salad

Prep time: 10 minutes
Cook time: 25 minutes
Yield: 8 servings

Ingredients

4 ears corn, husks removed
½ cup mayonnaise
¼ cup fresh lime juice
½ tsp. chili powder
½ cup crumbled cotija cheese
¼ cup chopped fresh cilantro
Salt and pepper, to taste

Directions

1. Heat a grill or grill pan over medium heat. Cook the corn until it is charred on all sides. Remove from the grill and allow it to cool. Once cooled, cut the kernels off the cob and place them in a large bowl.

2. In a separate bowl, mix together the mayonnaise, lime juice, and chili powder.

3. Pour the dressing over the grilled corn kernels and mix until they are well coated.

4. Add the cotija cheese and cilantro to the bowl. Mix well.

5. Season the salad with salt and pepper, to taste.

6. Serve the salad immediately or refrigerate it for an hour to allow the flavors to meld.

Greek Yogurt Chicken Salad with Apples and Almonds

This dish is versatile and can be enjoyed in several ways. It's a great way to use up leftover chicken and perfect for those warmer days when you want something light and satisfying. You can serve it on crackers or warm pita bread for a quick and easy lunch. For a lighter option, you could serve it atop a bed of mixed greens. Pair the chicken salad with some fresh grapes on the side for a refreshing and balanced meal!

Prep Time: 15 minutes
Yield: 4 servings

Ingredients

2 cups leftover chicken, shredded
Juice of 1 lemon
1½ cups nonfat Greek yogurt
1 T. honey
½ tart apple, chopped
½ cup slivered almonds
½ cup dried cranberries
Salt and pepper, to taste
Optional: Crackers, warm pita bread, and grapes for serving

Directions

1. Place the shredded chicken in a large mixing bowl.

2. Squeeze the juice of the lemon over the chicken. This will not only add a tangy freshness to the salad but will also keep the chicken moist.

3. Add the Greek yogurt and honey to the bowl. Stir until the chicken is evenly coated.

4. Next, add the apple, almonds, and dried cranberries to the bowl. Stir to combine all the ingredients well.

5. Season with salt and pepper, to taste. Your chicken salad is now ready to serve with crackers, pita, grapes, or however you like it!

A Prayer for the Spring Season

Lord, I welcome spring
to my home and to my table.
I open my heart and my hands
to the rhythms
You have created.

Lord, help me to see the gifts
of this season.

I ask that spring brings
a fresh creative
spark through
the first harvests of spring
in quiches, salads,
and bright broths.

As more light
fills our days,
please make me aware
of how You are working
in me, and in my home.

Help me to see
the seeds You plant
and teach me how to water
what You desire to grow,
so that I may partner with You.

May all who eat at this table
be reminded
of Your constant provision,
in this season,
and in seasons to follow.

Week Fifteen
Soul Satisfaction

Cooking with hearty, aromatic ingredients delivers satisfaction to our senses, bodies, and families. As the Sabbath day practices around your mealtimes become second nature, take time to notice how you are experiencing a greater contentment—peace. Are you and your spouse more content? Are you and your family more peaceful? Is there less stress in bringing everyone together? Do you feel less harried as you place food on the table and sit down to nourish yourself? Appreciating these changes—big or small—will serve up a soul satisfaction that lingers long into the week.

Week 15 Menu

Saturday

Chili-Sauced Bacon Meatloaf
Creamy Yukon Gold Mashed
   Potatoes
Zucchini and Mushroom
   Stir-Fry

Dessert:
Nutella-Stuffed Brownies

Sunday

Breakfast:
Quiche (Bacon and Cheese)

Lunch:
Enchilada Soup
Southwest Chopped Salad
Cheese and Veggie Quesadillas

Dinner:
Charcuterie Board
Overnight Soup Bread
Green Salad (no recipe)

Monday

Remixed Meatloaf Spaghetti
Caesar Salad

Tuesday

Enchilada Soup
Southwest Chopped Salad

Wednesday

Leftovers or frozen meal of choice

Thursday

Dinner out

Friday

Pizza night!

Sabbath Soup

Enchilada Soup

Prep Time: 20 minutes • Cook Time: 45 minutes • Yield: 4 bowls or 8 cups

Ingredients

2 T. olive oil or avocado oil

1 medium onion, diced

2 celery ribs, sliced

1 large red bell pepper, diced

3 cloves garlic, minced

1½ tsp. ground cumin

1 T. chili powder

1 tsp. dried oregano

1 (15 oz.) can diced fire-roasted tomatoes

¼ cup tomato paste

5 cups low-sodium chicken broth

2 lbs. boneless skinless chicken breasts

1 (15 oz.) can red kidney beans, drained and rinsed

1 (15 oz.) can black beans, drained and rinsed

1 (15.25 oz.) can whole kernel corn, drained

1½ cups enchilada sauce

1 cup shredded cheddar cheese

1 cup shredded Monterey Jack cheese

Salt and pepper, to taste

Directions

1. Heat the oil in a large Dutch oven or stockpot over medium heat. Add the onion, celery, and red bell pepper. Sauté until they begin to soften, about 5 minutes.
2. Add the garlic, cumin, chili powder, and oregano. Cook for another minute, until the spices are well integrated and fragrant.
3. Add the tomatoes, tomato paste, and chicken broth to the pot. Stir well to combine and bring the mixture to a simmer.
4. Once simmering, add the chicken breasts to the pot. Allow them to cook for about 20 minutes, or until fully cooked through.
5. Remove the chicken from the pot and place on a large platter. Use two forks to shred it, then set it aside for now.
6. Add the kidney beans, black beans, corn, and enchilada sauce to the pot. Stir well and return the mixture to a simmer.
7. Return the shredded chicken to the pot. Stir well to combine and allow the soup to simmer for another 10 to 15 minutes. This will allow the flavors to meld.
8. Reduce the heat to low, and gradually add the shredded cheddar and Monterey Jack cheese, stirring well to ensure it melts evenly into the soup.
9. Season the soup to taste with salt and pepper. Ladle the soup into bowls, top with additional cheese if desired, and serve hot.

Chili-Sauced Bacon Meatloaf

Prep Time: 15 minutes
Cook Time: 1 hour
Yield: 4 to 6 servings

Ingredients

Meatloaf

- 1 medium yellow onion, diced
- 1 tsp. unsalted butter
- 2 large eggs (or 3 small)
- ¾ cup whole milk
- ¾ cup Italian breadcrumbs
- 2 lbs. (80/20) ground beef
- 1 T. chili sauce (or ketchup, but the chili sauce gives it a mild kick without spice)
- 1 tsp. Italian seasoning
- 2 tsp. dried parsley
- 1 tsp. kosher salt
- 1 tsp. black pepper, or to taste

Meatloaf Topping

- ½ cup chili sauce
- 1 tsp. Worcestershire sauce
- ½ cup ketchup
- 2 T. brown sugar
- 3 strips bacon

Directions

1. Preheat the oven to 350°F. Line a rimmed baking pan with aluminum foil and spray with cooking spray.
2. In a small pan, cook the onion in butter over medium-low heat until browned and tender. Let it cool completely.
3. In a medium bowl, combine the eggs, milk, and breadcrumbs. Let the mixture sit for 5 minutes to thicken.
4. Add the ground beef, cooked onion, chili sauce, Italian seasoning, parsley, and salt and pepper to the bowl. Mix until just combined.
5. Mound an 8 × 4-inch loaf in the center of the prepared baking pan and bake for 40 minutes.
6. While the meatloaf is cooking, combine the chili sauce, Worcestershire sauce, ketchup, and brown sugar. Spread the mixture over the meatloaf and top with the bacon. Bake for an additional 10 to 15 minutes or until the meatloaf is cooked through and reaches an internal temperature of 160°F. Broil for 1 to 2 minutes, if desired, to crisp the bacon.
7. Let the meatloaf rest for 10 minutes before slicing and serving.

Creamy Yukon Gold Mashed Potatoes

Prep Time: 15 minutes
Cook Time: 20 minutes
Yield: 8 servings

Ingredients

- 3 lbs. Yukon Gold potatoes
- 1 cup whole milk (or half-and-half for a richer texture)
- ½ cup unsalted butter
- Salt and freshly ground black pepper, to taste
- Optional: minced garlic, fresh herbs (like chives or parsley) for garnish

Directions

1. Start by washing and peeling the potatoes. Cut them into uniform chunks, about 2 inches in size.
2. Place the potato chunks in a large pot and fill with enough water to cover them. Add a generous pinch of salt to the water. Bring the water to a boil over high heat, then reduce to a simmer. Cook the potatoes until they are fork-tender, usually around 15 to 20 minutes.
3. While the potatoes are boiling, gently heat the milk and butter in a small saucepan over low heat. Stir occasionally until the butter is melted. Keep this mixture warm.
4. Once the potatoes are cooked, drain the water and return the potatoes to the pot.
5. Slowly add the warm milk and butter mixture to the potatoes while mashing. Use a potato masher or ricer for best results.
6. Season with salt and pepper, to taste. If you're using minced garlic, you can add it here.
7. Gently mix all the ingredients until you achieve a creamy texture. If the mixture seems too dry, you can add a little more milk.
8. Transfer the mashed potatoes to a serving bowl. If desired, garnish with freshly chopped herbs.

Zucchini and Mushroom Stir-Fry

Prep Time: 5 minutes
Cook Time: 12 minutes
Yield: 4 servings

Ingredients

2 T. vegetable oil or olive oil
3 cloves garlic, minced
1 small onion, thinly sliced
1 cup sliced mushrooms (any variety you prefer)
2 medium zucchinis, sliced into half-moons
Salt and freshly ground black pepper, to taste
1 T. soy sauce
Dash of sesame oil (optional)

Directions

1. Place a large skillet or wok over medium-high heat. Add the oil and let it heat up.
2. Once the oil is hot, add the garlic and onion. Stir-fry for 1 to 2 minutes, until the onion becomes translucent and the garlic is fragrant.
3. Add the mushrooms to the pan and stir-fry for about 3 to 4 minutes, until they start to soften.
4. Incorporate the sliced zucchini into the pan. Stir-fry for an additional 4 to 5 minutes, or until the zucchini is tender but still crisp.
5. Season with salt and black pepper, to taste. Drizzle the soy sauce over the vegetables and stir well to combine.
6. If you're using sesame oil, add it at this point for added flavor. Stir-fry for another minute to make sure all the ingredients are well coated with the sauce.
7. Remove from heat and transfer to a serving dish. Serve immediately as a side or incorporate it into a main course.

Nutella-Stuffed Brownies

Prep Time: 10 minutes
Cook Time: 40 to 45 minutes
Yield: 12 servings

Ingredients

Brownie Batter
1 cup unsalted butter
2 cups granulated sugar
4 large eggs
1 tsp. vanilla extract
1 cup all-purpose flour
½ cup cocoa powder
¼ tsp. salt
½ tsp. baking powder
Nutella Filling
1 cup Nutella
½ cup cream cheese, softened
1 egg
2 T. sugar

Directions

1. Preheat your oven to 350°F. Grease a 9 × 13-inch baking dish or line it with parchment paper.
2. Start by making the brownie batter: In a medium saucepan, melt the butter over low heat. Remove from heat and stir in the sugar. Once the sugar is incorporated, stir in the eggs and vanilla extract.
3. In a separate bowl, combine the flour, cocoa powder, salt, and baking powder. Gradually add this to the butter mixture and stir until well combined.
4. Make the Nutella filling: In a separate bowl, combine the Nutella, cream cheese, egg, and sugar. Stir until everything is smooth and well mixed.
5. Pour half of the brownie batter into the prepared baking dish. Spread the Nutella filling over the batter, then pour the rest of the brownie batter on top, spreading it to cover the Nutella filling as best as you can.
6. Using a butter knife, gently swirl the layers together to create a marbled effect.
7. Bake for about 40 to 45 minutes, or until a

toothpick inserted into the center comes out with a few moist crumbs.

8. Let the brownies cool completely in the baking dish before cutting them into squares.

Quiche (Bacon and Cheese)

Prep Time: 20 minutes
Cook Time: 45 minutes
Yield: 8 servings

Ingredients

4 large eggs
⅔ cup whole milk
½ cup heavy cream (or heavy whipping cream)
¼ tsp. salt
¼ tsp. pepper
1 cup shredded or crumbled cheese (feta, cheddar, blue cheese, goat cheese, or Gruyère)
1 cup cooked, crumbled bacon
1 cup cooked vegetable of choice
1 store-bought frozen pastry pie shell, defrosted overnight
¼ cup grated Parmesan cheese

Directions

1. Preheat oven to 350°F.
2. In a large bowl, beat the eggs, milk, cream, salt, and pepper on high speed, approximately 1 minute.
3. Fold in your choice of cheese, along with the bacon, and cooked vegetables. (I love asparagus, mushrooms, onions, and broccoli, but any leftover vegetable would be great.) Pour mixture into the crust.
4. Sprinkle the Parmesan cheese on top.
5. Cover the edges of the pie shell with aluminum foil to keep them from burning.
6. Bake quiche until the center is set and a toothpick comes out clean, about 45 minutes.
7. Let the quiche cool for 10 minutes before serving.

Southwest Chopped Salad

Prep time: 30 minutes
Yield: 4 main servings or 8 side servings

Ingredients

6 cups chopped romaine lettuce
1 cup cooked black beans (if canned, be sure to drain and rinse)
1 cup corn kernels
1 red bell pepper, diced
1 avocado, diced
½ cup cherry tomatoes, halved
½ cup crumbled queso fresco or feta cheese
Cilantro Dressing

Directions

1. In a large salad bowl, combine the romaine lettuce, black beans, corn, red bell pepper, avocado, cherry tomatoes, and cheese.
2. Drizzle the dressing over the salad and gently toss to combine. Serve immediately.

Cilantro Dressing

Ingredients

1 cup loosely packed fresh cilantro
½ cup Greek yogurt
2 T. fresh lime juice
1 clove garlic
2 T. olive oil
½ tsp. salt
¼ tsp. black pepper

Directions

Combine all ingredients in a blender or food processor and blend until smooth.

Be still, and know that I am God.

PSALM 46:10

Cheese and Veggie Quesadillas

Prep Time: 10 minutes
Cook Time: 15 minutes
Yield: 4 servings

Ingredients

4 large flour tortillas
2 cups shredded cheddar cheese
1 red bell pepper, diced
1 green bell pepper, diced
1 onion, diced

Directions

1. Preheat a large skillet over medium heat.
2. Spread ½ cup of cheese on half of each tortilla.
3. Sprinkle the peppers and onion over the cheese.
4. Fold the empty half of each tortilla over the filled half.
5. Cook the quesadillas in the skillet for 2 to 3 minutes on each side, until the cheese is melted and the tortillas are crispy. Cook in batches, if needed, to keep the quesadillas in a single layer in your skillet.
6. Cut into triangles and serve hot.

Charcuterie Board

A charcuterie board is a great option for parties, but it's also great for an easy dinner treat. Don't let the fancy reputation scare you away. Just remember to include a few items from each of the categories below.

Prep Time: 10 minutes
Yield: customizable

Ingredients

Base
Crackers, pita bread, pretzels
Slices of cucumber

Substance
Hard cheeses: cheddar, Swiss, smoked gouda
Soft cheeses: goat, brie, crema, spreadable cheeses, Havarti
Cured meats: ham, sausage, salami, prosciutto, pepperoni
Hard-boiled eggs

Flavor
Nuts, pickles, olives, sliced apples, cocktail onions

Extras

    Dips, tapenades, jams
    Fruit: strawberries, grapes, dried apricots
    Dark chocolate

Directions

1. Get a nice tray, platter, or wooden cutting board to hold your spread. Gather serving tools: toothpicks, small tongs, a small knife for spreading soft cheese, and spoons for dips or jams.

2. Choose two or more options from each category and lay them out in bite-size slices or chunks, grouped together on your serving tray. Be sure to offer and label gluten-free items for those with sensitivities or allergies and consider separating them from any gluten-containing items by placing them in their own bowl or tray. You may also want to separate nuts or other potential allergens into their own bowls. Enjoy!

Overnight Soup Bread

Who knew that this life-changing recipe would come from, of all places, TikTok! I have come to see it many places since, and it really is one of the simplest recipes for amazing, warm bread that complements soup perfectly.

One warning: This is not spur-of-the-moment bread. This bread, while it takes very little effort, does take a little forethought. But that's okay, because if you're prepping your soup on Saturday, just mix up this dough Saturday evening and then forget about it until about an hour before "Soup's On!" Your dough needs between 12 and 16 hours to rise, and then another hour of forming and baking. But trust me. It's easy, and it's worth it.

Prep Time: 10 minutes, plus 12 to 16 hours to rise
Cook Time: 45 minutes
Yield: 8 to 12 servings

Ingredients

    1 ½ cups water, room temperature to warm
    ½ tsp. yeast
    3 cups flour
    1 ½ tsp. salt

Directions

1. Mix all ingredients together in an ovenproof bowl (not plastic). One option is to use the stand mixer to mix the dough and leave it in that bowl to rise.

2. Cover the bowl with a kitchen towel and place it in the oven with the oven light on. Let it sit undisturbed for 12 to 16 hours.

3. Remove the bowl from the oven and preheat the oven to 450°F.

4. Line a Dutch oven with parchment paper. You may find it helpful to first crinkle the parchment as this will help it stay in place inside your Dutch oven.

5. Flour a surface and place the dough on that surface. Stretch and fold the dough ball, then place it in the parchment-lined Dutch oven.

6. Use kitchen shears to make three snips on the top of the bread, allowing the bread to expand. Cover the Dutch oven with its lid.

7. Cook the bread in the covered Dutch oven for 30 minutes.

8. After 30 minutes, remove the Dutch oven lid and continue cooking for 15 more minutes.

9. Serve warm, accompanied by salted butter or a mix of oil and balsamic vinegar.

He refreshes my soul.
He guides me
along the right paths
for his name's sake.

PSALM 23:3

Remixed Meatloaf Spaghetti

This Remixed Meatloaf Spaghetti is a fun twist on traditional spaghetti and meat sauce, and a clever way to transform leftover meatloaf into a whole new meal. Enjoy!

Prep Time: 10 minutes
Cook Time: 20 minutes
Yield: 4 servings

Ingredients

16 oz. dried spaghetti
2 to 4 slices leftover bacon meatloaf
1 (26 oz.) jar marinara sauce (your favorite kind)
Salt and pepper, to taste
Grated Parmesan cheese, for serving
Optional: Fresh basil leaves for garnish, crushed red pepper flakes for a spicy kick

Directions

1. Fill a large pot with water, add a generous pinch of salt, and set it over high heat. Once your pot of water is boiling, add your spaghetti and cook until al dente. This typically takes around 8 to 10 minutes.
2. Meanwhile, chop up your leftover meatloaf into fine pieces. This will not only help it mix well with the sauce, but will also help it reheat evenly.
3. In a large skillet over medium heat, combine the chopped meatloaf and the marinara sauce. Stir together until well mixed. Allow the mixture to come to a simmer, stirring occasionally to prevent sticking.
4. After your spaghetti is cooked, reserve one cup of the cooking water and then drain the pasta well.
5. Transfer the cooked and drained spaghetti into a large serving bowl. Pour the meatloaf marinara sauce over the spaghetti and toss everything together until the spaghetti is evenly coated with sauce. If the sauce appears too thick, add a bit of the reserved pasta water.
6. Season with salt and pepper (I think freshly ground black pepper is best here), then top with a generous sprinkle of grated Parmesan cheese.
7. For those who like a bit of heat, sprinkle on some crushed red pepper flakes. Garnish with fresh basil leaves for a pop of color and added freshness. Serve the Remixed Meatloaf Spaghetti immediately, with extra Parmesan cheese on the side for sprinkling.

Caesar Salad

Prep Time: 15 minutes
Yield: 4 main servings or 8 side servings

Ingredients

1 head romaine lettuce, torn into bite-size pieces
1 cup croutons
½ cup freshly grated Parmesan cheese
½ cup Creamy Caesar Dressing

Directions

1. In a large salad bowl, combine the romaine lettuce, croutons, and Parmesan cheese.
2. Pour the dressing over the salad and toss until well coated.
3. Serve immediately, with additional Parmesan cheese on top if desired.

Creamy Caesar Dressing

Ingredients

¾ cup mayonnaise
2 T. fresh lemon juice
2 garlic cloves, minced
1 tsp. Worcestershire sauce
1 tsp. Dijon mustard
¼ cup grated Parmesan cheese
Salt and freshly ground pepper, to taste

Directions

Combine all ingredients in a blender or food processor and blend until smooth.

A Prayer Over a Simple Meal

The ingredients before me
are too simple,
and I fear it's possible
it won't be enough.
Lord, I admit I am curious
how this modest soup will be a meal.

And then I consider how
the onion came to be:
the germination of the seed,
the first leaves,
the formation of the bulb,
the harvest.
Now it sits before me to flavor my soup.
What a wonder the onion is.

Lord, thank You for
each extravagant ingredient
and for all of the hands
that took part in bringing these
items to my kitchen.

Thank You for this simple bowl of
soup that will fuel my body.

This lavish soup is a
miraculous wonder.

What a wonder You are.

What a wonder.

Thank You for this feast.

Week Sixteen

Italian Countryside Retreat

H ere is a week of some of my favorite meals inspired by Italian flavors (except the donut cake, which is not Italian, but is amazing). If you want a Sabbath state of mind, I figure you can't get much closer than when you envision sitting on a terrace and looking out over the vast rolling hills of Tuscany with the afternoon sun warming your skin.

May this week's lineup, and the soup in particular, transport you to your happy place, whether it's an Italian villa or your back porch.

Week 16 Menu

Saturday

Chicken Manicotti
Cucumber, Tomato, and
   Avocado Salad

Dessert:
Old-Fashioned
   Donut Cake

Sunday

Breakfast:
Overnight Oatmeal with Apples
   and Apricots

Lunch:
 Italian Wedding Soup
Italian Chopped Salad
Overnight Soup Bread

Dinner:
Slow Cooker Ham with Pineapple
   Glaze
Cheesy Scalloped Yukon Gold
   Potatoes
Asparagus (no recipe)
Rolls

Monday

Pasta Salad with Shredded
   Chicken

Tuesday

Italian Wedding Soup
Italian Chopped Salad
Cheesy Garlic Bread

Wednesday

Leftovers or frozen meal of choice

Thursday

Dinner out

Friday

Pizza night!

Sabbath Soup

Italian Wedding Soup

Prep Time: 10 minutes • Cook Time: 45 minutes • Yield: 4 bowls or 8 cups

Ingredients

- 2 lbs. frozen Italian style meat-balls
- 2 quarts chicken broth
- ⅓ cup chopped fresh spinach
- 1 tsp. onion powder
- 1 tsp. dried parsley flakes
- ¾ tsp. salt
- 1 ¼ tsp. pepper
- 1 ¼ tsp. garlic powder
- 1 ¼ cups cooked medium pasta shells
- Optional: Parmesan cheese, grated, to serve

Directions

1. In a Dutch oven or large pot, brown the frozen meatballs in small batches over medium heat. Drain any excess fat.
2. Add the chicken broth to the pot with the meatballs.
3. Add the spinach, onion powder, dried parsley flakes, salt, pepper, and garlic powder. Stir well to combine.
4. Bring the mixture to a boil over high heat, then reduce the heat to low, cover the pot, and let it simmer for about 20 to 30 minutes. This will allow the flavors to meld and the meatballs to heat thoroughly.
5. Stir in the cooked pasta shells and heat through for about 5 more minutes.
6. Taste the soup and adjust seasoning if necessary. Serve hot and enjoy! You can garnish with some grated Parmesan cheese if desired.

Chicken Manicotti

This Chicken Manicotti is a delicious and satisfying dish, perfect for a weekend family dinner. The creamy cheese and savory chicken are a wonderful combination. Enjoy this special treat!

Prep Time: 30 minutes
Cook Time: 1 hour
Yield: 6 servings

Ingredients

14 manicotti shells
3 cups cooked, shredded chicken breasts (or 1 lb. raw chicken breasts, with 1 T. butter)
2 cups low-fat ricotta cheese
½ cup shredded mozzarella or Parmesan cheese
1 tsp. dried parsley
2 eggs, lightly beaten
4 cups marinara sauce

Directions

1. Preheat your oven to 350°F.
2. Set a pot of water on the stove over high heat. Bring the water to a boil and then drop in the manicotti noodles for just 1 to 2 minutes to parboil them. You want them only slightly softened and still holding a firm shape. Drain and set the noodles aside.
3. If using raw chicken: Melt the butter in a large skillet over medium heat. Brown the chicken in the butter for about 5 to 7 minutes per side, until it is no longer pink in the center. Set it aside to cool, then shred the meat.
4. In a large bowl, mix together the chicken, ricotta cheese, mozzarella or Parmesan cheese, parsley, and eggs until well combined.
5. Spread about 1 cup of tomato sauce in the bottom of a 9 × 13-inch baking dish.
6. Fill each parboiled manicotti shell with the chicken and cheese mixture. Arrange the filled shells in a single layer in the baking dish.
7. Pour the remaining tomato sauce over the manicotti, making sure all the pasta is covered.
8. Cover the dish with aluminum foil and bake in the preheated oven for 45 minutes.
9. Remove the foil and bake for an additional 10 to 15 minutes, or until the cheese is bubbly and golden.
10. Allow the manicotti to cool for a few minutes before serving.

Cucumber, Tomato, and Avocado Salad

Prep Time: 15 minutes
Yield: 4 main servings or 8 side servings

Ingredients

2 cucumbers, diced
2 tomatoes, diced
2 avocados, diced
¼ red onion, thinly sliced
¼ cup chopped fresh cilantro
¼ cup olive oil
2 T. fresh lime juice
1 tsp. honey
Salt and pepper, to taste

Directions

1. In a large salad bowl, combine the cucumbers, tomatoes, avocados, red onion, and cilantro.
2. In a small bowl, whisk together the olive oil, lime juice, and honey.
3. Drizzle the dressing over the salad, season with a dash of salt and pepper, and gently toss to combine. Serve immediately.

Note: This salad is best consumed the day it is made to prevent the avocados from browning.

Old-Fashioned Donut Cake

Prep Time: 15 minutes
Cook Time: 55 to 60 minutes
Yield: 8 servings

Ingredients

Cake

3 cups all-purpose flour
1 T. baking powder
½ tsp. baking soda
½ tsp. salt
2 tsp. ground nutmeg
1 cup unsalted butter, room temperature
2 cups granulated sugar
4 large eggs

2 tsp. pure vanilla extract

1 cup buttermilk

Glaze

2 cups powdered sugar

¼ cup whole milk

1 tsp. pure vanilla extract

Directions

1. Preheat your oven to 350°F. Grease and lightly flour a Bundt pan.

2. In a bowl, whisk together the flour, baking powder, baking soda, salt, and nutmeg.

3. In another large bowl, cream together the butter and sugar until light and fluffy. This should take about 2 to 3 minutes using an electric mixer on medium speed.

4. Beat in the eggs, one at a time, making sure each is incorporated before adding the next. Stir in the vanilla extract.

5. Add the dry ingredients to the butter mixture in three parts, alternating with the buttermilk, starting and ending with the dry ingredients. Mix just until combined after each addition. Do not overmix.

6. Pour the batter into the prepared Bundt pan and smooth the top with a spatula. Bake for 50 to 60 minutes, or until a toothpick inserted into the center comes out clean.

7. Let the cake cool in the pan for 10 minutes, then invert it onto a wire rack to cool completely.

8. While the cake is cooling, prepare the glaze: In a bowl, whisk together the powdered sugar, milk, and vanilla extract until smooth.

9. Once the cake has cooled, pour the glaze evenly over the top, allowing it to drip down the sides.

Overnight Oatmeal with Apples and Apricots

Some days I need my breakfast to be waiting for me—amazing, hot, and ready to go. What I don't eat on the first day I just refrigerate and then reheat throughout the week. I also like to put a little sweetener in the oatmeal. Dealer's choice! You can add it into the slow cooker with the raw oats, or add it as a topping once the oats are cooked.

Prep Time: 5 minutes

Cook Time: 8 hours in a slow cooker

Yield: 6 servings

Ingredients

1½ cups steel-cut oats

4 cups water

2 cups milk, any kind you like (I use nonfat)

1 large tart apple, peeled and chopped

1 cup chopped dried apricots

2 tsp. pure vanilla extract

1½ tsp. ground cinnamon

½ tsp. ground nutmeg

½ tsp. kosher salt

Sweetener of your choice: brown sugar, white sugar, honey, or agave.

Toppings of your choice: blueberries, raspberries, blackberries, granola, shredded coconut, sliced almonds, chopped pecans, Greek yogurt

Directions

1. Place all the ingredients except the toppings in the bottom of a 4- to 6-quart slow cooker, then stir to combine. Cover and cook on low for 8 hours. Remove the cover and stir. Taste and see if you need to add anything else, like more vanilla or cinnamon.

2. I like to keep oatmeal in the fridge for up to a week. Place it in a big tub, and reheat individual servings in the microwave for 2 minutes and 30 seconds.

Italian Chopped Salad

Prep Time: 20 minutes

Yield: 4 main servings or 8 side servings

Ingredients

1 head iceberg lettuce, chopped

1 red onion, thinly sliced

1 cup cherry tomatoes, halved

1 (15 oz.) can chickpeas, drained and rinsed

1 cup pearl mozzarella balls

1 cup cubed provolone cheese

½ cup sliced pepperoncini

½ cup cubed genoa salami

½ cup chopped sun-dried tomatoes

½ cup Italian dressing

Salt and pepper, to taste

Directions

1. In a large salad bowl, combine the lettuce, red onion, cherry tomatoes, chickpeas, pearl mozzarella, provolone cheese, pepperoncini, salami, and sun-dried tomatoes.
2. Drizzle the dressing over the salad, season with a dash of salt and pepper, and gently toss to combine. Serve immediately.

Italian Dressing

Ingredients

½ cup extra-virgin olive oil
¼ cup red wine vinegar
1 tsp. honey
1 tsp. dried oregano
1 tsp. dried basil
½ tsp. garlic powder
Salt and freshly ground pepper, to taste

Directions

Shake all ingredients together in a jar until well combined.

Overnight Soup Bread

Who knew that this life-changing recipe would come from, of all places, TikTok! I have come to see it many places since, and it really is one of the simplest recipes for amazing, warm bread that complements soup perfectly.

One warning: This is not spur-of-the-moment bread. This bread, while it takes very little effort, does take a little forethought. But that's okay, because if you're prepping your soup on Saturday, just mix up this dough Saturday evening and then forget about it until about an hour before "Soup's On!" Your dough needs between 12 and 16 hours to rise, and then another hour of forming and baking. But trust me. It's easy, and it's worth it.

Prep Time: 10 minutes, plus 12 to 16 hours to rise
Cook Time: 45 minutes
Yield: 8 to 12 servings

Ingredients

1½ cups water, room temperature to warm
½ tsp. yeast
3 cups flour
1½ tsp. salt

Directions

1. Mix all ingredients together in an ovenproof bowl (not plastic). One option is to use the stand mixer to mix the dough and leave it in that bowl to rise.
2. Cover the bowl with a kitchen towel and place it in the oven with the oven light on. Let it sit undisturbed for 12 to 16 hours.
3. Remove the bowl from the oven and preheat the oven to 450°F.
4. Line a Dutch oven with parchment paper. You may find it helpful to first crinkle the parchment as this will help it stay in place inside your Dutch oven.
5. Flour a surface and place the dough on that surface. Stretch and fold the dough ball, then place it in the parchment-lined Dutch oven.
6. Use kitchen shears to make three snips on the top of the bread, allowing the bread to expand. Cover the Dutch oven with its lid.
7. Cook the bread in the covered Dutch oven for 30 minutes.
8. After 30 minutes, remove the Dutch oven lid and continue cooking for 15 more minutes.
9. Serve warm, accompanied by salted butter or a mix of oil and balsamic vinegar.

Slow Cooker Ham with Pineapple Glaze

Prep Time: 15 minutes
Cook Time: 4 to 6 hours
Yield: 8 to 10 servings

Ingredients

2 cups pineapple juice
1 (5 to 7 lb.) fully-cooked ham
10 whole cloves
1 cup brown sugar
1 T. Dijon mustard
1 T. balsamic vinegar
1 T. honey
2 T. cornstarch

Directions

1. Using a sharp knife, score the ham in a diamond pattern, making cuts about ¼ inch deep. Insert the whole cloves into the intersections of the cuts.
2. Place the ham flat side down in the slow cooker. Pour the pineapple juice over the ham, making sure it coats all sides and gets into the cuts that you made.
3. In a small bowl, combine the brown sugar, Dijon mustard, balsamic vinegar, and honey. Using a spatula or your hands (I like to keep disposable gloves on hand—no pun intended—for just such jobs), spread the glaze evenly over the top and sides of the ham.
4. Cover the slow cooker with the lid and cook on low for 4 to 6 hours, basting the ham with the juices every 2 hours, if possible. The ham is done when it reaches an internal temperature of 140°F when measured with a meat thermometer.
5. Carefully remove the ham from the slow cooker and transfer it to a serving dish. Tent the ham loosely with aluminum foil and let it rest for 15 to 20 minutes to allow the juices to redistribute.
6. Meanwhile, pour the juices from the slow cooker into a saucepan (you can use a strainer to get all the big chunks). Bring the juices to a boil. Remove 2 tablespoons of the juice to a small bowl, and whisk in the cornstarch to create a slurry. Gradually pour it back into the boiling juices, whisking constantly to prevent lumps and form nice glaze. Once the slurry is fully incorporated, reduce the heat to low and simmer, stirring occasionally, for about 5 minutes or until it thickens to your desired consistency.
7. Discard the cloves, transfer the ham to a cutting board, and thinly slice the ham. Arrange the slices back on the serving dish, and drizzle the warm pineapple glaze over the ham, keeping a little extra on the side for guests to add as desired.

Cheesy Scalloped Yukon Gold Potatoes

Prep Time: 20 minutes
Cook Time: 90 minutes
Yield: 6 servings

Ingredients

4 to 5 medium Yukon Gold potatoes, peeled and thinly sliced
2 cups heavy cream
1 cup shredded sharp cheddar cheese, divided
½ cup grated Parmesan cheese
1 tsp. olive oil
1 small onion, finely chopped
2 to 3 cloves garlic, minced
1 tsp. salt, or to taste
½ tsp. freshly ground black pepper
½ tsp. paprika (optional, for color)
Optional: fresh thyme or parsley, for garnish

Directions

1. Preheat the oven to 350°F. Grease a 9 × 13-inch baking dish and set it aside.
2. Peel and thinly slice the potatoes using a mandoline slicer or a sharp knife. Aim for slices about ⅛ inch thick.
3. In a saucepan over medium heat, combine the heavy cream, half of the cheddar cheese, and the Parmesan. Whisk until the cheese is mostly melted and the mixture is smooth. Remove from heat.
4. In a small pan, heat the oil and sauté the onion and garlic until the onion is translucent. Add this to the cheese sauce.
5. Add salt and black pepper to the cheese sauce, adjusting to taste.
6. In the prepared baking dish, start by layering half of the sliced potatoes. Pour half of the cheese sauce over the potatoes. Repeat with another layer of potatoes and the remaining cheese sauce. Sprinkle the rest of the cheddar cheese on top.
7. If using, sprinkle paprika over the top layer for a splash of color.
8. Cover the baking dish with aluminum foil and bake in the preheated oven for 45 minutes.
9. Remove the foil and continue to bake for

another 20 to 25 minutes, or until the potatoes are tender and the top is golden and bubbly.

10. Let the potatoes rest for a few minutes before serving. If desired, garnish with thyme or parsley.

Rolls

The ingredients for rolls and sandwich bread dough are the same, so feel free to double the recipe to get both rolls for dinner and sliced bread for sandwiches for the week. Look at you being so clever!

Prep Time: 10 minutes, plus 2 hours to rise
Cook Time: 30 minutes
Yield: 6 Rolls

Ingredients

1 cup warm water
½ T. active dry yeast
2 T. honey
2¾ cups all-purpose flour, divided
1 tsp. salt
2 T. melted butter, divided

Directions

1. Mix the water, yeast, and honey together. Add 2 cups of flour, salt, and 1 tablespoon melted butter and mix.
2. Put dough on a surface with ¼ cup of flour and knead it for about 5 minutes, adding in the other half cup of flour to get a doughy texture.
3. Take your dough ball and put it in a bowl. Cover it with a dishcloth and stick it in the oven with the oven light on for an hour (it should approximately double in size).
4. Preheat the oven to 350°F.
5. Butter a pie tin. Cut the dough into six pieces and form the pieces into rolls.
6. Place the rolls in the pie tin and let the dough double again, covered.
7. Bake for 30 minutes.
8. Remove from oven and brush with the other tablespoon of melted butter.

Pasta Salad

Prep Time: 15 minutes
Cook Time: 10 minutes
Yield: 8 servings

Ingredients

1 (16 oz.) box Rotini pasta
2 cups cherry tomatoes, halved
1 cucumber, sliced
1 red bell pepper, diced
½ cup red onion, diced
1 cup feta cheese, crumbled
1 cup Italian dressing

Directions

1. Cook the pasta according to the package directions, then drain and rinse under cold water until cool.
2. In a large bowl, combine the cooled pasta, tomatoes, cucumber, bell pepper, red onion, feta cheese, and Italian dressing.
3. Toss until all ingredients are well mixed and coated with dressing.
4. Serve chilled.

Cheesy Garlic Bread

Prep Time: 10 minutes
Cook Time: 15 minutes
Yield: 8 servings

Ingredients

½ cup unsalted butter, softened
3 cloves garlic, minced
1 loaf French bread, halved lengthwise
2 cups shredded mozzarella cheese
¼ cup chopped fresh parsley

Directions

1. Preheat the oven to 375°F.
2. In a small bowl, mix together the butter and garlic.
3. Spread the garlic butter evenly over the cut sides of the bread.
4. Sprinkle the shredded mozzarella over the butter.
5. Place the bread on a baking sheet and bake for 10 minutes, or until the cheese is melted.
6. Switch the oven to broil and cook for another 2 to 3 minutes, until the cheese is bubbly and golden.
7. Sprinkle with parsley before serving.

Week Seventeen
Easy, Breezy Spring

This week I share a chili recipe that may be the meal that I've made most in my life. It provides a great way of using leftover chicken or turkey, freezes beautifully, and makes for a delicious, quickly prepared Sabbath meal or a dinner after a long workday. I never make one batch on its own; it's truly too good to make just one.

Allowing ourselves stress-free weeks on the home front doesn't mean we can't eat well. Each time you plan and prepare, even a little, you give yourself a future moment (or two or three) to take it easy.

Week 17 Menu

Saturday

One-Sheet Salmon with Potatoes
   and Asparagus
Dessert:
Apple Cake

Sunday

Breakfast:
Amazing Mix-In Muffins
   (Banana and Chocolate Chip)

Lunch:

Turkey Chili
Taco Salad
Corn Bread

Dinner:
Italian Zucchini and
   Sausage Bake
Risotto

Monday

Italian Chopped Salad
   with Salmon
Toasted Baguette (no recipe)

Tuesday

Turkey Chili
Bagged Salad (no recipe)

Wednesday

Leftovers or frozen meal of choice

Thursday

Dinner out

Friday

Pizza night!

Sabbath Soup

Turkey Chili

Prep Time: 20 minutes • Cook Time: 1 hour and 25 minutes
Yield: 4 bowls or 8 cups

Ingredients

1 T. vegetable oil

1 cup onion, chopped

1 clove garlic, minced

1 (16 oz.) can stewed tomatoes, undrained

1 (16 oz.) can kidney beans, drained

1 (16 oz.) can tomato sauce

3 tsp. chili powder

½ tsp. basil

1 (6 oz. can) tomato paste

¾ lb. leftover turkey (or you can use chicken), shredded

Shredded cheddar cheese, to serve

Sour cream, to serve

Directions

1. In a large soup pot, heat the vegetable oil and sauté the onion and garlic until the onion is translucent. Drain.

2. Add in the tomatoes, kidney beans, tomato sauce, chili powder, basil, and tomato paste.

3. Simmer on low for at least an hour, so the flavors can meld. Add the leftover chicken or turkey and heat until warm (about 15 minutes). Top with cheese and sour cream. Serve with corn bread and a salad.

I always double this recipe to feed friends and neighbors or put some in the freezer for homemade fast food.

One-Sheet Salmon with Potatoes and Asparagus

Prep Time: 15 minutes
Cook Time: 30 minutes
Yield: 4 servings

Ingredients

6 T. olive oil, divided
2 cloves garlic, minced
Juice of 1 lemon
1 tsp. dried thyme or oregano
4 (4 to 6 oz.) salmon fillets
1½ lbs. Yukon Gold potatoes, sliced into ¼-inch-thick rounds
Salt and pepper, to taste
1 bunch asparagus, ends trimmed

Directions

1. Preheat the oven to 400°F. Line a large baking sheet with parchment paper or aluminum foil for easy cleanup.
2. For the salmon marinade, in a large bowl mix 2 tablespoons of the olive oil with the garlic, lemon juice, and herbs. Place the salmon fillets in the marinade and let sit for at least 15 minutes.
3. Toss the potatoes in 2 tablespoons of olive oil, salt, and pepper. Arrange them in a single layer on the baking sheet.
4. Place the baking sheet in the oven and roast the potatoes for 15 minutes.
5. While the potatoes are roasting, toss the asparagus in 1 tablespoon of olive oil, salt, and pepper.
6. After the potatoes have roasted for 15 minutes, remove the sheet from the oven. Push the potatoes to one side of the pan and arrange the marinated salmon fillets and asparagus on the other side of the sheet.
7. Place the sheet back into the oven and roast for another 12 to 15 minutes, or until the salmon is cooked through and flakes easily with a fork.
8. Once everything is cooked, remove the baking sheet from the oven. Check the seasoning and adjust if necessary.
9. Drizzle the remaining 1 tablespoon of olive oil over the salmon, potatoes, and asparagus before serving.

Apple Cake

This cake is amazing both on its own or served with ice cream (or any kind of cream) and strong coffee. If you are serving this to guests, time it to finish baking right while they are coming through the door. Half the delight of this cake is the smell wafting through your house.

Prep Time: 15 minutes
Cook Time: 60 minutes
Yield: 16 servings

Ingredients

2 cups sugar
½ cup oil
2 eggs
4 cups peeled and diced apples
2 cups flour
2 tsp. baking soda
1 tsp. nutmeg
2 tsp. cinnamon
1 tsp. salt

Directions

1. Preheat your oven to 350°F. Grease a 9 × 13-inch pan.
2. Combine sugar, oil, and eggs in a large bowl, stirring until well mixed.
3. Stir in apples. Sift together flour, baking soda, nutmeg, cinnamon, and salt, then add to the bowl.
4. Stir all ingredients together to form a batter until the flour mixture is thoroughly mixed into the wet ingredients. Pour into greased pan. Bake one hour, or until golden and cake is set.

A generous person will prosper; whoever refreshes others will be refreshed.

PROVERBS 11:25

Amazing Mix-In Muffins (Banana and Chocolate Chip)

Prep Time: 10 minutes
Cook Time: 25 minutes
Yield: 12 muffins

Ingredients

2 cups all-purpose flour
¾ cup granulated sugar
½ tsp. salt
2 tsp. baking powder
⅓ cup vegetable oil
1 large egg, room temperature
1 tsp. vanilla extract
¾ cup milk
1 cup mashed ripe banana (about 2 to 3 medium bananas)
1 cup semi-sweet chocolate chips

Directions

1. Preheat your oven to 400°F. Line a 12-cup muffin tin with paper liners or grease the cups with nonstick cooking spray.
2. In a large bowl, whisk together the flour, sugar, salt, and baking powder.
3. In a separate medium bowl, combine the vegetable oil, egg, vanilla extract, and milk. Stir well.
4. Gently pour the wet ingredients into the dry ingredients and mix until just combined. Be careful not to overmix, as this can result in tough muffins.
5. Fold in the mashed banana and chocolate chips until evenly distributed throughout the batter.
6. Divide the batter evenly among the 12 muffin cups, filling each about two-thirds full.
7. Bake for 20 to 25 minutes, or until a toothpick inserted into the center of a muffin comes out clean.
8. Remove the muffins from the oven and allow them to cool in the tin for 5 minutes before transferring to a wire rack to cool completely.

Taco Salad

Prep Time: 30 minutes
Cook Time: 10 minutes
Yield: 4 main servings or 8 side servings

Ingredients

1 lb. ground beef
1 packet taco seasoning (about 1 oz. or 3 T.)
6 cups chopped romaine lettuce
1 (15 oz.) can black beans, drained and rinsed
1 cup corn kernels
1 cup cherry tomatoes, halved
1 cup shredded cheddar cheese
¼ cup sliced black olives (optional)
1 avocado, diced
½ cup sour cream
½ cup salsa
Salt and pepper, to taste

Directions

1. In a large skillet, cook the ground beef over medium heat until browned. Drain off any excess fat.
2. Stir in the taco seasoning, following the package directions.
3. In a large salad bowl, arrange the romaine lettuce. Top with the cooked beef, black beans, corn, cherry tomatoes, cheddar cheese, black olives, and avocado.
4. In a small bowl, combine the sour cream and salsa to create a dressing. Drizzle the dressing over the salad, sprinkle with a dash of salt and pepper, and gently toss to combine. Serve immediately.

Corn Bread

Prep Time: 10 minutes
Cook Time: 20 minutes
Yield: 9 servings

Ingredients

1 cup cornmeal
1 cup all-purpose flour
¼ cup sugar
1 T. baking powder
½ tsp. salt
1 cup milk
¼ cup vegetable oil
2 large eggs

Directions

1. Preheat the oven to 400°F and grease a
   9 × 9-inch baking pan.
2. In a large bowl, combine the cornmeal, flour,
   sugar, baking powder, and salt.
3. In a separate bowl, whisk together the milk,
   vegetable oil, and eggs.
4. Add the wet ingredients to the dry and stir until
   just combined.
5. Pour the batter into the prepared pan and bake
   for 20 minutes, or until a toothpick inserted in
   the center comes out clean.
6. Allow to cool slightly before cutting into squares
   to serve.

*The law of the LORD
is perfect,
refreshing the soul.
The statutes of the LORD
are trustworthy,
making wise the simple.*

PSALM 19:7

Italian Zucchini and Sausage Bake

Prep Time: 20 minutes
Cook Time: 35 minutes
Yield: 8 servings

Ingredients

4 medium zucchini
2 T. olive oil
1 lb. Italian sausage
1 large onion, chopped
3 cloves garlic, minced
1 (15 oz.) can diced tomatoes
1 tsp. dried basil
1 tsp. dried oregano
Salt and pepper, to taste
2 cups shredded mozzarella cheese
¼ cup grated Parmesan cheese

Directions

1. Preheat your oven to 375°F and lightly grease a
   baking sheet or dish.
2. Cut each zucchini in half lengthwise and use a
   spoon or melon baller to hollow out the centers,
   making a "boat" with sides that are about ¼ inch
   thick. Place the zucchini on the baking sheet.
3. In a large skillet, heat the olive oil over medium-
   high heat. Add the Italian sausage (removing any
   skin) and cook until browned, breaking it up
   with a wooden spoon as it cooks. Remove the
   sausage from the skillet and set it aside.
4. In the same skillet, add the onion and minced
   garlic, cooking until the onion is translucent.
5. Add the tomatoes, basil, oregano, and a pinch
   of salt and pepper. Stir well and cook for a few
   more minutes.
6. Add back the sausage and cook for another 2 to
   3 minutes until everything is well combined.
7. Spoon the sausage mixture into each zucchini
   boat, pressing it down and filling to the top.
8. Top each zucchini boat with a generous amount
   of mozzarella and Parmesan cheese.
9. Bake in the preheated oven for 25 to 30 minutes,
   or until the cheese is melted and bubbly and the
   zucchini is tender.
10. Remove from the oven and allow to cool for a
    few minutes before serving.

Risotto

Prep time: 15 minutes
Cook time: 25 minutes
Yield: 8 servings

Ingredients

7 cups chicken stock
2 T. olive oil
1 large shallot, finely chopped
2 cloves garlic, minced
Salt and pepper, to taste
1 cup sliced mushrooms
1 bay leaf
5 T. unsalted butter, divided
2 cups arborio rice
1 cup white wine or 1 additional cup chicken stock
1 T. fresh herbs (I like basil, but parsley, tarragon, and chives are all wonderful)
¾ cup grated Parmesan, plus more for garnish
Lemon wedges

Directions

1. Warm the chicken stock in a large saucepan on medium-low heat. Keep it covered and warm.
2. In another saucepan or Dutch oven, heat the olive oil over medium heat. Add the shallot and garlic. Add salt and pepper to your own taste, also considering any salt and pepper that may already be in your stock. Cook for 3 to 4 minutes, stirring occasionally, until softened. Add mushrooms and sauté for 2 minutes.
3. Add bay leaf and 3 tablespoons of butter to the mixture. Stir until butter melts, around 1 minute.
4. Add rice and toast it for 3 to 4 minutes, stirring once. The rice should smell nutty and turn light golden brown.
5. Add the wine (or 1 cup of additional stock) and let it simmer until it evaporates completely, around 2 to 3 minutes.
6. Add 1 cup of warm stock to the rice, stirring gently until it's absorbed. This takes around 2 to 3 minutes.
7. Continue adding stock, 1 cup or ladleful at a time, and keep stirring until the rice is al dente. This takes around 17 to 19 minutes total. You may have some stock left over. Remove the bay leaf and add your fresh herbs.
8. If you prefer a risotto with more sauce, add more stock in ¼ cup increments until desired consistency is reached.
9. Stir in Parmesan, 2 tablespoons of butter, 1 teaspoon salt, and more black pepper. Serve with lemon wedges and extra Parmesan.

Italian Chopped Salad

Prep Time: 20 minutes
Yield: 4 main servings or 8 side servings

Ingredients

1 head iceberg lettuce, chopped
1 red onion, thinly sliced
1 cup cherry tomatoes, halved
1 (15 oz.) can chickpeas, drained and rinsed
1 cup pearl mozzarella balls
1 cup cubed provolone cheese
½ cup sliced pepperoncini
½ cup cubed genoa salami
½ cup chopped sun-dried tomatoes
½ cup Italian dressing
Salt and pepper, to taste

Directions

1. In a large salad bowl, combine the lettuce, red onion, cherry tomatoes, chickpeas, pearl mozzarella, provolone cheese, pepperoncini, salami, and sun-dried tomatoes.
2. Drizzle the dressing over the salad, season with a dash of salt and pepper, and gently toss to combine. Serve immediately.

Italian Dressing

Ingredients

½ cup extra-virgin olive oil
¼ cup red wine vinegar
1 tsp. honey
1 tsp. dried oregano
1 tsp. dried basil
½ tsp. garlic powder
Salt and freshly ground pepper, to taste

Directions

Shake all ingredients together in a jar until well combined.

A Prayer for a Meal for One

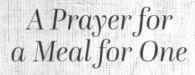

Lord, here I am
and here You are —
what a generosity
that I am never alone.
What is before me
at this table and
on this plate
is enough for me.

Let me be full
of thanks
for this moment
that nurtures
my body and soul.

Speak to me in the quiet.

Here I am.
Here You are.

This is a small moment
but You are here
with me
and that makes
it a moment of plenty.

My heart rejoices
in Your goodness to me.

Week Eighteen
Surprise Combinations

After speaking at my favorite church, La Casa de Cristo, I went with my friends Jennine and Michelle to the White Chocolate Grill in Scottsdale, Arizona, and had their tomato gin soup. I'd had it before and somehow talked the whole table into getting it. (This combination is not exactly the tomato soup in our mother's recipe box.) It was love at first slurp for everyone.

This week's Sabbath soup recipe is my version, which I just made, tasted, and declared as good—if not even a little bit better than the one at the restaurant. The fresh chives definitely leveled up this offering. My only recommendation? Double the recipe. You will want to have this with a grilled cheese sandwich for lunch later in the week. Promise.

Week 18 Menu

Saturday
Orange-Glazed Pork Chops
Risotto
Stir-Fried Zucchini
Dessert:
Spiced-Peach Cobbler

Sunday
Breakfast:
Overnight Egg, Sausage, and
   Hashbrown Casserole
Lunch:

Tomato Gin Soup
Asian Sesame Salad
Rolls
Dinner:
Air Fryer Chicken Wings
   with Lemon Pepper
Caesar Salad
French Fries (no recipe)

Monday
Pork Risotto and Zucchini Stir-Fry
Rolls

Tuesday
Tomato Gin Soup
Grilled Cheese sandwich
   (no recipe)

Wednesday
Leftovers or frozen meal of choice

Thursday
Dinner out

Friday
Pizza night!

Sabbath Soup

Tomato Gin Soup

Prep Time: 20 minutes • Cook Time: 25 to 30 minutes • Yield: 4 bowls or 8 cups

Ingredients

8 slices bacon, chopped

10 to 12 fresh tomatoes, peeled,
  or 1 (28 oz.) can whole peeled
  tomatoes

3 garlic cloves, chopped

½ tsp. paprika

¼ tsp. dried basil

⅛ tsp. dried thyme

⅛ tsp. sugar

¼ cup butter

4 oz. cremini mushrooms, sliced

⅓ cup gin*

Salt and pepper, to taste

½ cup heavy cream

2 T. diced fresh chives

Directions

1. Heat a heavy soup pot or Dutch oven over medium heat. Add the chopped bacon and cook until crisp. Using a slotted spoon, transfer the bacon to a paper towel-lined plate to drain, but be sure to keep the flavorful drippings in the pot.

2. While the bacon cooks, create your tomato soup base by combining the following in a blender: tomatoes, garlic, paprika, basil, thyme, and sugar. Puree until smooth.

3. Once the bacon is removed from your Dutch oven, add the butter to the bacon drippings and let it melt, melding the flavors together. Toss in the mushrooms and sauté them until they turn a beautiful golden color and release their earthy aroma, about 5 minutes.

4. Use the gin to deglaze the pot, and allow the alcohol to cook off and the flavors to infuse the mushrooms. Return the bacon to the pan and pour in the pureed tomato mixture. Let the soup simmer for 15 minutes for a fuller flavor to develop.

5. Add salt and pepper to taste. Just before serving, stir in the heavy cream. Taste again and adjust the seasoning to your liking. Ladle the soup into individual bowls and garnish with a sprinkle of fresh green chives for a pop of color and added flavor.

*If you'd prefer not to use alcohol for this soup, substitute the gin with a combination of white grape juice or apple juice and a splash of white vinegar to mimic the acidity and depth of flavor.

Orange-Glazed Pork Chops

Prep Time: 5 minutes
Cook Time: 30 minutes
Yield: 4 servings

Ingredients

4 pork chops
Salt and pepper, to taste
2 T. olive oil
½ cup orange marmalade
¼ cup orange juice
2 cloves garlic, minced
1 T. soy sauce
1 tsp. dried rosemary

Directions

1. Season the pork chops with salt and pepper on both sides.
2. Heat the olive oil in a skillet over medium-high heat. Add the pork chops and cook until browned on both sides, about 5 to 7 minutes each side. Remove the chops and set them aside.
3. In the same skillet, add the orange marmalade, orange juice, garlic, soy sauce, and rosemary. Stir well to combine and heat until bubbling.
4. Return the pork chops to the skillet, coating them in the glaze. Reduce the heat to medium-low and simmer for another 5 minutes, or until the pork chops are cooked through.
5. Serve the pork chops with the remaining glaze from the pan.

Risotto

Prep time: 15 minutes
Cook time: 25 minutes
Yield: 8 servings

Ingredients

7 cups chicken stock
2 T. olive oil
1 large shallot, finely chopped
2 cloves garlic, minced
Salt and pepper, to taste
1 cup sliced mushrooms
1 bay leaf
5 T. unsalted butter, divided
2 cups arborio rice
1 cup white wine or 1 additional cup chicken stock
1 T. fresh herbs (I like basil, but parsley, tarragon, and chives are all wonderful)
¾ cup grated Parmesan, plus more for garnish
Lemon wedges

Directions

1. Warm the chicken stock in a large saucepan on medium-low heat. Keep it covered and warm.
2. In another saucepan or Dutch oven, heat the olive oil over medium heat. Add the shallot and garlic. Add salt and pepper to your own taste, also considering any salt and pepper that may already be in your stock. Cook for 3 to 4 minutes, stirring occasionally, until softened. Add mushrooms and sauté for 2 minutes.
3. Add bay leaf and 3 tablespoons of butter to the mixture. Stir until butter melts, around 1 minute.
4. Add rice and toast it for 3 to 4 minutes, stirring once. The rice should smell nutty and turn light golden brown.
5. Add the wine (or 1 cup of additional stock) and let it simmer until it evaporates completely, around 2 to 3 minutes.
6. Add 1 cup of warm stock to the rice, stirring gently until it's absorbed. This takes around 2 to 3 minutes.
7. Continue adding stock, 1 cup or ladleful at a time, and keep stirring until the rice is al dente. This takes around 17 to 19 minutes total. You may have some stock left over. Remove the bay leaf and add your fresh herbs.
8. If you prefer a risotto with more sauce, add more stock in ¼ cup increments until desired consistency is reached.
9. Stir in Parmesan, 2 tablespoons of butter, 1 teaspoon salt, and more black pepper. Serve with lemon wedges and extra Parmesan.

Stir-Fried Zucchini

Prep Time: 10 minutes
Cook Time: 10 minutes
Yield: 4 servings

Ingredients

1 small onion
3 cloves garlic
2 medium zucchinis
2 T. vegetable oil or olive oil
Salt and pepper, to taste
1 T. soy sauce

Directions

1. Thinly slice the onion, mince the garlic, and slice the zucchini into ¼-inch-thick half-moon shapes (cut the zucchini in half lengthwise and then slice).
2. Place a large skillet or wok over medium-high heat. Add the oil and let it heat up.
3. Once the oil is hot, add the garlic and onion. Stir-fry for 1 to 2 minutes, or until the onion starts to soften and the garlic becomes aromatic.
4. Add the zucchini to the pan, and stir-fry for 4 to 6 minutes, stirring occasionally, until the zucchini starts to soften and brown slightly.
5. Season with salt and black pepper.
6. Add the soy sauce. Stir well to combine all the ingredients.
7. Continue to stir-fry for another 1 to 2 minutes, making sure the zucchini is well coated with the sauce.

*Your love has given me
great joy and encouragement,
because you, brother,
have refreshed the hearts
of the Lord's people.*

PHILEMON 1:7

Spiced-Peach Cobbler

Prep Time: 20 minutes
Cook Time: 35 to 40 minutes
Yield: 6 servings

Ingredients

Filling
6 to 8 ripe peaches, pitted and sliced (approximately 4 cups)
1 cup granulated sugar
1 T. cornstarch
1 tsp. vanilla extract
½ tsp. cinnamon
¼ tsp. nutmeg
Pinch of salt

Cobbler Topping
1 cup all-purpose flour
¼ cup granulated sugar
1 tsp. baking powder
½ tsp. baking soda
¼ tsp. salt
4 T. unsalted butter, chilled and cut into small pieces
⅔ cup buttermilk

Directions

1. Preheat your oven to 375°F. Lightly grease a 9-inch baking dish.
2. Start with the peach filling: In a large bowl, combine the sliced peaches, sugar, cornstarch, vanilla extract, cinnamon, nutmeg, and a pinch of salt. Stir gently until well combined, then transfer to the prepared baking dish.
3. For the cobbler topping: In a medium bowl, whisk together the flour, sugar, baking powder, baking soda, and salt. Add the butter and use your fingers or a pastry cutter to incorporate it into the flour until the mixture looks like coarse crumbs.
4. Pour in the buttermilk and stir until just combined. Don't overmix; it's okay if there are a few lumps.
5. Drop spoonfuls of the cobbler topping over the peach filling. It's okay if some of the peaches are peeking through; the topping will spread as it bakes.

6. Bake for 35 to 40 minutes, or until the topping is golden brown and the peaches are bubbling.

7. Remove the cobbler from the oven and allow it to cool for about 10 minutes before serving.

8. Serve warm and with a scoop of vanilla ice cream. Divine.

Overnight Egg, Sausage, and Hash-brown Casserole

Prep Time: 30 minutes, the night before
Cook Time: 1 hour, plus 20 minutes to rest before and after baking
Yield: 6 to 8 servings

Ingredients

1 lb. breakfast sausage
½ cup diced green bell pepper
½ cup diced red bell pepper
1 small onion, diced
8 large eggs
1 cup whole milk
1 tsp. salt
½ tsp. black pepper
1 tsp. dried thyme
1 tsp. smoked paprika
½ tsp. garlic powder
1 (20 oz.) package refrigerated hash browns
2 cups shredded cheddar cheese, divided
Optional: chopped green onions or parsley for garnish

Directions

1. Brown the sausage in a large skillet over medium heat, breaking it up into small crumbles. Once cooked through, remove it from the pan and set it aside.

2. In the same skillet, add the peppers and onion. Sauté until the vegetables are tender and the onion is translucent.

3. In a large bowl, whisk together the eggs, milk, salt, pepper, thyme, smoked paprika, and garlic powder until well combined.

4. Add the cooked sausage, sautéed vegetables, hash browns, and 1½ cups of the shredded cheddar cheese to the egg mixture. Stir well to combine.

5. Grease a 9 × 13-inch baking dish, then pour the egg and sausage mixture into the dish. Sprinkle the remaining ½ cup of cheese on top.

6. Cover the dish with aluminum foil and place it in the refrigerator overnight.

7. The next morning, preheat your oven to 350°F.

8. Remove the casserole from the refrigerator and let it sit at room temperature while the oven is preheating.

9. Bake the casserole, covered, for 45 minutes. Then remove the foil and bake for an additional 15 minutes, or until the cheese on top is bubbly and starting to brown.

10. Remove the casserole from the oven and let it rest for 10 minutes before cutting into it.

11. Serve hot, garnished with green onion or parsley if desired.

Asian Sesame Salad

This is a great side salad, or you can turn it into a main dish with the addition of cooked, shredded chicken. The addition of sesame seeds, mandarin oranges, and wonton strips takes it to the next level.

Prep Time: 15 minutes
Yield: 4 main servings or 8 side servings

Ingredients

6 cups mixed greens
1 cup shredded carrots
1 cucumber, sliced
¼ cup Asian Salad Dressing
Optional additions
2 cups cooked, shredded chicken
2 cups wonton strips
Sesame seeds for garnish
Canned mandarin oranges

Directions

1. In a large salad bowl, combine the mixed greens, carrots, and cucumber.

2. Toss with the Asian Salad Dressing and serve immediately.

3. If desired, add chicken, wonton strips, sesame seeds, and mandarin oranges in desired amounts per plate. You may want a little extra dressing if you include a lot of additions.

Asian Salad Dressing

Ingredients

¼ cup soy sauce

2 T. sesame oil

2 T. rice vinegar

1 tsp. sugar

1 garlic clove, minced

1 tsp. finely grated fresh ginger

1 T. lime juice

Optional: 1 tsp. sesame seeds for garnish

Directions

1. In a bowl, whisk together soy sauce, sesame oil, rice vinegar, and sugar until the sugar is completely dissolved.
2. Add the garlic and ginger and whisk again to combine everything.
3. Squeeze in the lime juice—this will add a tangy freshness to the dressing.
4. Once everything is well mixed, taste and adjust as needed. For example, if it's too salty, you can add more vinegar or lime juice. If it's too tangy, add a bit more sugar.

Rolls

The ingredients for rolls and sandwich bread dough are the same, so feel free to double the recipe to get both rolls for dinner and sliced bread for sandwiches for the week. Look at you being so clever!

Prep Time: 10 minutes, plus 2 hours to rise
Cook Time: 30 minutes
Yield: 6 Rolls

Ingredients

1 cup warm water

½ T. active dry yeast

2 T. honey

2¾ cups all-purpose flour, divided

1 tsp. salt

2 T. melted butter, divided

Directions

1. Mix the water, yeast, and honey together. Add 2 cups of flour, salt, and 1 tablespoon melted butter and mix.
2. Put dough on a surface with ¼ cup of flour and

knead it for about 5 minutes, adding in the other half cup of flour to get a doughy texture.
3. Take your dough ball and put it in a bowl. Cover it with a dishcloth and stick it in the oven with the oven light on for an hour (it should approximately double in size).
4. Preheat the oven to 350°F.
5. Butter a pie tin. Cut the dough into six pieces and form the pieces into rolls.
6. Place the rolls in the pie tin and let the dough double again, covered.
7. Bake for 30 minutes.
8. Remove from oven and brush with the other tablespoon of melted butter.

Note: For sandwich bread, at step 5, butter a loaf pan instead of the pie tin and shape the dough to fit. Allow the dough to rise and bake as above. Allow just a few more minutes to bake, until the loaf is golden and sounds hollow when tapped. Brush with butter, then let it cool on a wire rack before slicing.

Air Fryer Chicken Wings with Lemon Pepper

These Lemon Pepper Chicken Wings offer a tangy and spicy twist on the classic chicken wing—perfect for a snack, appetizer, or main course. Enjoy!

Prep Time: 15 minutes
Cook Time: 25 minutes
Yield: 4 to 5 servings

Ingredients

2½ lbs. chicken wings

Salt, to taste

4 T. olive oil, divided

1 lemon, zested and juiced (2 T. juice and 2 tsp. zest)

2 T. ground black pepper

1 T. garlic powder

Directions

1. Preheat your air fryer to 400°F.
2. Pat the chicken wings dry and season them with salt.
3. In a large bowl, mix 2 tablespoons of the olive oil with the lemon juice, lemon zest, pepper, and garlic powder.

4. Add the wings to the bowl and toss to coat them in the lemon-pepper mixture.

5. Place the wings in the air fryer basket, making sure not to crowd the basket. You may need to cook the wings in batches.

6. Cook the wings for 12 minutes, then flip the wings and cook for another 12 minutes, or until the wings are golden brown and crispy.

7. Drizzle the cooked wings with the remaining 2 tablespoons of olive oil and toss to coat.

8. Serve the wings immediately.

Caesar Salad

Prep Time: 15 minutes
Yield: 4 main servings or 8 side servings

Ingredients

1 head romaine lettuce, torn into bite-size pieces
1 cup croutons
½ cup freshly grated Parmesan cheese
½ cup Creamy Caesar Dressing

Directions

1. In a large salad bowl, combine the romaine lettuce, croutons, and Parmesan cheese.

2. Pour the dressing over the salad and toss until well coated.

3. Serve immediately, with additional Parmesan cheese on top if desired.

Creamy Caesar Dressing

Ingredients

¾ cup mayonnaise
2 T. fresh lemon juice
2 garlic cloves, minced
1 tsp. Worcestershire sauce
1 tsp. Dijon mustard
¼ cup grated Parmesan cheese
Salt and freshly ground pepper, to taste

Directions

Combine all ingredients in a blender or food processor and blend until smooth.

Pork Risotto and Zucchini Stir-Fry

Prep time: 15 minutes
Cook time: 25 minutes
Yield: 8 servings

Ingredients

1 T. vegetable oil
1 onion, sliced
2 cloves garlic, minced
1 to 2 zucchini, sliced
Leftover cooked pork chops, sliced into thin strips
Leftover risotto (about 1 to 2 cups, see recipe on page 95)
1 T. soy sauce
1 T. oyster sauce (optional)
Salt and pepper, to taste
Optional: Fresh herbs (such as parsley or cilantro) for garnish

Directions

1. Heat vegetable oil in a large skillet or wok over medium-high heat.

2. Add the onion and garlic to the skillet and sauté for a few minutes until fragrant and translucent.

3. Add the zucchini to the skillet and continue to stir-fry for about 3 to 4 minutes, until the zucchini starts to soften.

4. Push the vegetables to one side of the skillet and add the pork to the other side. Cook the pork for a couple of minutes until it is heated through.

5. Add the risotto to the skillet and stir-fry with the vegetables and pork. Break up any clumps of risotto and mix well to combine with the other ingredients.

6. Drizzle the soy sauce and oyster sauce into the skillet and continue to stir-fry for another 2 to 3 minutes until everything is well coated and heated through.

7. Taste the stir-fry and season with salt and pepper according to your preference.

8. Remove from heat and garnish with fresh herbs, if desired.

A Prayer for an Expansive Heart

Lord, Your creativity
is on display through
the food we eat:
the colors,
the flavors,
the myriad of ways
we use a singular ingredient,
are all reflections of
the grandness of
Your creative nature.

We are tethered to You,
to this world, to our family,
and to our culture through food.
What a joyfully diverse
world You have created;
it is remarkable and
I am in awe of You.

God, I ask that You would
teach me more about
this world You have
made through the
food traditions of
different cultures.

I want to be a student
of Your creative force
that is present all around me;
a force as close as the
food on my plate.

Summer

What if the Meal
Is the Ministry?

*Lift up your heart to Him during your meals and in company;
the least little remembrance will always be the most pleasing to Him.
One need not cry out very loudly; He is nearer to us than we think.*

BROTHER LAWRENCE

What if we realized that the dinner table was holy ground?

What if we could feel and lean into His presence whenever we break bread with others?

What if in addition to looking for ways to serve outside of our homes, we looked at all that God could accomplish with our family, our friends, our neighbors, within our four walls?

As a part of a teen mission trip in England, my team would be given a strict 15 minutes to eat because, after all, it was a mission trip and we needed to get out and do the work of connecting with people. We needed to eat fast so we could get to the real ministry.

It wasn't until later in my life that I noticed that most of the best, deepest conversations I've ever had were around a table—actually, a kitchen table.

I realized the way I wanted to connect wouldn't look like going up to random people on the streets and trying to engage them in a conversation about Jesus. (Which rarely worked and seemed a bit weird.) Instead, from that day forward, almost every conversation about Jesus I've had has been one shared warmly and authentically over food.

A cup of coffee and a scone.

A BBQ in a friend's backyard.

Early in the morning around our kitchen table after a friend had spent the night at our house.

And here is what I've discovered: The meal *is* the ministry.

Sharing a meal does something mystical. It breaks down walls and gives our hands something to focus on (the food) so that our heads and hearts can be put at ease. There are times we need to quickly nourish ourselves in order to get down to the business of whatever needs to be accomplished, but more often the meal is where the real connection, teaching, joy, and hope are found.

I remember spending a lot of time as a teenager and young adult trying to evangelize my friends and neighbors by getting them to come to an outreach event, a church service, or some other situation where I knew God would be present.

But is there any space more holy than where there is just enough room between the salad and the dinner rolls to squeeze the scalloped potatoes?

What if we started to look a little differently at that sack lunch at work, that pot roast with family, the breakfast eaten on the way to school? What if we saw these as opportunities for ministry, service, compassion?

What if every time we opened up a cookbook, made a shopping list, or turned on the stove, we realized we were participating in holy work?

Yes, we have big examples of Jesus using food to show the miracles of God (the feeding of the five thousand comes to mind), but then there are smaller, more intimate stories of Jesus using food to know and be known by others.

The story of the Emmaus meal takes place in Luke 24:13-35. Two disciples were walking from Jerusalem to a village called Emmaus, discussing the recent crucifixion of Jesus and the reports of His resurrection. As they walked and talked, Jesus Himself (whom they did not recognize) approached and walked along with them.

During their walk, Jesus explained the Scriptures to them, focusing on the prophecies about Himself. Despite His teaching, the two disciples still didn't recognize Him. But they were moved by His words and asked Him to stay with them as it was getting late.

> *When he was at the table with them, he took bread, gave thanks, broke it and began to give it to them.*
> LUKE 24:30

It was in this moment, at their meal, that their eyes were opened, and they finally recognized Him. But then He immediately disappeared from their sight. The disciples noted how their hearts burned within them as He spoke to them and opened the Scriptures. The disciples hurried back to Jerusalem that very night to share their experience with the others.

In this story that many of us may have read but not remembered (I know I didn't until I reread it recently and saw it through the light of sharing a meal), we're given so many insights into how important to Jesus was the act of sharing a meal.

He never shamed people for wanting to be fed physically and spiritually at the same time.

He ate not just with those He loved but also with those who were set against Him.

He cared deeply about the physical needs of those around Him.

He knew that in order to learn, people needed to be fed. You can't fill the hearts when the stomachs are empty.

Jesus's love transformed each moment of a simple meal into a meaningful ritual:

The Breaking of Bread: There was nothing unusual about the breaking of bread, but in this instance, it harkened back to the Last Supper. Just as Jesus broke the bread, the disciples' eyes were opened to who He was and the significance of that moment.

Teaching and Revelation: I know that I absorb more of the conversation when I'm lingering over the table. Jesus used the walk to explain Scriptures, and the meal provided a moment of reflection that allowed them to fully absorb His teachings.

Community: Jesus not only shared a meal and Scripture, He shared Himself with these followers.

Resurgence of Hope: The revelation of Jesus's resurrection brought hope and joy to the disciples, fueling them to return to Jerusalem despite the late hour. They hurried to go and tell the other disciples.

Look at all that came from that time around the table with Jesus. They were fed in every way imaginable. No matter what you are serving, the meal becomes holy ground to serve the bodies, minds, spirits, and hearts of those we gather.

A Season for Salads

As you've probably noticed throughout this book, we love a good salad. Not only do we have a "fancy" salad once a week or so for one of our main meals (usually with soup), but about half of our lunches are salads as well. So clearly, I don't view a bowl of yummy greens as a summer-only meal. But summer especially is a time when many people desire to include refreshing options because of warm weather or because they stand in awe of their garden's summer offerings and want to make the most of them when meal planning.

But we're not talking tiny-little-limp-lettuce-with-a-side-of-celery salads. We're talking hearty, fill-you-up salads that stand in as a full meal. We're talking a restaurant salad with meat, loads of veggies, starch, and cheese. (We don't play when it comes to salads.)

Prep Like a Pro

With my Sabbath soup and weekly menu goals, I prep my salad and vegetables on Thursday and Monday, because trying to keep prepped produce fresh for a week can be stretching it. And I do like to have all my veggies ready to go, so when it's time to make our salads or create that soup on Saturday, the cleaning and chopping is done and I can just grab and go.

Cleaning and prepping vegetables

Supplies I find helpful when cleaning and prepping vegetables—and fruits for that matter:

1. **Produce Wash.** You can buy one (like Fit Organic) or make your own: Take 4 cups water to 1 cup vinegar and 1 tablespoon lemon juice and mix it all in a large spray bottle. Spray your produce (or soak for 3 minutes) and then rinse under running water.

2. **Salad Spinner.** This is for your lettuces and fresh herbs and such. After washing your produce, spin it to remove as much moisture as possible.

3. **Kitchen Towels.** (Choose ones you won't mind getting stained.) After washing and cutting/tearing your produce, let it sit on a kitchen towel for a couple of hours to remove as much moisture as possible. Moisture makes your fruits and vegetables go bad quicker. Let everything dry before you pack it up.

4. **Plastic or glass containers.** A vegetable that can't be seen is one that will never get eaten in my house. I need to see it to eat it.

5. **Paper towels or fabric napkins.** Whisk away as much moisture as possible, and before you put your produce in its storage container, put a napkin or towel at the bottom. This will absorb condensation and keep your fruit and vegetables fresh longer.

While I'm prepping these goodies for our salads and other main dishes, I also create two little snack trays: a fruit tray and a vegetable tray. If I prep them (and make a Greek yogurt dip for the veg), we go for those at least half the time when we want snacks. Check out the lists that follow, or consider what's in your fridge or fresh at the farmer's market, and think about which vegetables you and others might enjoy with a dip as well as in a salad.

Everyday Veggies

We always have at least one kind of salad green on hand. Our favorite is romaine, but we also will occasionally eat spinach or whatever our garden is offering. In addition, I have a few all-star veggies that are around all the time:

Red onions	Mushrooms	Cucumbers	Peppers
Yellow onions	Tomatoes	Carrots	

I also keep frozen broccoli, frozen mixed vegetables, canned tomatoes, and canned corn on hand.

Side Vegetables

This is where I get too ambitious and overestimate the variety of veggies I need in a week. If I use a couple of the everyday veggies as side dishes, plus just one of the wild cards listed below, that is plenty of variety in a week. Then I don't have as many expiring veggies to feed to our chickens (don't worry, our girls are "treated" well).

Broccoli	Zucchini	Eggplant	Brussels sprouts
Asparagus	Yellow squash	Green beans	

Amazing Add-ons

I don't have most of these ingredients on hand at all times, but I am bummed when I make a salad and later realize I've forgotten the wonton strips or smoked salmon that would have made that salad amazing.

Unexpected Vegetables

Avocado	Sun-dried tomatoes	Marinated mushrooms
Olives	Crispy onion	Marinated carrots
Pickled red onion	Marinated artichoke hearts	Corn (canned or fresh)

Dried or Fresh Fruits

Cranberries	Mango	Apples
Cherries	Blueberries	Mandarin oranges

Seeds, Nuts, and Legumes

Sunflower seeds	Almonds	Pecans
Walnuts	Edamame	Hummus
Black beans	Crispy chickpeas	Kidney beans

Grains

Croutons	Wonton strips	Cooked rice

Protein

Tofu	Bacon	Shrimp
Hard-boiled eggs	Ham	Tuna
Shredded chicken	Taco meat	Smoked salmon
Turkey	Steak	Cheeses: Feta cheese, shredded cheese, Parmesan

Dress It Up for Any Occasion

When vegetables are a frequent guest for your Sabbath or everyday meals, you'll find yourself looking forward to growing or buying a broader variety, sampling new flavors and combinations, and cooking them in different ways. Whether you grill, sauté, roast, or serve them raw with a dip, they can become the colorful, flavorful star.

When you chop or layer your favorites into a salad, your choice of dressing is a variable that gives you nearly endless tastes and presentations. To help you start experimenting, there is a lineup of dressings under Dressings and Sauces in the recipe listings.

Summer
Sabbath Experiences

Rest is not idleness, and to lie sometimes on the grass under trees on a summer's day, listening to the murmur of the water, or watching the clouds float across the sky, is by no means a waste of time.

JOHN LUBBOCK, *THE USE OF LIFE*

1. Make a summer Sabbath altar or centerpiece. Get creative with small river stones, fresh fruit, reeds from the lake, written prayers or poetry, and discoveries from those summer strolls.

2. Go on a bike ride. Don't have a bike? Rent one, borrow one. Experience the wind blowing through your hair.

3. Get your toes dirty. Walk outside barefoot like you're a kid again. Stop to pick up a pretty rock or a dandelion (and make a wish while you're at it).

4. Take a summer nap outside…in a hammock or a lounge chair in a favorite spot.

5. Light a candle and say a prayer for people in a different part of the world.

6. Sing. Play music. Have a family impromptu music session or choose a hymn or praise song to sing together before the Sabbath day meal. Even out-of-tune melodies bless God, and this could become a very special ritual as you gather around the table.

7. Take your phone with you on a walk and snap pictures of scenes, objects, and settings that lift your spirit. Use the photos as prompts for journaling or to send as "thinking of you" texts to friends.

8. Remember the tea or coffee ceremony in winter? Immerse yourself in a ritual of noticing as you make fresh lemonade. Take delight as you squeeze the citrus, sprinkle the sugar, stir the mixture, add slices of lemon and a colorful paper straw, and then sip. Ahh.

9. Sabbath journaling for summer: Spend moments this season writing about delight. Make lists of what has given you joy in the past and what you might want to add back to your days now.

10. I often think of my activities on Sabbath as a "delight in" instead of a "need to." So while I don't usually cook on the Sabbath, during the summer I "delight in" baking pies, crisps, and cobblers with the fresh fruits of summer.

Week Nineteen
Tomato Time

Tomatoes are my favorite thing to grow in our garden and one of my absolute favorite things to cook with, especially in the summer. I hope you'll enjoy some of the varied ways to use this fruit disguised as a vegetable. If you have tomatoes growing in your garden or in a planter on the deck, you'll understand how the simple acts of watching them deepen in color as they ripen and then selecting one for a fresh salad, sauce, or soup are acts of meditation.

During this season, give yourself time in the garden, time appreciating the miracle of the colorful food on your plate or on the vine. Living with a Sabbath mindset means we can ditch the guilt and actually enjoy our front-row seats to the beauty surrounding us.

Week 19 Menu

Saturday

Pesto Chicken
Air Fryer Smashed Baby Potatoes
Roasted Tomatoes (no recipe)

Dessert:
Banana Cake with
    Citrus Glaze

Sunday

Breakfast:
Blueberry Lemon-Glaze Muffins

Lunch:
Chill Chili
Southwest Chopped Salad

Dinner:
Pulled Pork Quesadillas
Tortilla Chips and Salsa
    (no recipe)

Monday

Caesar Salad topped with
    Pesto Chicken

Tuesday

Chill Chili
Cheese and Veggie Quesadillas

Wednesday

Leftovers or frozen meal of choice

Thursday

Dinner out

Friday

Pizza night!

Sabbath Soup

Chill Chili

Prep Time: 10 minutes • Cook Time: 50 minutes • Yield: 4 bowls or 8 cups

Ingredients

¾ lb. ground beef
1 cup chopped onion
1 clove garlic, minced
1 (16 oz.) can stewed tomatoes, drained
1 (16 oz.) can kidney beans, drained

1 (16 oz.) can tomato sauce
3 tsp. chili powder
½ tsp. dried basil
1 (6 oz.) can tomato paste
2 cups chicken broth

Directions

1. In a large saucepan, cook the ground beef, onion, and garlic until the onion is translucent and the meat is brown. Drain the fat.

2. Stir in the stewed tomatoes, kidney beans, tomato sauce, chili powder, basil, tomato paste, and chicken broth. Bring to a boil.

3. Reduce heat and simmer, covered, for 30 minutes. Taste and adjust seasoning if needed before serving.

This is a less spicy version that even kids will like.

Pesto Chicken

This is a simple yet flavorful dish that can be prepared in no time. The pesto provides a fresh, herby taste, while the mozzarella cheese gives it a nice, gooey finish. It's a perfect weeknight meal when you're short on time but still want something delicious and satisfying.

Prep Time: 10 minutes
Cook Time: 30 to 40 minutes
Yield: 6 servings

Ingredients

6 boneless skinless chicken breasts
½ cup prepared pesto sauce
6 slices mozzarella cheese
Cooking spray

Directions

1. Preheat your oven to 350°F. Spray a baking dish with a light coating of cooking spray.
2. Place the chicken breasts in the prepared baking dish. Pour the pesto sauce evenly over each chicken breast, making sure each piece is well coated.
3. Bake the chicken for 25 to 30 minutes, or until the chicken is almost cooked through.
4. Take the dish out of the oven and place one slice of mozzarella cheese on top of each chicken breast.
5. Return the dish to the oven and continue baking for an additional 5 to 10 minutes, or until the cheese is melted and bubbly and the chicken is no longer pink in the center.
6. Serve the Pesto Chicken hot, ideally with a side of pasta, roasted vegetables, or a fresh salad. Enjoy!

Then God blessed the seventh day and made it holy, because on it he rested from all the work of creating that he had done.

GENESIS 2:3

Air Fryer Smashed Baby Potatoes

Prep Time: 5 minutes
Cook Time: 45 minutes
Yield: 6 servings

Ingredients

1 lb. baby potatoes
2 T. olive oil
2 cloves garlic, minced
1 tsp. dried rosemary
Salt and black pepper
Optional: ¼ cup Parmesan cheese, for serving

Directions

1. Wash and dry the baby potatoes. Place them in a large pot and cover with water. Bring the water to a boil and cook the potatoes for 10 to 15 minutes, or until they are fork-tender.
2. Drain the potatoes and let them cool for a few minutes. Preheat the air fryer to 400°F.
3. In a small bowl, mix together the olive oil, garlic, rosemary, salt, and black pepper.
4. Place enough of the potatoes to cover the bottom of the basket of the air fryer, spaced apart, and smash them down slightly with the bottom of a glass or a fork. (Depending on the size of your air fryer, you may have to do a couple of batches. If so, place the cooked potatoes on a plate and cover with foil to keep warm.)
5. Brush the tops of the potatoes with the olive oil mixture.
6. Place the basket in the air fryer and cook for 8 minutes, flip, and then cook for another 8 minutes, or until the potatoes are golden and crispy on the outside.
7. Serve the smashed potatoes hot, garnished with grated Parmesan cheese, if desired.

Banana Cake with Citrus Glaze

Prep Time: 25 minutes
Cook Time: 70 minutes
Yield: 16 servings

Ingredients

Cake

    2½ T. lemon juice, divided (adjust to 3 T. for more lemon flavor)

    1⅜ cups milk

    1⅓ cups ripe, mashed bananas

    1 cup white sugar

    ¾ cup brown sugar

    ⅔ cup butter, room temperature

    3 large eggs

    1 tsp. vanilla

    3 cups flour

    1½ tsp. baking soda

    1 tsp. ground cinnamon

    ¼ tsp. ground nutmeg

    ¼ tsp. salt

    ½ cup shredded coconut (optional)

Frosting

    8 oz. cream cheese, room temperature

    ⅓ cup butter, room temperature

    1 lemon

    3 to 3½ cups powdered sugar

Citrus Glaze (optional but oh so amazing...)

    1 cup powdered sugar

    2 to 3 T. lemon juice or orange juice

Directions

For the Cake:

1. Preheat your oven to 350°F. Grease a 9 × 13-inch baking pan with butter, then dust it with flour, tapping out the excess. This will ensure your cake doesn't stick to the pan.
2. Stir 1½ tablespoons of lemon juice into the milk and let it sit for a few minutes to create a buttermilk-like texture.
3. Mash the bananas with a fork in a bowl, and stir in the remaining lemon juice. The lemon juice prevents the bananas from turning brown and adds a subtle tang to the cake.
4. In a large mixing bowl, use an electric mixer to cream together the sugars and the butter. Mix

for about 3 to 4 minutes until light and fluffy. Add the eggs one at a time, mixing well after each addition. Stir in the vanilla.
5. In another bowl, whisk together the flour, baking soda, cinnamon, nutmeg, and salt. Slowly add about a third of the dry mixture to the wet ingredients, then half the milk, and alternately add more of each, ending with the dry ingredients, and mixing until just combined. Be careful not to overmix, as this can lead to a tough cake. Gently fold in the mashed bananas and shredded coconut, if using.
6. Pour the batter into the prepared pan and smooth the top with a spatula. Bake for 60 to 70 minutes, or until a toothpick inserted into the center of the cake comes out clean. Let the cake cool in the pan for 10 minutes before transferring it to a wire rack to cool completely.

For the Frosting:

7. In a large bowl, beat together the cream cheese and softened butter until smooth and creamy. Mix the zest and some of the juice from your fresh lemon, using about 1½ teaspoons zest and 1 teaspoon juice. Gradually add the powdered sugar, a half cup at a time, mixing well after each addition until you reach your desired consistency. Spread the frosting evenly over the cooled cake.

For the Citrus Glaze (optional):

8. In a small bowl, whisk the powdered sugar with about half the lemon or orange juice until smooth. Add more juice until the glaze is the desired consistency. If it becomes too thin, add more powdered sugar. Drizzle the glaze over the frosted cake, creating a beautiful pattern.
9. Slice the cake into squares and serve.

Blueberry Lemon-Glaze Muffins

Prep Time: 10 minutes
Cook Time: 25 minutes
Yield: 12 muffins

Ingredients

Muffins

    2 cups all-purpose flour

    1½ tsp. baking powder

½ tsp. baking soda

¼ tsp. salt

2 large eggs

1 cup granulated sugar

½ cup unsalted butter, melted and cooled

1 cup buttermilk

Zest and juice of 1 large lemon

1½ cups fresh or frozen blueberries*

Lemon Glaze

1 cup powdered sugar

2 to 3 T. fresh lemon juice

Directions

1. Preheat your oven to 375°F and line a 12-cup muffin tin with paper liners.
2. In a large bowl, whisk together the flour, baking powder, baking soda, and salt. Set aside.
3. In another bowl, whisk the eggs and granulated sugar together until well combined. Add the melted butter, buttermilk, lemon zest, and lemon juice, stirring until the mixture is smooth.
4. Gradually add the wet ingredients to the dry ingredients, stirring just until combined. Don't overmix, or the muffins will become dense.
5. Gently fold in the blueberries.
6. Using a large scoop or spoon, divide the batter evenly among the prepared muffin cups, filling each about two-thirds full.
7. Bake for about 20 to 25 minutes, or until the tops are lightly golden and a toothpick inserted into the center comes out clean.
8. Allow the muffins to cool in the tin for 5 minutes, then transfer them to a wire rack to cool completely.
9. While the muffins are cooling, prepare the glaze. In a small bowl, whisk together the powdered sugar and 2 tablespoons of the lemon juice until smooth. If necessary, add more lemon juice, a little at a time, until the glaze is pourable but still thick.
10. Drizzle the glaze over the cooled muffins. Allow the glaze to set for a few minutes before serving.
11. Enjoy these light and tangy blueberry lemon muffins! They are perfect for breakfast or a mid-afternoon snack.

*Note: If you are using frozen blueberries, there is no need to thaw them. Just fold them into the batter while still frozen.

Southwest Chopped Salad

Prep time: 30 minutes

Yield: 4 main servings or 8 side servings

Ingredients

6 cups chopped romaine lettuce

1 cup cooked black beans (if canned, be sure to drain and rinse)

1 cup corn kernels

1 red bell pepper, diced

1 avocado, diced

½ cup cherry tomatoes, halved

½ cup crumbled queso fresco or feta cheese

Cilantro Dressing

Directions

1. In a large salad bowl, combine the romaine lettuce, black beans, corn, red bell pepper, avocado, cherry tomatoes, and cheese.
2. Drizzle the dressing over the salad and gently toss to combine. Serve immediately.

Cilantro Dressing

Prep Time: 5 minutes

Yield: 8 servings

Ingredients

1 cup loosely packed fresh cilantro

½ cup Greek yogurt

2 T. fresh lime juice

1 clove garlic

2 T. olive oil

½ tsp. salt

¼ tsp. black pepper

Directions

Combine all ingredients in a blender or food processor and blend until smooth.

Pulled Pork Quesadillas

Enjoy these Pulled Pork Quesadillas as a delicious and satisfying way to use up leftover pulled pork.

Prep Time: 10 minutes

Yield: 4 servings

Ingredients

- 1 yellow onion, chopped
- 8 flour tortillas
- 2 cups leftover pulled pork
- 2 cups Mexican blend shredded cheese
- Sour cream and salsa, for serving

Directions

1. Heat a nonstick pan over medium heat and add a little bit of cooking spray or olive oil. Sauté the onion until it becomes translucent and slightly caramelized, about 5 to 7 minutes. Remove the onion from the pan and set aside.
2. Place one tortilla in the same pan and top it evenly with a quarter of the pork.
3. Sprinkle a quarter of the onion over the pork.
4. Spread a quarter of the cheese over the onion.
5. Place another tortilla on top and press it down gently.
6. Cook the quesadilla on medium heat until the bottom tortilla is golden brown and crispy, about 3 to 4 minutes.
7. Carefully flip the quesadilla over and cook on the other side until it is also golden brown and the cheese is melted, about 3 to 4 minutes more.
8. Remove the quesadilla from the pan and let it cool for a couple of minutes before cutting it into quarters.
9. Repeat the process with the remaining tortillas, pork, onion, and cheese.
10. Serve the quesadillas with sour cream and salsa on the side for dipping.

Caesar Salad

Prep Time: 15 minutes
Yield: 4 main servings or 8 side servings

Ingredients

- 1 head romaine lettuce, torn into bite-size pieces
- 1 cup croutons
- ½ cup freshly grated Parmesan cheese
- ½ cup Creamy Caesar Dressing

Directions

1. In a large salad bowl, combine the romaine lettuce, croutons, and Parmesan cheese.
2. Pour the dressing over the salad and toss until well coated.
3. Serve immediately, with additional Parmesan cheese on top if desired.

Creamy Caesar Dressing

Ingredients

- ¾ cup mayonnaise
- 2 T. fresh lemon juice
- 2 garlic cloves, minced
- 1 tsp. Worcestershire sauce
- 1 tsp. Dijon mustard
- ¼ cup grated Parmesan cheese
- Salt and freshly ground pepper, to taste

Directions

Combine all ingredients in a blender or food processor and blend until smooth.

Cheese and Veggie Quesadillas

Prep Time: 10 minutes
Cook Time: 15 minutes
Yield: 4 servings

Ingredients

- 4 large flour tortillas
- 2 cups shredded cheddar cheese
- 1 red bell pepper, diced
- 1 green bell pepper, diced
- 1 onion, diced

Directions

1. Preheat a large skillet over medium heat.
2. Spread ½ cup of cheese on half of each tortilla.
3. Sprinkle the peppers and onion over the cheese.
4. Fold the empty half of each tortilla over the filled half.
5. Cook the quesadillas in the skillet for 2 to 3 minutes on each side, until the cheese is melted and the tortillas are crispy. Cook in batches, if needed, to keep the quesadillas in a single layer in your skillet.
6. Cut into triangles and serve hot.

Week Twenty
World Market Delights

H ere comes the sun! Enjoy the long summer days without worrying about what you'll eat for dinner. Keep this week simple and flavorful as you savor the simple joys of Tuscan cuisine with this week's hearty Meatball Soup—an effortlessly charming meal to prepare. Indulge in the comforting blend of succulent meatballs, fresh vegetables, and robust herbs—all swimming in a rich chicken broth. Using premade, frozen meatballs saves you time without compromising the taste.

Perfect for a cozy dinner with loved ones, this soup brings a piece of Tuscany to your table, promising both warmth and delight in every spoonful.

Week 20 Menu

Saturday

Air Fryer Honey Soy Beef Kebabs
Rice Pilaf with Toasted Almonds
Bacon and Broccoli Salad

Dessert:
Fresh Fruit Galette
(Berry)

Sunday

Breakfast:
Quiche (Sausage and
Mushroom)

Lunch:
Tuscan Meatball Soup
Caprese Salad
Cheesy Garlic Bread

Dinner:
Charcuterie Board

Monday

Air Fryer Twice-Baked Potatoes
topped with beef and horseradish
Red House Salad

Tuesday

Tuscan Meatball Soup
Caesar Salad
Cheesy Garlic Bread

Wednesday

Leftovers or frozen meal of choice

Thursday

Dinner out

Friday

Pizza night!

Sabbath Soup

Tuscan Meatball Soup

Prep Time: 10 minutes • Cook Time: 30 minutes • Yield: 4 bowls or 8 cups

Ingredients

Extra-virgin olive oil
1 medium onion, diced
2 cloves garlic, minced
2 carrots, peeled and diced
2 ribs celery, diced
1 red bell pepper, diced
1 bag (approx. 1 to 1½ lbs.)
   frozen meatballs, any brand
4 cups low-sodium chicken
   broth
1 (15 oz.) can diced tomatoes

1 (15 oz.) can cannellini beans,
   drained and rinsed
1 tsp. dried basil
1 tsp. dried oregano
Salt and pepper, to taste
2 cups roughly chopped fresh
   spinach or kale
Fresh basil leaves for garnishing
Freshly grated Parmesan cheese,
   for serving

Directions

1. Heat a large pot or Dutch oven over medium heat. Add a splash of olive oil, followed by the onion, garlic, carrots, celery, and bell pepper. Sauté until the vegetables are tender and the onion is translucent, about 5 to 7 minutes.

2. Stir in the frozen meatballs, chicken broth, diced tomatoes, cannellini beans, dried basil, dried oregano, and salt and pepper. Bring the mixture to a simmer.

3. Once simmering, reduce the heat to low, cover the pot, and let it simmer for about 15 to 20 minutes, or until the meatballs are heated through.

4. Stir in the spinach or kale and let it cook for an additional 2 to 3 minutes, or until the greens are wilted.

5. Taste the soup and adjust the seasoning if needed. Top with fresh basil leaves and serve with grated Parmesan.

Air Fryer Honey Soy Beef Kebabs

Prep Time: 15 minutes, plus 30 minutes or up to 24 hours to marinate
Cook Time: 10 minutes
Yield: 4 servings

Ingredients

¼ cup low-sodium soy sauce
2 T. honey
2 T. olive oil
2 cloves garlic, minced
1 tsp. grated fresh ginger
1 T. sesame seeds
Salt and pepper, to taste
1 lb. beef sirloin, cut into 1-inch cubes
Bamboo skewers, soaked in water for 30 minutes

Directions

1. In a large bowl, combine soy sauce, honey, olive oil, garlic, ginger, sesame seeds, salt, and pepper. Stir well to combine.
2. Add the beef cubes to the bowl and toss them in the marinade until well coated. Let it marinate for at least 30 minutes or refrigerate overnight for best results.
3. Preheat your air fryer to 400°F for 5 minutes.
4. Thread the marinated beef onto the soaked bamboo skewers, leaving a small space between each piece.
5. Place the beef skewers in a single layer inside the air fryer basket. You may need to cook them in batches depending on the size of your air fryer.
6. Cook the beef kebabs in the air fryer for 8 to 10 minutes, flipping them halfway through the cooking time. The exact cooking time may vary based on the thickness of the beef and the desired level of doneness.
7. Once the beef is cooked to your liking, remove the kebabs from the air fryer and let them rest for a few minutes.

Rice Pilaf with Toasted Almonds

Prep time: 10 minutes
Cook time: 25 minutes
Yield: 8 servings

Ingredients

2 cups basmati rice
3 T. olive oil
1 onion, finely chopped
2 garlic cloves, minced
1 tsp. ground cumin
½ tsp. ground turmeric
½ tsp. ground coriander
4 cups chicken or vegetable broth
Salt and pepper, to taste
½ cup sliced almonds, toasted
2 T. chopped fresh parsley

Directions

1. Rinse the basmati rice under cold water until the water runs clear. Set aside to drain.
2. Heat the olive oil in a large saucepan over medium heat. Add the onion and cook until it starts to soften and become translucent, about 5 minutes.
3. Add the garlic, cumin, turmeric, and coriander. Stir and cook for another minute until fragrant.
4. Add the rice to the saucepan. Stir until the rice is well coated in the oil and spices.
5. Pour in the chicken or vegetable broth. Season with salt and pepper, to taste.
6. Bring the mixture to a boil, then reduce the heat to low, cover, and simmer for 15 to 20 minutes, or until the rice is tender and the liquid is absorbed.
7. Remove from heat and let the rice sit, covered, for 5 minutes.
8. Fluff the rice with a fork and mix in the toasted almonds and parsley. Serve the rice pilaf warm.

Bacon and Broccoli Salad

Prep Time: 20 minutes
Yield: 4 main servings or 8 side servings

Ingredients

4 cups broccoli florets, cut into bite-size pieces
8 slices bacon, cooked and crumbled
½ cup finely chopped red onion
½ cup shredded cheddar cheese
¼ cup sunflower seeds (optional)
½ cup mayonnaise
2 T. apple cider vinegar
1 T. sugar
Salt and pepper, to taste

Directions

1. In a large salad bowl, combine the broccoli, bacon, onion, cheddar, and sunflower seeds.
2. In a small bowl, whisk together the mayonnaise, apple cider vinegar, and sugar.
3. Drizzle the dressing over the salad, season with a dash of salt and pepper, and gently toss to combine.
4. Refrigerate the salad for at least one hour before serving to allow the flavors to meld.
5. Serve chilled.

Fresh Fruit Galette (Berry)

Prep Time: 20 minutes
Cook Time: 15 to 25 minutes
Yield: 8 servings

Ingredients

1 (10 × 15-inch) layer frozen puff pastry, thawed
½ cup granulated sugar
1 tsp. cornstarch
1 cup fresh berries
1 T. lemon juice
1 small egg, for brushing on pastry
Turbinado sugar

Directions

1. Heat oven to 375°F.
2. Place a frozen puff pastry sheet on a baking sheet lined with parchment paper and let it defrost: either on the kitchen counter for 4 hours, or overnight in the fridge (then set out on the counter for one hour before baking).
3. In a bowl, whisk together sugar and cornstarch. Add in the berries and lemon juice and stir to coat.
4. Pour berry mixture into the center of the puff pastry. Fold the edges of the puff pastry toward the border of the fruit mixture to form an outer crust. There should be a rustic circle of fruit visible in the center of the galette.
5. Whisk the egg in a small bowl and brush the exposed pastry with the egg using a pastry brush.
6. Sprinkle with the turbinado sugar.
7. Bake for 15 to 25 minutes or until the pastry is golden brown. (Check often after the 15 minute mark.)
8. When done, remove the galette from the oven and let the pastry sit for at least 10 minutes, allowing the fruit juices to firm up slightly.

Note: You can make many variations of this galette. Sliced fresh pears, peaches, apricots, and apples are my favorites to use in place of berries.

Quiche (Sausage and Mushroom)

Prep Time: 20 minutes
Cook Time: 45 minutes
Yield: 8 servings

Ingredients

4 large eggs
⅔ cup whole milk
½ cup heavy cream (or heavy whipping cream)
¼ tsp. salt
¼ tsp. pepper
½ cup shredded cheddar cheese
½ cup crumbled feta cheese
1 cup cooked, crumbled breakfast sausage
1 cup cooked, sliced mushrooms
1 store-bought frozen pastry pie shell, defrosted overnight
¼ cup grated Parmesan cheese

Directions

1. Preheat oven to 350°F.
2. In a large bowl, beat the eggs, milk, cream, salt, and pepper on high speed, approximately 1 minute.
3. Fold in the cheeses, sausage, and mushrooms.

Pour mixture into the crust.

4. Sprinkle the Parmesan cheese on top.
5. Cover the edges of the pie shell with aluminum foil to keep them from burning.
6. Bake quiche until the center is set and a toothpick comes out clean, about 45 minutes.
7. Let the quiche cool for 10 minutes before serving.

Caprese Salad

Prep Time: 15 minutes
Yield: 4 main servings or 8 side servings

Ingredients

4 large tomatoes, sliced
1 lb. fresh mozzarella cheese, sliced
1 cup loosely packed fresh basil leaves
¼ cup olive oil
2 T. balsamic vinegar
Salt and pepper, to taste

Directions

1. Arrange the tomato slices, mozzarella slices, and basil leaves on a large platter, alternating and overlapping them.
2. In a small bowl, whisk together the olive oil and balsamic vinegar.
3. Drizzle the dressing over the arranged ingredients on the platter. Season the salad with a dash of salt and pepper. Serve immediately.

Cheesy Garlic Bread

Prep Time: 10 minutes
Cook Time: 15 minutes
Yield: 8 servings

Ingredients

½ cup unsalted butter, softened
3 cloves garlic, minced
1 loaf French bread, halved lengthwise
2 cups shredded mozzarella cheese
¼ cup chopped fresh parsley

Directions

1. Preheat the oven to 375°F.
2. In a small bowl, mix together the butter and garlic.
3. Spread the garlic butter evenly over the cut sides of the bread.
4. Sprinkle the shredded mozzarella over the butter.
5. Place the bread on a baking sheet and bake for 10 minutes, or until the cheese is melted.
6. Switch the oven to broil and cook for another 2 to 3 minutes, until the cheese is bubbly and golden.
7. Sprinkle with parsley before serving.

Charcuterie Board

A charcuterie board is a great option for parties, but it's also great for an easy dinner treat. Don't let the fancy reputation scare you away. Just remember to include a few items from each of the categories below.

Prep Time: 10 minutes
Yield: customizable

Ingredients

Base
    Crackers, pita bread, pretzels
    Slices of cucumber
Substance
    Hard cheeses: cheddar, Swiss, smoked gouda
    Soft cheeses: goat, brie, crema, spreadable cheeses, Havarti
    Cured meats: ham, sausage, salami, prosciutto, pepperoni
    Hard-boiled eggs
Flavor
    Nuts, pickles, olives, sliced apples, cocktail onions
Extras
    Dips, tapenades, jams
    Fruit: strawberries, grapes, dried apricots
    Dark chocolate

Directions

1. Get a nice tray, platter, or wooden cutting board to hold your spread. Gather serving tools: tooth-

picks, small tongs, a small knife for spreading soft cheese, and spoons for dips or jams.

2. Choose two or more options from each category and lay them out in bite-size slices or chunks, grouped together on your serving tray. Be sure to offer and label gluten-free items for those with sensitivities or allergies and consider separating them from any gluten-containing items by placing them in their own bowl or tray. You may also want to separate nuts or other potential allergens into their own bowls. Enjoy!

Air Fryer Twice-Baked Potatoes

Prep Time: 10 minutes
Cook Time: 50 minutes
Yield: 8 servings

Ingredients

4 large russet potatoes
1 T. olive oil
Salt and pepper, to taste
1 cup sour cream
2 cups shredded cheddar cheese, divided
Leftover cooked beef, chopped
2 green onions, sliced
Horseradish sauce

Directions

1. Preheat your air fryer to 400°F.
2. Pierce your potatoes with a fork several times, and coat with the olive oil, salt, and pepper. Place the potatoes on the trivet and air fry for 20 minutes.
3. With a pair of tongs, flip the potatoes over and continue to air fry for another 20 minutes. Remove from the air fryer and let sit for 5 minutes to cool slightly.
4. Once the potatoes are cooked, cut in half lengthwise and scoop out the middle, leaving a thin layer of potato in the skin.
5. Mix the scooped potato with the sour cream, 1 cup of cheddar cheese, beef, and green onion.
6. Stuff the potato skins with this mixture, then top with the remaining cheddar cheese.
7. Cook the potatoes in the air fryer at 375°F for 10 minutes, or until cheese is melted and bubbly. Serve hot with horseradish sauce.

Red House Salad

This is the signature salad here at our house, The Red House, which is also a writing retreat center. Returning guests ask for it by name, and we make sure it's on the menu whenever the ingredients are in season.

Prep Time: 15 minutes
Yield: 4 main servings or 8 side servings

Ingredients

6 cups mixed greens
1 cup fresh strawberries, hulled and sliced
1 cup fresh blueberries
½ red onion, thinly sliced
½ cup crumbled feta cheese
¼ cup balsamic vinaigrette

Directions

1. In a large salad bowl, combine the mixed greens, strawberries, blueberries, red onion, and feta cheese.
2. Drizzle the dressing over the salad and gently toss to combine. Serve immediately.

Caesar Salad

Prep Time: 15 minutes
Yield: 4 main servings or 8 side servings

Ingredients

1 head romaine lettuce, torn into bite-size pieces
1 cup croutons
½ cup freshly grated Parmesan cheese
½ cup Creamy Caesar Dressing

Directions

1. In a large salad bowl, combine the romaine lettuce, croutons, and Parmesan cheese.
2. Pour the dressing over the salad and toss until well coated.
3. Serve immediately, with additional Parmesan cheese on top if desired.

Creamy Caesar Dressing

Ingredients

¾ cup mayonnaise

2 T. fresh lemon juice

2 garlic cloves, minced

1 tsp. Worcestershire sauce

1 tsp. Dijon mustard

¼ cup grated Parmesan cheese

Salt and freshly ground pepper, to taste

Directions

Combine all ingredients in a blender or food processor and blend until smooth.

Cheesy Garlic Bread

Prep Time: 10 minutes

Cook Time: 15 minutes

Yield: 8 servings

Ingredients

½ cup unsalted butter, softened

3 cloves garlic, minced

1 loaf French bread, halved lengthwise

2 cups shredded mozzarella cheese

¼ cup chopped fresh parsley

Directions

1. Preheat the oven to 375°F.
2. In a small bowl, mix together the butter and garlic.
3. Spread the garlic butter evenly over the cut sides of the bread.
4. Sprinkle the shredded mozzarella over the butter.
5. Place the bread on a baking sheet and bake for 10 minutes, or until the cheese is melted.
6. Switch the oven to broil and cook for another 2 to 3 minutes, until the cheese is bubbly and golden.
7. Sprinkle with parsley before serving.

A Prayer for the Summer Season

Lord, I welcome summer
to my home and to my table.
I open my heart and my hands
to the rhythms that
You have created.

Lord, help me to see the gifts
of this season.

I ask that summer brings
a fresh creative spark
through strawberries,
watermelon, and
fresh-from-the-farm vegetables.

Summer always seems
to go quickly, and I ask
that You might show me
where to focus my
attention in this full season.

Please help me find joy in
unexpected guests,
a simple meal, and
cool treats on warm days.

May all who
eat at this table
be reminded
of Your constant provision,
in this season,
and in seasons to follow.

Week Twenty-One
Mediterranean Summer

Enjoy this menu inspired by a Mediterranean summer soiree. Start your journey with the Oven-Roasted Chicken, reminiscent of traditional Greek rotisserie, accompanied by heartwarming baked potatoes and the Stir-Fried Zucchini for a homestyle touch. Indulge in the Lemon-Infused Blackberry Cobbler, a delightful nod to the region's love for fresh, seasonal fruits. Wake up to this Cinnamon French Toast, a sweet fusion of Mediterranean flavors, followed by the tangy Greek Lemon Soup and the refreshing Greek Salad, perfectly capturing the spirit of Greek cuisine.

You may very well want to hit repeat on this one!

Week 21 Menu

Saturday

Oven-Roasted Chicken
Air Fryer Baked Potatoes
Stir-Fried Zucchini

Dessert:
Lemon-Infused
    Blackberry Cobbler

Sunday

Breakfast:
Baked Cinnamon French Toast

Lunch:
Greek Lemon Soup
Greek Salad
Corn Bread

Dinner:
Italian Zucchini and
    Sausage Bake
Cheesy Garlic Bread

Monday

Pita Sandwich with Chicken
    Caesar Salad
Lemon Dill Greek Yogurt Dip
    with Veggies

Tuesday

Greek Lemon Soup
Greek Salad
Corn Bread

Wednesday

Leftovers or frozen meal of choice

Thursday

Dinner out

Friday

Pizza night!

Sabbath Soup

Greek Lemon Soup

Prep Time: 5 minutes • Cook Time: 30 to 40 minutes • Yield: 4 bowls or 8 cups

Ingredients

4 cups chicken broth
½ cup uncooked orzo or rice
Salt and pepper, to taste
3 eggs
Juice of 2 lemons (about ⅓ to ½
   cup, depending on taste)

Optional: 1 cup shredded cooked
   chicken, and fresh chopped
   parsley or dill for garnish

Directions

1. In a large pot, bring the chicken broth to a boil.
2. Add the orzo or rice, reduce heat, and simmer until tender. (This will take about 10 minutes for orzo or about 18 minutes for rice.) Season with salt and pepper.
3. While the orzo or rice is cooking, whisk together the eggs in a separate bowl until well beaten. Continue to whisk and gradually add in the lemon juice.
4. Once the orzo or rice is cooked, reduce the heat to low. Take a ladle full of hot broth and slowly add it to the egg-lemon mixture, whisking continuously. This process is called tempering and prevents the eggs from scrambling when added to the hot soup.
5. Continue to slowly add another 2 to 3 ladles of broth into the egg-lemon mixture, making sure to keep whisking.
6. Once the egg-lemon mixture is warmed, slowly pour it back into the soup pot, stirring the soup as you pour.
7. Add in the shredded chicken.
8. Stir the soup over low heat for 2 to 3 minutes until heated through. Do not let it come to a boil.
9. Taste and adjust the seasoning if needed.
10. Ladle the soup into bowls, garnish with fresh parsley or dill, and serve immediately.

Oven-Roasted Chicken

Prep Time: 10 minutes
Cook Time: 1 hour and 40 minutes
Yield: 4 to 6 servings

Ingredients

1 whole chicken, giblets removed, rinsed and
    patted dry
Cooking spray
Salt (1 tsp. per pound of chicken)
Pepper (⅓ tsp. per pound of chicken)
6 garlic cloves, cut in half
4 T. butter
Garlic salt and pepper

Directions

1. Preheat your oven to 425°F.
2. Place the chicken in a roasting pan covered in
   cooking spray, breast side up. Season the chicken
   cavity with salt and pepper, then place the
   garlic inside. Adjust the suggested levels if you
   like a more seasoned chicken. Chop the butter
   into pats and place them all over the top of the
   chicken. Sprinkle with garlic salt and pepper.
3. Roast until the chicken's internal temperature
   reaches 165°F. Let it roast for an hour and then
   keep checking the internal temperature until it
   reaches 165°F. Let it sit for 20 minutes before
   serving.

Air Fryer Baked Potatoes

Prep Time: 5 minutes
Cook Time: 40 minutes
Yield: 4 servings

Ingredients

4 baking potatoes
Olive oil
Sea salt
Pepper

Directions

1. Preheat your air fryer to 400°F.
2. Pierce your potatoes with a fork several times.
   Rub the outsides with olive oil, salt, and pepper.
   Place the potatoes on the trivet and air fry for
   20 minutes.

3. With a pair of tongs, flip the potatoes over and
   continue to air fry for another 20 minutes. Remove from the air fryer and let sit for 5 minutes
   before serving.
4. Serve with your choice of toppings.

Stir-Fried Zucchini

Prep Time: 10 minutes
Cook Time: 10 minutes
Yield: 4 servings

Ingredients

1 small onion
3 cloves garlic
2 medium zucchinis
2 T. vegetable oil or olive oil
Salt and pepper, to taste
1 T. soy sauce

Directions

1. Thinly slice the onion, mince the garlic, and
   slice the zucchini into ¼-inch-thick half-moon
   shapes (cut the zucchini in half lengthwise and
   then slice).
2. Place a large skillet or wok over medium-high
   heat. Add the oil and let it heat up.
3. Once the oil is hot, add the garlic and onion.
   Stir-fry for 1 to 2 minutes, or until the onion
   starts to soften and the garlic becomes aromatic.
4. Add the zucchini to the pan, and stir-fry for 4 to
   6 minutes, stirring occasionally, until the zucchini
   starts to soften and brown slightly.
5. Season with salt and black pepper.
6. Add the soy sauce. Stir well to combine all the
   ingredients.
7. Continue to stir-fry for another 1 to 2 minutes,
   making sure the zucchini is well coated with the
   sauce.

Lemon-Infused Blackberry Cobbler

Prep Time: 20 minutes
Cook Time: 35 to 40 minutes
Yield: 6 servings

Ingredients

Filling

    4 cups fresh blackberries
    1 cup granulated sugar
    1 T. cornstarch
    Zest and juice of 1 small lemon
    Pinch of salt

Cobbler Topping

    1 cup all-purpose flour
    ¼ cup granulated sugar
    1 tsp. baking powder
    ½ tsp. baking soda
    ¼ tsp. salt
    4 T. unsalted butter, chilled and cut into small
       pieces
    ⅔ cup buttermilk

Directions

1. Preheat your oven to 375°F. Lightly grease a 9-inch baking dish.
2. Make the blackberry filling: In a large bowl, combine the blackberries, sugar, cornstarch, lemon zest, lemon juice, and a pinch of salt. Stir gently until well combined, then transfer to the prepared baking dish.
3. For the cobbler topping: In another bowl, whisk together the flour, sugar, baking powder, baking soda, and salt. Add the butter and use your fingers or a pastry cutter to incorporate it into the flour until the mixture looks like coarse crumbs. Pour in the buttermilk and stir until just combined. Don't overmix; it's okay if there are a few lumps.
4. Drop spoonfuls of the cobbler topping over the blackberry filling. It's okay if some of the blackberries are peeking through; the topping will spread as it bakes.
5. Bake for 35 to 40 minutes, or until the topping is golden brown and the blackberries are bubbling.
6. Remove the cobbler from the oven and allow it to cool for about 10 minutes before serving. Serve warm. (This is a great time to break out a scoop of ice cream to put on top.)

Baked Cinnamon French Toast

Prep Time: Overnight
Cook Time: 1 hour
Yield: 12 servings

Ingredients

French Toast

    1 T. butter, room temperature
    1 loaf crusty unsliced bread
    8 whole eggs
    2 cups whole milk
    ½ cup heavy cream
    ¾ cup sugar
    2 T. vanilla extract
    ¼ tsp. nutmeg

Topping

    ½ cup all-purpose flour
    ½ cup firmly packed brown sugar
    1 tsp. cinnamon
    ¼ tsp. salt
    ¼ tsp. nutmeg
    1 stick (8 T.) chilled unsalted butter

Optional Toppings

    Sliced fruit (we like bananas, blueberries,
       strawberries, and peaches)
    Powdered sugar
    Maple syrup

Directions

1. Begin by generously buttering a 9 × 13-inch baking pan, making sure to coat every corner and crevice.
2. Next, take your chosen loaf of bread (we like this with sourdough, challah, or French bread) and tear it into rustic, bite-sized chunks. If you prefer a more uniform look, you can also cut the bread into cubes. Arrange the pieces in the prepared pan, ensuring an even distribution.
3. In a medium-sized bowl, create the custard by whisking together the eggs, milk, cream, sugar, vanilla, and nutmeg. Pour the mixture over the bread, making sure each piece is thoroughly

coated. Cover the pan tightly with plastic wrap or aluminum foil and place it in the refrigerator to rest overnight, allowing the bread to soak up all the flavors.

4. When you are ready to bake the casserole, preheat your oven to 350°F. Remove the French toast from the refrigerator and let it sit at room temperature while the oven warms up.

5. Prepare the topping: Combine all the dry topping ingredients in a medium mixing bowl. Cut the chilled butter into small pieces and add it to the mix. Using a pastry blender or two knives, work the butter into the mixture until it resembles coarse, pebble-like crumbs. (You can also prepare the topping in advance and store it in an airtight container in the refrigerator overnight.) Sprinkle the topping over the bread, creating a delightful streusel-like layer.

6. Place the dish in the preheated oven and bake for a full hour. This extended baking time ensures that the custard sets firmly and the top develops a beautiful golden-brown crust. Once done, remove from the oven and let it cool slightly.

7. To serve, cut the Baked Cinnamon French Toast into generous squares and transfer them to individual plates. Top with fruit and dust each serving with a sprinkle of powdered sugar, if desired. Serve alongside a pitcher of warm maple syrup.

By the seventh day
God had finished the work
he had been doing;
so on the seventh day
he rested from all his work.

GENESIS 2:2

Greek Salad

Prep Time: 15 minutes
Yield: 4 main servings or 8 side servings

Ingredients

4 large tomatoes, cut into wedges
1 cucumber, sliced
½ red onion, thinly sliced
1 cup crumbled feta cheese
½ cup pitted kalamata olives
¼ cup Greek Dressing

Directions

1. In a large salad bowl, combine the tomatoes, cucumber, red onion, feta cheese, and kalamata olives.

2. Drizzle the dressing over the salad and gently toss to combine.

3. Serve immediately or chill in the refrigerator for an hour to allow the flavors to meld.

Greek Dressing

Ingredients

½ cup extra-virgin olive oil
¼ cup red wine vinegar
2 garlic cloves, minced
1 tsp. dried oregano
Salt and freshly ground pepper, to taste

Directions

Shake all ingredients together in a jar until well combined.

Corn Bread

Prep Time: 10 minutes
Cook Time: 20 minutes
Yield: 9 servings

Ingredients

1 cup cornmeal
1 cup all-purpose flour
¼ cup sugar
1 T. baking powder
½ tsp. salt
1 cup milk
¼ cup vegetable oil
2 large eggs

Directions

1. Preheat the oven to 400°F and grease a 9 × 9-inch baking pan.
2. In a large bowl, combine the cornmeal, flour, sugar, baking powder, and salt.
3. In a separate bowl, whisk together the milk, vegetable oil, and eggs.
4. Add the wet ingredients to the dry and stir until just combined.
5. Pour the batter into the prepared pan and bake for 20 minutes, or until a toothpick inserted in the center comes out clean.
6. Allow to cool slightly before cutting into squares to serve.

Italian Zucchini and Sausage Bake

Prep Time: 20 minutes
Cook Time: 35 minutes
Yield: 8 servings

Ingredients

4 medium zucchini
2 T. olive oil
1 lb. Italian sausage
1 large onion, chopped
3 cloves garlic, minced
1 (15 oz.) can diced tomatoes
1 tsp. dried basil
1 tsp. dried oregano
Salt and pepper, to taste
2 cups shredded mozzarella cheese
¼ cup grated Parmesan cheese

Directions

1. Preheat your oven to 375°F and lightly grease a baking sheet or dish.
2. Cut each zucchini in half lengthwise and use a spoon or melon baller to hollow out the centers, making a "boat" with sides that are about ¼ inch thick. Place the zucchini on the baking sheet.
3. In a large skillet, heat the olive oil over medium-high heat. Add the Italian sausage (removing any skin) and cook until browned, breaking it up with a wooden spoon as it cooks. Remove the sausage from the skillet and set it aside.

4. In the same skillet, add the chopped onion and minced garlic, cooking until the onion is translucent.
5. Add the tomatoes, basil, oregano, and a pinch of salt and pepper. Stir well and cook for a few more minutes.
6. Add back the sausage and cook for another 2 to 3 minutes until everything is well combined.
7. Spoon the sausage mixture into each zucchini boat, pressing it down and filling to the top.
8. Top each zucchini boat with a generous amount of mozzarella and Parmesan cheese.
9. Bake in the preheated oven for 25 to 30 minutes, or until the cheese is melted and bubbly and the zucchini is tender.
10. Remove from the oven and allow to cool for a few minutes before serving.

Cheesy Garlic Bread

Prep Time: 10 minutes
Cook Time: 15 minutes
Yield: 8 servings

Ingredients

½ cup unsalted butter, softened
3 cloves garlic, minced
1 loaf French bread, halved lengthwise
2 cups shredded mozzarella cheese
¼ cup chopped fresh parsley

Directions

1. Preheat the oven to 375°F.
2. In a small bowl, mix together the butter and garlic.
3. Spread the garlic butter evenly over the cut sides of the bread.
4. Sprinkle the shredded mozzarella over the butter.
5. Place the bread on a baking sheet and bake for 10 minutes, or until the cheese is melted.
6. Switch the oven to broil and cook for another 2 to 3 minutes, until the cheese is bubbly and golden.
7. Sprinkle with parsley before serving.

Pita Sandwich with Chicken Caesar Salad

Prep Time: 10 minutes
Yield: 4 servings

Ingredients

4 pitas
1 Caesar salad kit (store-bought)
1 rotisserie chicken, cut into chunks
Optional: chopped tomato, sliced cucumber, or other fresh vegetables.

Directions

1. Cut pitas in half and open up the pocket. Toast the pita halves in a toaster, then remove and let cool.
2. Meanwhile, mix together the ingredients from the salad kit (except for the croutons) with the chicken chunks.
3. Stuff the toasted pita with chicken Caesar salad mix.
4. If using, garnish with extra goodies, such as tomatoes and cucumbers.

Lemon Dill Greek Yogurt Dip

This dip is delicious served with fresh vegetables, pita bread, or as a sauce for grilled meats or fish. It is best served chilled, so be sure to refrigerate it for an hour or so before serving. It should keep in the fridge for up to 1 week. Just give it a good stir before using if any water separates out. Enjoy!

Prep Time: 5 minutes
Yield: 8 servings

Ingredients

2 cups plain Greek yogurt
1 garlic clove, minced
Zest and juice of 1 lemon
2 T. finely chopped fresh dill
½ tsp. sea salt, or to taste
¼ tsp. freshly ground black pepper
Optional: 1 T. extra-virgin olive oil for drizzling

Directions

1. In a bowl, combine the Greek yogurt, garlic, lemon zest, and lemon juice. Stir until well combined.
2. Add the dill, salt, and pepper. Stir again until all the ingredients are evenly distributed.
3. Taste the dip and adjust the seasoning if necessary.
4. If desired, drizzle a bit of extra-virgin olive oil on top of the dip before serving.

*"Let me get you something
to eat, so you can be refreshed
and then go on your way—
now that you have
come to your servant."
"Very well," they answered,
"do as you say."*

GENESIS 18:5

Week Twenty-Two
Sweet and Savory Summer

W elcome the joys of warm weather this week. Begin with BBQ Sausages, perfectly charred for an authentic taste of summer. Savor the medley of grilled veggies imbued with smoky flavors. The Angel Food Cake with berries perfectly encapsulates summer in dessert form.

I'm letting you know now that if you're gathering a few friends and family for any of this week's sweet and savory meals, you will be hearing a lot of yums, mm-hmms, and amens.

Week 22 Menu

Saturday

BBQ Sausages
Grilled Veggies (no recipe)
Mac 'n' Cheese
Dessert:
Angel Food Cake

Sunday
Breakfast:
Air Fryer Sugar and
    Cinnamon Donuts
Lunch:
French Onion Soup
BLT Salad
Dinner:
Air Fryer Chicken Wings
    with BBQ Sauce
Side Salad (no recipe)

Monday

Quiche (Sausage, Spinach,
    and Gruyère)

Tuesday

French Onion Soup
Apple Almond Salad

Wednesday

Leftovers or frozen meal of choice

Thursday

Dinner out

Friday

Pizza night!

Sabbath Soup

French Onion Soup

Prep Time: 15 minutes • Cook Time: 90 minutes • Yield: 4 bowls or 8 cups

Ingredients

4 T. unsalted butter

2 T. extra-virgin olive oil

4 large red or yellow onions, peeled
and thinly sliced

1 tsp. sugar

1 tsp. salt

½ tsp. pepper

3 cloves garlic, minced

½ cup dry sherry

6 cups beef broth (or a mix of beef and
chicken broth for a lighter taste)

2 bay leaves

1 tsp. fresh thyme leaves, or ½ tsp.
dried thyme

1 tsp. Worcestershire sauce

French bread or baguette

2 cups grated Gruyère cheese

½ cup grated Parmesan cheese

Directions

1. In a large heavy-bottomed stockpot, melt the butter with olive oil over medium heat.

2. Add the onion slices and toss to coat with the butter and oil. Turn the heat down to medium low. Cook the onion, stirring often, until it has softened, about 15 to 20 minutes.

3. Sprinkle with sugar, salt, and pepper. Continue to cook, stirring frequently, until the onions are well caramelized, about 20 to 30 more minutes.

4. Add the garlic and cook for a minute more.

5. Stir in the sherry, scraping up any browned bits on the bottom of the pot. Cook for 2 to 3 minutes until the sherry has mostly evaporated.

6. Add the broth, bay leaves, thyme, and Worcestershire sauce. Bring to a simmer, cover the pot, and lower the heat to maintain a low simmer. Cook for about 30 minutes.

7. Meanwhile, preheat your oven to 400°F. Cut the baguette into 8 slices (about 1 inch thick) and arrange them in a single layer on a baking sheet. Bake for 6 to 8 minutes, until the bread is toasted and golden around the edges. Set aside.

8. Taste the soup and adjust seasoning with more salt and pepper if needed. Discard the bay leaves.

9. Switch the oven to the broiler. Ladle the soup into oven-safe bowls, place a slice of toasted baguette on top, then sprinkle generously with both Gruyère and Parmesan cheese.

10. Place the bowls on a baking sheet for easy handling and broil in the oven until the cheese is melted and bubbly, 2 to 3 minutes.

BBQ Sausages

We love Aidell's Italian Style Smoked Chicken and Mozzarella Sausage. These sausages are precooked and just need to be heated through. We also sometimes use this recipe with Polish or pork sausages.

Prep Time: 5 minutres
Cook Time: 10 minutes
Yield: 4 servings

Ingredients

4 sausages of choice
1 cup BBQ sauce

Directions

1. Heat your grill to medium-high heat and lightly oil the grates.
2. Grill the sausages for about 6 to 7 minutes per side, or until they are nearly done.
3. Brush the BBQ sauce on the sausages, then continue to grill for another 2 to 3 minutes per side, until the sausages are cooked through and the sauce is caramelized.

Mac 'n' Cheese

The BEST I've ever eaten.

Prep Time: 30 minutes
Cook Time: 30 minutes
Yield: 8 servings

Ingredients

1 (16 oz.) package penne pasta
2 cups shredded Gruyère cheese
4 cups shredded sharp cheddar cheese
1 T. extra-virgin olive oil
6 T. unsalted butter
⅓ cup all-purpose flour
3 cups whole milk
1 cup heavy whipping cream
1½ tsp. salt
½ tsp. black pepper
½ tsp. dry mustard
½ tsp. garlic powder
¼ tsp. nutmeg
1½ cups panko breadcrumbs
½ cup shredded Parmesan cheese
¼ tsp. smoked paprika
4 T. butter, melted

Directions

1. Preheat the oven to 350°F. Lightly grease a 9 × 13-inch baking dish.
2. Cook the pasta according to package directions, and drain.
3. In a large bowl, combine the Gruyère and cheddar cheese. Reserve 2 cups of the cheese mixture for later use.
4. Place the cooked pasta in a large bowl and drizzle it with the olive oil while still warm. Stir to coat the pasta, then set it aside to cool.
5. In a large saucepan, melt the butter over medium heat. Whisk in the flour and continue whisking for about 1 minute, until bubbly.
6. Gradually whisk in the milk and heavy cream until smooth. Continue whisking until the mixture bubbles again, then whisk for an additional 2 minutes.
7. Season the sauce with salt, pepper, dry mustard, garlic powder, and nutmeg. Stir to combine.
8. Gradually add handfuls of the cheese mixture to the sauce, whisking until smooth between each addition. (Do not stir in the 2 reserved cups of cheese.)
9. Pour the cheese sauce over the cooled pasta, stirring to fully coat the pasta in the sauce.
10. Spread half of the pasta in the prepared baking dish, sprinkle with the reserved 2 cups of cheese, then top with the remaining pasta.
11. In a small bowl, combine the panko crumbs, Parmesan cheese, melted butter, and smoked paprika. Sprinkle this mixture evenly over the pasta.
12. Bake for about 30 minutes, or until the topping is golden brown and the cheese is bubbly.

Angel Food Cake

Prep Time: 15 minutes
Cook Time: 55 minutes
Yield: 12 servings

Ingredients

1 cup cake flour, sifted
1½ cups sugar, divided
9 egg whites
¼ tsp. salt
1 tsp. cream of tartar
1½ tsp. vanilla
2 cups berries of choice
Whipped cream (optional)

Directions

1. Preheat the oven to 330°F.
2. Sift together the flour and ½ cup of sugar. (I use a mesh colander since I keep breaking my sifters.)
3. In a large bowl (a stand mixer works well for this), beat the egg whites until foamy. Add the salt and cream of tartar and continue beating until the whites form soft peaks. Beat in the remaining cup of sugar and the vanilla until stiff peaks form.
4. Fold the flour mixture into the beaten egg whites.
5. Turn out the mixture into an ungreased angel food cake pan. (I prefer a tube pan that has a removable bottom to make it easier to get the cake out.)
6. Bake 45 to 55 minutes, until an inserted toothpick comes out clean.
7. Invert the cake on a cooling rack. If the cake needs a little persuasion to come out, run a rubber spatula around the sides of the pan.
8. To serve, slice the cake into 8 or 12 portions (depending on how many servings you need). We top the cake with whatever berries we have on hand. Strawberries, blueberries, blackberries, and raspberries are our favorites. In the winter we will drizzle the cake with dark chocolate syrup and top it with bananas and slivered almonds. You can also slice the cake in half horizontally. (I use unflavored dental floss and leave it on the tube part of the cake pan while slicing.) Set the bottom half of the cake on a platter, top it with berries, add the top half, and frost it with whipped cream. This works only if you are serving the whole cake immediately.

Air Fryer Sugar and Cinnamon Donuts

Prep Time: 5 minutes
Cook Time: 10 minutes
Yield: 6 servings

Ingredients

1 (16.3 oz) can Pillsbury Grands! Flaky Layers Original Biscuits (from the refrigerated section of the supermarket)
Cooking spray (preferably butter-flavored)
½ cup granulated sugar
2 tsp. ground cinnamon
¼ cup unsalted butter, melted

Directions

1. Open the can of biscuits and separate each biscuit.
2. Use a very small round biscuit cutter (or the cap from a plastic water bottle) to cut out the center of each biscuit to create a donut shape. Save the cutouts to make donut holes.
3. Fully preheat your air fryer to 350°F (if your air fryer requires preheating).
4. Lightly spray the air fryer basket with the cooking spray to prevent sticking. Place the donuts and donut holes into the basket, ensuring they are not touching. You may need to do this in batches depending on the size of your air fryer.
5. Cook for about 5 minutes or until they're golden brown and cooked through. Repeat this process until all the donuts and donut holes have been cooked.
6. While the donuts are cooking, mix together the sugar and cinnamon in a shallow bowl or plate.
7. Once the donuts are cooked, allow them to cool slightly and then lightly brush each one with the melted butter. Immediately dip each buttered donut into the cinnamon sugar mixture, turning to coat evenly.
8. Serve the donuts warm for best flavor.

BLT Salad

Prep Time: 20 minutes
Yield: 4 main servings or 8 side servings

Ingredients

8 slices bacon, cooked and crumbled
4 cups chopped romaine lettuce
2 tomatoes, diced
½ cup bread croutons
¼ cup mayonnaise
1 T. lemon juice
Salt and pepper, to taste

Directions

1. In a large salad bowl, combine the bacon, romaine lettuce, tomatoes, and bread croutons.
2. In a small bowl, whisk together the mayonnaise and lemon juice.
3. Drizzle the dressing over the salad, season with a dash of salt and pepper, and gently toss to combine. Serve immediately.

Air Fryer Chicken Wings with BBQ Sauce

Prep Time: 10 minutes
Cook Time: 24 minutes
Yield: 4 to 5 servings

Ingredients

2½ lbs. chicken wings
1 cup Homemade BBQ sauce
1 cup ranch dressing

Directions

1. Preheat the air fryer to 400°F.
2. Rinse the wings in cold water and pat them dry with paper towels.
3. Spray the basket of the air fryer with cooking spray. Arrange the wings in the fryer basket, spacing them evenly. Cook the wings in batches if necessary.
4. Air fry for 12 minutes, then flip the wings using tongs and cook for an additional 12 minutes.
5. Meanwhile, warm up the BBQ sauce in the microwave for 60 seconds in a large, microwavable bowl. Add the cooked wings and toss to coat them in the sauce.
6. Serve immediately with ranch dressing.

Homemade BBQ Sauce

This sauce can be stored in the refrigerator in an airtight container for up to a week. It's perfect for brushing on grilled meats or using as a dipping sauce.

Prep Time: 10 minutes
Cook Time: 20 minutes
Yield: about 2 cups

Ingredients

1 cup ketchup
½ cup apple cider vinegar
½ cup firmly packed brown sugar
¼ cup honey
1 T. Worcestershire sauce
1 T. lemon juice
2 tsp. stone ground mustard
½ tsp. garlic powder
½ tsp. onion powder
¼ tsp. cayenne pepper (optional)
Salt and pepper, to taste

Directions

1. In a medium saucepan, combine the ketchup, apple cider vinegar, brown sugar, honey, Worcestershire sauce, lemon juice, mustard, garlic powder, onion powder, and optional cayenne pepper.
2. Bring the mixture to a simmer over medium heat.
3. Reduce the heat to low and let the sauce simmer for 15 to 20 minutes, stirring occasionally.
4. Season the sauce with salt and pepper, to taste. Remove the sauce from the heat and let it cool. It will thicken further as it cools.

Quiche (Sausage, Spinach, and Gruyère)

Prep Time: 20 minutes
Cook Time: 45 minutes
Yield: 8 servings

Ingredients

4 large eggs
⅔ cup whole milk
½ cup heavy cream (or heavy whipping cream)
¼ tsp. salt
¼ tsp. pepper
1 cup shredded Gruyère cheese
1 cup cooked, crumbled breakfast sausage
1 (10 oz.) package frozen, chopped spinach, thawed and squeezed dry
1 store-bought frozen pastry pie shell, defrosted overnight
¼ cup grated Parmesan cheese

Directions

1. Preheat oven to 350°F.
2. In a large bowl, beat the eggs, milk, cream, salt, and pepper on high speed, approximately 1 minute.
3. Fold in the cheese, sausage, and spinach. Pour mixture into the crust.
4. Sprinkle the Parmesan cheese on top.
5. Cover the edges of the pie shell with aluminum foil to keep them from burning.
6. Bake quiche until the center is set and a toothpick comes out clean, about 45 minutes.
7. Let the quiche cool for 10 minutes before serving.

Apple Almond Salad

Prep Time: 15 minutes
Yield: 4 main servings or 8 side servings

Ingredients

6 cups mixed greens
2 apples, cored and thinly sliced
½ cup almonds, sliced and toasted
¼ cup dried cranberries
¼ cup blue cheese or feta cheese, crumbled
¼ cup Balsamic Vinaigrette

Directions

1. In a large salad bowl, combine the mixed greens, apples, almonds, and dried cranberries.
2. Sprinkle the blue cheese or feta cheese on top.
3. Drizzle the balsamic vinaigrette dressing over the salad and gently toss to combine. Serve immediately.

Balsamic Vinaigrette

Ingredients

½ cup extra-virgin olive oil
¼ cup balsamic vinegar
1 tsp. honey
1 tsp. Dijon mustard
Salt and freshly ground pepper, to taste

Directions

Combine all ingredients in a jar with a tight-fitting lid and shake until well combined.

*On the Sabbath we went
outside the city gate to the river,
where we expected to find
a place of prayer.
We sat down and began to speak to
the women who had gathered there.*

Acts 16:13

A Prayer for Provision in Good Times and Hard Times

Lord, I know You are aware
that my trust in Your provision
falters at times.
When things are hard
I try not to panic
but sometimes I do.

I know You
see my circumstances.

Lord, impress upon me
that You do not change
even when chaos is close.

I will trust Your provision
when the cupboards are
full of lack
and when they overflow.

I will rejoice
in Your provision in
times of abundance
and when
all I have is belief in
who You are
and a bunch
of questions and prayers.

Week Twenty-Three
Grandma's Kitchen

I s there anything more comforting than a bowl of chicken noodle soup? Whether it's to ease a cold, a broken arm, a broken heart, or just for a great meal, this week's soup recipe is one you will break out over and over again for years to come. This is not your average chicken soup! With the special addition of ginger for additional warmth and turmeric for color and added health benefits, it could very well become a family favorite. As you ladle the soup into the bowls, let it remind you of all that comforts you and the ways you comfort others. Sabbath time gives us the space and the ritual to pause and savor more than we might on a rushed Wednesday. Enjoy.

Week 23 Menu

Saturday

Oven-Roasted Chicken
Pasta Salad
Green Beans (no recipe)

Dessert:
Old-Fashioned
   Donut Cake

Sunday

Breakfast:
Overnight French Toast

Lunch:
Chicken Noodle Soup
Caesar Salad

Dinner:
Pulled Pork Lettuce Wraps
Grilled Veggies (no recipe)

Monday

Pasta Salad with Chicken
Rolls

Tuesday

Chicken Noodle Soup
Italian Chopped Salad

Wednesday

Leftovers or frozen meal of choice

Thursday

Dinner out

Friday

Pizza night!

Sabbath Soup

Chicken Noodle Soup

Prep Time: 20 minutes • Cook Time: 20 minutes • Yield: 4 bowls or 8 cups

Ingredients

1 T. olive oil

1 medium onion, finely chopped

2 carrots, peeled and sliced into
  thin rounds

2 celery ribs, sliced

3 garlic cloves, minced

1 tsp. freshly grated ginger

½ tsp. turmeric

6 cups chicken stock or broth

1 bay leaf

Salt and pepper, to taste

2 cups dried egg noodles

2 cups shredded cooked
  chicken

2 T. chopped fresh parsley

1 T. fresh thyme leaves

1 T. chopped fresh dill

½ lemon, juiced (about 1 T.
  juice)

Directions

1. Heat the olive oil over medium heat in a large soup pot.

2. Add the onion, carrots, celery, garlic, ginger, and turmeric and sauté for 5 minutes, or until the vegetables are tender.

3. Add the chicken stock or broth to the pot, followed by the bay leaf, salt, and pepper. Bring the broth to a boil.

4. Add the egg noodles to the pot and cook according to the package directions until tender.

5. Add the chicken to the pot.

6. Stir in the fresh herbs and lemon juice, and adjust the seasonings if necessary.

Oven-Roasted Chicken

Prep Time: 10 minutes
Cook Time: 1 hour and 40 minutes
Yield: 4 to 6 servings

Ingredients

1 whole chicken, giblets removed, rinsed and
  patted dry
Cooking spray
Salt (1 tsp. per pound of chicken)
Pepper (⅓ tsp. per pound of chicken)
6 garlic cloves, cut in half
4 T. butter
Garlic salt and pepper

Directions

1. Preheat your oven to 425°F.
2. Place the chicken in a roasting pan covered in
   cooking spray, breast side up. Season the chicken
   cavity with salt and pepper, then place the
   garlic inside. Adjust the suggested levels if you
   like a more seasoned chicken. Chop the butter
   into pats and place them all over the top of the
   chicken. Sprinkle the skin with garlic salt and
   pepper.
3. Roast until the chicken's internal temperature
   reaches 165°F. Let it roast for an hour and then
   keep checking the internal temperature until it
   reaches 165°F. Let it sit for 20 minutes before
   serving.

*They feast on the
abundance of your house; you
give them drink from your
river of delights.*

PSALM 36:8

Pasta Salad

Prep Time: 15 minutes
Cook Time: 10 minutes
Yield: 8 servings

Ingredients

1 (16 oz.) box Rotini pasta
2 cups cherry tomatoes, halved
1 cucumber, sliced
1 red bell pepper, diced
½ cup red onion, diced
1 cup feta cheese, crumbled
1 cup Italian dressing

Directions

1. Cook the pasta according to the package directions, then drain and rinse under cold water
   until cool.
2. In a large bowl, combine the cooled pasta,
   tomatoes, cucumber, bell pepper, red onion, feta
   cheese, and Italian dressing.
3. Toss until all ingredients are well mixed and
   coated with dressing.
4. Serve chilled.

Old-Fashioned Donut Cake

Prep Time: 15 minutes
Cook Time: 55 to 60 minutes
Yield: 8 servings

Ingredients

Cake
3 cups all-purpose flour
1 T. baking powder
½ tsp. baking soda
½ tsp. salt
2 tsp. ground nutmeg
1 cup unsalted butter, room temperature
2 cups granulated sugar
4 large eggs
2 tsp. pure vanilla extract
1 cup buttermilk
Glaze
2 cups powdered sugar
¼ cup whole milk
1 tsp. pure vanilla extract

Directions

1. Preheat your oven to 350°F. Grease and lightly flour a Bundt pan.
2. In a bowl, whisk together the flour, baking powder, baking soda, salt, and nutmeg.
3. In another large bowl, cream together the butter and sugar until light and fluffy. This should take about 2 to 3 minutes using an electric mixer on medium speed.
4. Beat in the eggs, one at a time, making sure each is incorporated before adding the next. Stir in the vanilla extract.
5. Add the dry ingredients to the butter mixture in three parts, alternating with the buttermilk, starting and ending with the dry ingredients. Mix just until combined after each addition. Do not overmix.
6. Pour the batter into the prepared Bundt pan and smooth the top with a spatula. Bake for 50 to 60 minutes, or until a toothpick inserted into the center comes out clean.
7. Let the cake cool in the pan for 10 minutes, then invert it onto a wire rack to cool completely.
8. While the cake is cooling, prepare the glaze: In a bowl, whisk together the powdered sugar, milk, and vanilla extract until smooth.
9. Once the cake has cooled, pour the glaze evenly over the top, allowing it to drip down the sides.

*Better a dry crust
with peace and quiet
than a house full of feasting,
with strife.*

Proverbs 17:1

Overnight French Toast

This recipe is great to make with a crusty bread. Sourdough or French breads are great, but my favorite is brioche. For an extra special treat, serve this French toast with fresh berries and a side of bacon.

Prep Time: 10 minutes, plus 4 hours or overnight in the fridge
Cook Time: 45 to 60 minutes
Yield: 8 servings

Ingredients

1 loaf crusty bread
8 large eggs
2 cups whole milk
½ cup heavy cream
2 T. vanilla extract
1 tsp. cinnamon
½ tsp. nutmeg
½ tsp. salt
¼ cup sugar
½ cup brown sugar

Topping
½ cup all-purpose flour
½ cup packed light brown sugar
1 tsp. ground cinnamon
¼ tsp. salt
½ cup cold unsalted butter, diced
Warm maple syrup and butter, for serving

Directions

1. Grease a 9 × 13-inch pan with cooking spray. Cut bread into 1-inch chunks and spread evenly in pan.
2. In a medium bowl, mix together eggs, milk, cream, vanilla, cinnamon, nutmeg, salt, and sugars. Pour evenly over bread. Gently squish down the bread (using a food prep glove if you like) so that it's completely soaked in the mixture.
3. Cover the pan with plastic wrap and place in the fridge overnight (or for at least 4 hours).
4. Combine all the topping ingredients except butter in a medium bowl. Using a pastry blender or a large fork, cut the butter into the mixture until it resembles small pebbles. Cover and refrigerate overnight.
5. The next day, preheat the oven to 350°F.

6. Uncover the baking dish and place the topping evenly over the bread.
7. Bake for 45 to 60 minutes or until a clean toothpick comes out.

Caesar Salad

Prep Time: 15 minutes
Yield: 4 main servings or 8 side servings

Ingredients

1 head romaine lettuce, torn into bite-size pieces
1 cup croutons
½ cup freshly grated Parmesan cheese
½ cup Creamy Caesar Dressing

Directions

1. In a large salad bowl, combine the romaine lettuce, croutons, and Parmesan cheese.
2. Pour the dressing over the salad and toss until well coated.
3. Serve immediately, with additional Parmesan cheese on top if desired.

Creamy Caesar Dressing

Ingredients

¾ cup mayonnaise
2 T. fresh lemon juice
2 garlic cloves, minced
1 tsp. Worcestershire sauce
1 tsp. Dijon mustard
¼ cup grated Parmesan cheese
Salt and freshly ground pepper, to taste

Directions

Combine all ingredients in a blender or food processor and blend until smooth.

Pulled Pork Lettuce Wraps

Enjoy these refreshing and flavorful Pulled Pork Lettuce Wraps, a healthier alternative to traditional wraps and buns.

Prep time: 15 minutes
Cook time: 10 minutes
Yield: 4 servings

Ingredients

¼ cup hoisin sauce

1 T. soy sauce
1 T. rice vinegar
1 T. honey
1 T. vegetable oil
1 tsp. minced fresh ginger
2 cloves garlic, minced
2 cups leftover pulled pork (or shredded cooked pork loin)
1 head butter lettuce or iceberg lettuce, leaves separated and washed
½ cup shredded carrots
½ red bell pepper, thinly sliced
¼ cup chopped fresh cilantro
2 green onions, thinly sliced
¼ cup unsalted roasted peanuts or cashews, chopped
Optional: Lime wedges, sriracha, or other hot sauce, for serving

Directions

1. In a small bowl, whisk together the hoisin sauce, soy sauce, rice vinegar, and honey. Set it aside.
2. In a large skillet, heat the vegetable oil over medium heat. Add the ginger and garlic, and sauté until fragrant, about 1 minute.
3. Add the pork to the skillet, stirring to combine. Cook for 3 to 4 minutes, until heated through.
4. Stir in the sauce, ensuring the pork is well coated. Cook for another 2 to 3 minutes, until the sauce has slightly thickened.
5. Remove the skillet from the heat and allow the pork mixture to cool slightly.
6. To assemble the lettuce wraps, place a spoonful of the pork mixture onto each lettuce leaf. Top with carrots, red bell pepper, cilantro, and green onion. Sprinkle with peanuts or cashews.
7. Serve the lettuce wraps with lime wedges, and sriracha or other hot sauce on the side for those who like a little extra heat.

Rolls

The ingredients for rolls and sandwich bread dough are the same, so feel free to double the recipe to get both rolls for dinner and sliced bread for sandwiches for the week. Look at you being so clever!

Prep Time: 10 minutes, plus 2 hours to rise
Cook Time: 30 minutes
Yield: 6 Rolls

Ingredients

1 cup warm water
½ T. active dry yeast
2 T. honey
2¾ cups all-purpose flour, divided
1 tsp. salt
2 T. melted butter, divided

Directions

1. Mix the water, yeast, and honey together. Add 2 cups of flour, salt, and 1 tablespoon melted butter and mix.
2. Put dough on a surface with ¼ cup of flour and knead it for about 5 minutes, adding in the other half cup of flour to get a doughy texture.
3. Take your dough ball and put it in a bowl. Cover it with a dishcloth and stick it in the oven with the oven light on for an hour (it should approximately double in size).
4. Preheat the oven to 350°F.
5. Butter a pie tin. Cut the dough into six pieces and form the pieces into rolls.
6. Place the rolls in the pie tin and let the dough double again, covered.
7. Bake for 30 minutes.
8. Remove from oven and brush with the other tablespoon of melted butter.

Note: For sandwich bread, at step 5, butter a loaf pan instead of the pie tin and shape the dough to fit. Allow the dough to rise and bake as above. Allow just a few more minutes to bake, until the loaf is golden and sounds hollow when tapped. Brush with butter, then let it cool on a wire rack before slicing.

Italian Chopped Salad

Prep Time: 20 minutes
Yield: 4 main servings or 8 side servings

Ingredients

1 head iceberg lettuce, chopped
1 red onion, thinly sliced
1 cup cherry tomatoes, halved
1 (15 oz.) can chickpeas, drained and rinsed
1 cup pearl mozzarella balls
1 cup cubed provolone cheese
½ cup sliced pepperoncini
½ cup cubed genoa salami
½ cup chopped sun-dried tomatoes
½ cup Italian dressing
Salt and pepper, to taste

Directions

1. In a large salad bowl, combine the lettuce, red onion, cherry tomatoes, chickpeas, pearl mozzarella, provolone cheese, pepperoncini, salami, and sun-dried tomatoes.
2. Drizzle the dressing over the salad, season with a dash of salt and pepper, and gently toss to combine. Serve immediately.

Italian Dressing

Ingredients

½ cup extra-virgin olive oil
¼ cup red wine vinegar
1 tsp. honey
1 tsp. dried oregano
1 tsp. dried basil
½ tsp. garlic powder
Salt and freshly ground pepper, to taste

Directions

Shake all ingredients together in a jar until well combined.

A Prayer for the Ministry of Food

There are moments
when I feel like
I am surrounded
by grief and pain.
I want to help
and so often
it seems there's
nothing I can do
to help ease
the burdens of
my neighbors and friends.

Lord, I know You are near
to those who are in need
of Your comfort.
You sustain us all.

Prompt me and
guide me to be
Your hands in this world
full of need.

So often
there are no words,
and most times
a simple meal communicates
all that needs to be said
in that particular moment.

Equip me to be a
participant in
the ministry of food.

Week Twenty-Four
Ladle the Love

This week's soup, Chicken Tortilla, is a perfect choice to make in a pinch. It's also my go-to if I am delivering food to a friend. If you have shredded chicken in the freezer, you can grab everything else from your pantry and be at a friend's house with delicious soup in less than an hour. Because soup is such an easy meal to stretch into more servings, consider making a bigger batch of your Sabbath meal to bless a neighbor, someone from church, or an elderly friend. Perhaps even invite them to join you and your family around the table.

Week 24 Menu

Saturday
BBQ Chicken
Mac 'n' Cheese
Grilled Veggies (no recipe)
Dessert:
Chocolate Chip
   Cookies

Sunday
Breakfast:
Amazing Mix-In Muffins
   (Orange and Cranberry)

Lunch:
Chicken Tortilla Soup
Roasted Corn Salad
Corn Chips (no recipe)

Dinner:
Creamy Skillet Chicken
   Cacciatore
Caprese Salad

Monday
Greek Yogurt Chicken Salad with
   Apples and Almonds
French Bread (no recipe)

Tuesday
Chicken Tortilla Soup
Corn Chips (no recipe)

Wednesday
Leftovers or frozen meal of choice

Thursday
Dinner out

Friday
Pizza night!

Sabbath Soup

Chicken Tortilla Soup

Prep Time: 5 minutes • Cook Time: 20 minutes • Yield: 4 bowls or 8 cups

Ingredients

1 cup salsa (spiciness level is your choice)

2 (14.5 oz) cans chicken broth

4 cups water

1 packet taco seasoning (about 1 oz. or 3 T.)

4 cups shredded cooked chicken

1 (15 oz.) can corn

Optional toppings: Jack or cheddar cheese, tortilla chips, green onions

Directions

1. In a large soup pot, stir together the salsa, chicken broth, water, taco seasoning, chicken, and corn. Simmer for 20 minutes.

2. To serve, top with shredded cheese, chips, and sliced green onions.

BBQ Chicken

Prep Time: 5 minutes
Cook Time: 15 minutes
Yield: 4 servings

Ingredients

4 bone-in chicken breasts
Salt and pepper, to taste
1 T. smoked paprika
1 T. olive oil
1 cup BBQ sauce

Directions

1. Season the chicken breasts on both sides with smoked paprika and a good sprinkling of salt and pepper.
2. Heat your grill to medium-high heat and lightly oil the grates.
3. Grill the chicken for about 7 minutes per side, or until it is nearly done.
4. Brush the BBQ sauce on both sides of the chicken, then continue to grill for another 2 to 3 minutes per side, until the chicken is cooked through and the sauce is caramelized.
5. Let the chicken rest for a few minutes before serving.

*Therefore let us keep
the Festival,
not with the old bread
leavened with malice
and wickedness,
but with the unleavened
bread of sincerity
and of truth.*

1 CORINTHIANS 5:8

Mac 'n' Cheese

The BEST I've ever eaten.

Prep Time: 30 minutes
Cook Time: 30 minutes
Yield: 8 servings

Ingredients

1 (16 oz.) package penne pasta
2 cups shredded Gruyère cheese
4 cups shredded sharp cheddar cheese
1 T. extra-virgin olive oil
6 T. unsalted butter
⅓ cup all-purpose flour
3 cups whole milk
1 cup heavy whipping cream
1½ tsp. salt
½ tsp. black pepper
½ tsp. dry mustard
½ tsp. garlic powder
¼ tsp. nutmeg
1½ cups panko breadcrumbs
½ cup shredded Parmesan cheese
¼ tsp. smoked paprika
4 T. butter, melted

Directions

1. Preheat the oven to 350°F. Lightly grease a 9 × 13-inch baking dish.
2. Cook the pasta according to package directions, and drain.
3. In a large bowl, combine the Gruyère and cheddar cheese. Reserve 2 cups of the cheese mixture for later use.
4. Place the cooked pasta in a large bowl and drizzle it with the olive oil while still warm. Stir to coat the pasta, then set it aside to cool.
5. In a large saucepan, melt the butter over medium heat. Whisk in the flour and continue whisking for about 1 minute, until bubbly.
6. Gradually whisk in the milk and heavy cream until smooth. Continue whisking until the mixture bubbles again, then whisk for an additional 2 minutes.
7. Season the sauce with salt, pepper, dry mustard, garlic powder, and nutmeg. Stir to combine.
8. Gradually add handfuls of the cheese mixture to

the sauce, whisking until smooth between each addition. (Do not stir in the 2 reserved cups of cheese.)

9. Pour the cheese sauce over the cooled pasta, stirring to fully coat the pasta in the sauce.

10. Spread half of the pasta in the prepared baking dish, sprinkle with the reserved 2 cups of cheese, then top with the remaining pasta.

11. In a small bowl, combine the panko crumbs, Parmesan cheese, melted butter, and smoked paprika. Sprinkle this mixture evenly over the pasta.

12. Bake for about 30 minutes, or until the topping is golden brown and the cheese is bubbly.

Chocolate Chip Cookies

Hint: This dough can be frozen as pre-scooped balls or ready-to-slice logs.

Prep Time: 20 minutes
Cook Time: 10 minutes
Yield: 112 cookies (recipe may be halved)

Ingredients

5 cups oatmeal
2 cups butter, room temperature
2 cups granulated sugar
2 cups brown sugar
4 eggs
2 tsp. vanilla
4 cups flour
2 tsp. baking soda
2 tsp. baking powder
1 tsp. salt
24 oz. chocolate chips
1 8 oz. Hershey bar, grated
3 cups chopped nuts (your choice)

Directions

1. Preheat the oven to 375°F.
2. Measure the oatmeal and place it in a blender to blend into a fine powder.
3. In a large mixing bowl, cream together the butter and both sugars. Add the eggs and vanilla and stir to combine with the butter mixture, then stir in the flour, blended oatmeal, baking

powder, baking soda, and salt. Stir in the chocolate and nuts.

4. Scoop the dough into balls and place about 12 to a cookie sheet, evenly spaced, baking in batches. Bake for 10 minutes.

5. To freeze for later baking: Flash freeze scooped dough balls on a cookie sheet. Individually frozen dough balls are easier to handle and will keep their shape better when transferred to a freezer bag for longer-term storage. Alternately, form the dough into a log about 2 inches around and wrap in plastic wrap. Put the dough in the bag and write baking directions on the bag. I like to experiment with the cookies and find out what the baking time and temp is for frozen dough as well as thawed dough. Bake for 10 minutes, and then keep checking every 2 minutes to get them just perfect.

Amazing Mix-in Muffins (Orange and Cranberry)

Here is what I love about this recipe—I usually have all these main ingredients on hand, use whatever mix-ins I currently have, and I've got muffins. To make your own combination, use about 1½ cups total of your desired mix-ins as the last step in making the batter.

Prep Time: 10 minutes
Cook Time: 25 minutes
Yield: 12 muffins

Ingredients

2 cups all-purpose flour
¾ cup granulated sugar
½ tsp. salt
2 tsp. baking powder
⅓ cup vegetable oil
1 large egg, room temperature
1 tsp. vanilla extract
¾ cup milk (whole, low-fat, or non-dairy options all work)
1 cup dried cranberries
¼ cup fresh orange juice
1 T. orange zest

Directions

1. Preheat your oven to 400°F. Line a 12-cup muffin tin with paper liners or grease the cups with nonstick cooking spray.
2. In a large bowl, whisk together the flour, sugar, salt, and baking powder.
3. In a separate medium bowl, combine the vegetable oil, egg, vanilla extract, and milk. Stir well.
4. Gently pour the wet ingredients into the dry ingredients and mix until just combined. Be careful not to overmix, as this can result in tough muffins.
5. Fold in the cranberries, juice, and zest until evenly distributed throughout the batter.
6. Divide the batter evenly among the 12 muffin cups, filling each about two-thirds full.
7. Bake for 20 to 25 minutes, or until a toothpick inserted into the center of a muffin comes out clean.
8. Remove the muffins from the oven and allow them to cool in the tin for 5 minutes before transferring to a wire rack to cool completely.

Roasted Corn Salad

Prep time: 10 minutes
Cook time: 25 minutes
Yield: 8 servings

Ingredients

4 ears corn, husks removed
½ cup mayonnaise
¼ cup fresh lime juice
½ tsp. chili powder
½ cup crumbled cotija cheese
¼ cup chopped fresh cilantro
Salt and pepper, to taste

Directions

1. Heat a grill or grill pan over medium heat. Cook the corn until it is charred on all sides. Remove from the grill and allow it to cool. Once cooled, cut the kernels off the cob and place them in a large bowl.
2. In a separate bowl, mix together the mayonnaise, lime juice, and chili powder.
3. Pour the dressing over the grilled corn kernels

and mix until they are well coated.
4. Add the cotija cheese and cilantro to the bowl. Mix well.
5. Season the salad with salt and pepper, to taste.
6. Serve the salad immediately or refrigerate it for an hour to allow the flavors to meld.

Creamy Skillet Chicken Cacciatore

Enjoy this hearty and flavorful Creamy Skillet Chicken Cacciatore with a side of crusty bread or a green salad for a complete meal. This dish is a perfect way to use up leftover chicken, and it's sure to be a hit with your family!

Prep Time: 10 minutes
Cook Time: 25 minutes
Yield: 4 servings

Ingredients

1 T. olive oil
2 cloves garlic, minced
1 medium onion, coarsely chopped
8 oz. mushrooms, sliced
5 fresh tomatoes, diced, or 1 (14.5 oz.) can diced tomatoes
¼ cup heavy cream
½ cup chicken broth
1 T. Italian seasoning
2 cups leftover chicken, chopped
Salt and pepper, to taste
Hot pasta, for serving
Parmesan cheese and additional fresh basil, for topping
½ cup fresh basil leaves, roughly chopped

Directions

1. Heat olive oil in a large skillet over medium heat. Add garlic and onion and sauté for about 3 minutes until they start to soften.
2. Add mushrooms to the skillet and continue sautéing until onion is fully softened and mushrooms are browned.
3. Stir in the tomatoes, heavy cream, chicken broth, and Italian seasoning. Add salt and pepper, to taste.
4. Reduce heat to low and let the mixture simmer for about 10 to 15 minutes, or until the sauce

has thickened to your desired consistency.

5. Add the chicken to the skillet, stirring to mix it into the sauce. Let it cook for a few more minutes until the chicken is heated through.

6. Serve the creamy chicken cacciatore over hot pasta. Top with grated Parmesan cheese and fresh basil before serving.

Caprese Salad

Prep Time: 15 minutes
Yield: 4 main servings or 8 side servings

Ingredients

4 large tomatoes, sliced
1 lb. fresh mozzarella cheese, sliced
1 cup loosely packed fresh basil leaves
¼ cup olive oil
2 T. balsamic vinegar
Salt and pepper, to taste

Directions

1. Arrange the tomato slices, mozzarella slices, and basil leaves on a large platter, alternating and overlapping them.

2. In a small bowl, whisk together the olive oil and balsamic vinegar.

3. Drizzle the dressing over the arranged ingredients on the platter. Season the salad with a dash of salt and pepper. Serve immediately.

Greek Yogurt Chicken Salad with Apples and Almonds

This dish is versatile and can be enjoyed in several ways. It's a great way to use up leftover chicken and perfect for those warmer days when you want something light and satisfying. You can serve it on crackers or warm pita bread for a quick and easy lunch. For a lighter option, you could serve it atop a bed of mixed greens. Pair the chicken salad with some fresh grapes on the side for a refreshing and balanced meal!

Prep Time: 15 minutes
Yield: 4 servings

Ingredients

2 cups leftover chicken, shredded
Juice of 1 lemon
1½ cups nonfat Greek yogurt
1 T. honey
½ tart apple, chopped
½ cup slivered almonds
½ cup dried cranberries
Salt and pepper, to taste
Optional: Crackers, warm pita bread, and grapes for serving

Directions

1. Place the shredded chicken in a large mixing bowl.

2. Squeeze the juice of the lemon over the chicken. This will not only add a tangy freshness to the salad but will also keep the chicken moist.

3. Add the Greek yogurt and honey to the bowl. Stir until the chicken is evenly coated.

4. Next, add the apple, almonds, and dried cranberries to the bowl. Stir to combine all the ingredients well.

5. Season with salt and pepper, to taste. Your chicken salad is now ready to serve with crackers, pita, grapes, or however you like it!

A Prayer for Connection

Lord, help me
to remember
I am part of a whole.

My heart finds itself
tangled up
and tripping over
what is mine
and I end up
completely unaware
of my neighbors.

I am not proud of this.

In Your kingdom
there's always enough
and I want to be
part of
Your kingdom
here on this earth.
Open my eyes to
the need in my
community,
move my heart
to embrace
my neighborhood
as part of me.

I belong to my community
and my community belongs
to me.

Recipe Index

Kathi Lipp is the bestselling author of many books, including *The Accidental Homesteader* and *Clutter Free*. She is the host of the *Clutter Free Academy* podcast.

She and her husband, Roger, live in California and are parents of four young adults. Kathi shares her story at retreats, conferences, and women's events across the United States.

Connect with her at www.KathiLipp.com and on Facebook at www.Facebook.com/AuthorKathiLipp.